Economic Growth
in World Perspective

Economic Growth
in World Perspective

Edited by DENYS MUNBY

ASSOCIATION PRESS · NEW YORK

SCM PRESS · BLOOMSBURY STREET · LONDON

Economic Growth in World Perspective

Copyright © 1966 by
World Council of Churches

Published by Association Press, 291 Broadway, N. Y. 10007
and
SCM Press, Bloomsbury Street, London

Library of Congress catalog card number: 66-11796

Publisher's stock number: 1601.

 72

PRINTED IN THE UNITED STATES OF AMERICA

PREFACE

In 1962, the Central Committee of the World Council of Churches authorized the Department on Church and Society to begin preparations for a world conference to be held in 1966. The theme that was finally selected was "Christians in the Technical and Social Revolutions of Our Time." The department was also requested to undertake such preparatory studies as would help the conference in considering the central issues for Christian social ethics in contemporary society. In 1963, the Working Committee of the department recommended the preparation of four books of essays on the following subjects:

   I. *Christian Social Ethics in a Changing World*
  II. *Responsible Government in a Revolutionary Age*
 III. *Economic Growth in World Perspective*
 IV. *Man in Community*

We are pleased to commend these books to Christians around the world, and we invite them to share with us their reactions and opinions on the issues raised therein. Although the books are primarily intended as preparatory reading for the 1966 conference, it is hoped that they will also be used for discussion in local and regional groups around the world, after the conference as well as before.

Not since the Oxford World Conference on Church, Community and State, in 1937, has there been a similar worldwide effort to rethink Christian social responsibility. The study volumes for that conference dealt largely with the theological issues of social ethics within the context of the churches' encounter with the challenges of that time. Since then, new technical and social revolutions have overtaken societies all over the world, and new issues of social ethics have arisen as the churches have responded to them. The first of the present volumes deals with the theological problems of social ethics as such, while the others concentrate on relating theological insights to the actual problems of Christian responsibility in the contemporary situation of world political, economic and social change.

These symposia do not pretend to represent the full range of viewpoints held within the ecumenical fellowship on these questions. This is impossible in the space of four volumes on such large themes. The aim is rather to reveal the wide range of attitudes and opinions held, giving special attention to new and challenging points of view.

The responsibility for the structure and content of these volumes is shared by the international editorial committees, which met in 1963 and 1964 to prepare the outline of each book and to review the first drafts of the contributions, by the chairman or editorial conveners of these committees, who have since become the editors of the books, and by the staff of the Department on Church and Society, who necessarily had to undertake the large part of the detailed editorial work and correspondence. Each writer remains responsible for the content of his contribution.

We are grateful to all those who have contributed to the volumes and to those who have commented on the essays in draft form. We acknowledge with appreciation the contribution of the Church and Society staff—Professor Mauricio Lopez, the Reverend

Thomas Okuma and, in particular, Miss Margaret Sinclair, one of the early workers in the Universal Christian Council for Life and Work, who forsook her retirement for three months to assist us in preparing the manuscripts for publication. We depended throughout on our secretarial staff, Miss Audrey Smith, Miss Christa Stalschus, Miss Judith Brown, and Miss Karin Hock who typed the several drafts of these manuscripts.

M. M. THOMAS, *Chairman,*
Working Committee
Department on Church and Society

PAUL ABRECHT, *Executive Secretary*
Department on Church and Society

World Council of Churches
Division of Studies

CONTRIBUTORS TO
THIS VOLUME

MR. DENYS MUNBY Reader in transport economics, Oxford University; Fellow of Nuffield College, Oxford; consultant on social questions at the Second Assembly of the World Council of Churches, 1954, and vice-chairman of Committee on Church and Society, 1955/61. Author of *Christianity and Economic Problems,* 1956; *God and the Rich Society,* 1961; *The Idea of a Secular Society,* 1964; and of articles on transport, housing, nationalized industries and similar economic problems. (Church of England)

DR. PIETER KUIN Director, Unilever Company of the Netherlands; formerly professor of economics and industrial organization, Free University of Amsterdam; member of the Working Committee of the Department on Church and Society of the World Council of Churches. (Remonstrant Church of the Netherlands)

MONSIEUR CLAUDE GRUSON The Directeur Général of the Institut National de la Statistique et des Etudes Economiques. (Reformed Church of France)

DR. S. A. ALUKO Professor of economics, University of Nigeria (Nsukka); Ph.D. in economics from University of London. Author of *Christianity and Communism,* 1964. (Methodist Church of Nigeria)

PROF. MIKIO SUMIYA Professor of economics at Tokyo University; Member, Working Committee of the Department on Church and Society of the World Council of Churches. Author of *Christianity and the Formation of Modern Japan,* 1950; *Social Impact of In-*

9

dustrialization in Japan, 1964; *Labour Problems in Japan,* 1964. (United Church of Christ, Japan)

REV. RONALD PRESTON Canon residentiary of Manchester Cathedral and lecturer in Christian ethics in the University of Manchester. (Church of England)

PROF. JAC. P. THIJSSE Member of the faculty of the Institute of Social Studies in The Hague, Holland. (Lutheran Church)

MR. ROBERT THEOBALD An Englishman now living in the United States writing and lecturing on the problems of the modern technological society; studied at Cambridge University and the Graduate School of Public Administration at Harvard. Author of *The Rich and the Poor, The Challenge of Abundance* and other works. (Anglican)

PROF. HARVEY COX Associate professor of Christian ethics, Divinity School, Harvard University; until 1965 professor of theology and culture, Andover Newton Theological School. Author of *The Secular City,* 1965. (The American Baptist Church)

MR. CESAR ESPIRITU Vice-president of the Credit Corporation of the Philippines. Vice-president of the Executive Committee of the World Student Christian Federation. (United Church of Christ in the Philippines)

MR. MUSA NASIR Formerly foreign minister of Jordan; principal of Bir-Zeit College, Bir-Zeit, Jordan. (Episcopalian)

PROF. ROY BLOUGH Professor of international economics, Graduate School of Business, Columbia University, New York City (Church of the Brethren U.S.A.)

PROF. JAN TINBERGEN Professor of development planning; director of the Netherlands Economic Institute and chairman of the Council of the U.N. Research Institute for Social Development. (Remonstrant Church of the Netherlands)

PROF. S. L. PARMAR Professor of economics at the University of Allahabad on leave as visiting lecturer at the Ecumenical Institute, Geneva.

MR. CHARLES ELLIOTT Member of the Department of Economics, University of Nottingham and also ordained priest of the Anglican Church; at present undertaking special research in connection with the U.N. Research Institute for Social Development.

10

CONTRIBUTORS TO THIS VOLUME

ABBÉ FRANÇOIS HOUTART Professor of sociology at the University of Louvain and Director of the Centre de Recherches Socio-Religieuses, Louvain; general secretary of FERES. Author of many studies of the sociology of development, especially in Latin America; his recent books include *The Challenge to Change: The Church Confronts the Future,* 1964; *El Cambio Social en America Latina,* 1964; and, with E. Pin, *L'Eglise à l'heure de l'Amérique Latine,* 1965. (Roman Catholic Church)

MONSIEUR A. DELOBELLE Assistant to Professor A. E. Collard, Faculté Sciences Economiques Sociales, Université Catholique, Louvain. (Roman Catholic Church)

REV. PAUL ABRECHT Executive secretary, Department on Church and Society of the World Council of Churches; director of the WCC study on Rapid Social Change and author of *The Churches and Rapid Social Change,* 1961. (American Baptist Church)

CONTENTS

13

CONTENTS

PART II

Technology and the Control of Environment

14

PART III

The Needs of the Developing Countries

15

PART IV

Growth in the World Economy

16

PART V

Christian Valuation

CONTENTS

18

FOREWORD:
THE DEVELOPMENT OF THE ECUMENICAL CONCERN

by D. L. MUNBY (United Kingdom)

IT is nearly thirty years since the last great international church conference on social questions met at Oxford. The world then was very different. The Spanish Civil War had become the running sore of Europe. To those growing up, if not to their elders, it was clear that a world war would be an inevitable result of the aggressions of Germany and Italy, and the supine ineptitude of the statesmen of Britain and France. The old Europe and all that it stood for was dying, as Jews, Christians and Socialists were persecuted in Germany, and the Vatican more or less openly supported a bloodthirsty "crusade" by a ruthless general against principles and ideals which inspired many of the most sensitive, if misguided, youth of the West.[1] The United States remained aloof, determined on isolation, if not in fact indifferent.[2]

---

[1] See HUGH THOMAS, *The Spanish Civil War* (revised Penguin ed., 1965) for a full-scale reappraisal of this *kairos* of the West. Significant is the account of the mission of two Basque priests to the Vatican with a copy of a letter sent to the Pope about the bombing of Guernica with eye-witness accounts. The secretary of Cardinal Pacelli, then Secretary of State, "told them that they would be received provided that they said nothing about the matter, and that they did not mention the subject which had brought them to Rome. Pacelli received the two Basques standing up. They mentioned the letter to the Pope, and Pacelli, coldly remarking, 'The Church is persecuted in Barcelona,' showed them the door immediately" (p. 538). See also pp. 574–577, and the telegram sent to Franco by Pacelli as Pope in 1939 giving thanks to God for "Spain's Catholic victory" (p. 754). The final chapter of this book shows clearly that as the world has changed, so also has the Vatican.

[2] In 1936 the U. S. Ambassador warned the French Foreign Secretary "not to base his foreign policy . . . on an expectation that the United States would ever again send troops or warships or floods of munitions and money to Europe" (quoted Thomas, *op. cit.,* p. 422).

19

The isolation of America and the complacency of the political leaders of the western democracies were not the result of devoting their energies to expansion and improvement at home, or the debilitating effects of too much prosperity.[3] The year 1937 was the peak of the trade cycle, but it was still a year of massive unemployment in Britain and America. Britain had never been prosperous since the First World War; and her politicians appeared to be quite unconcerned about their incapacity to do anything about the glaring social problems which threatened to create unbridgeable divisions, even in the most stable of societies. In European countries where the political and social framework was less stable, the combined effects of unemployment, agricultural depression, the indifference of the rich and open armed support for disruptive groups from Moscow, Rome or Berlin threatened to precipitate civil war and revolution. The United States had not yet recovered from the shock which the Wall Street crash of 1929 and the subsequent prolonged depression had inflicted on the conviction of the 1920's that prosperity could never end. In Russia, on which many set their hopes, Stalin was painstakingly completing the massacre of his opponents, real or imaginary. Outside Russia, only in Germany was there full employment; it seemed that the only way to keep the ordinary man happy and to eliminate the absurdities of an outworn economic system was to make arms.

Outside the "western" world, there had been aggressive war in China, the rape of Abyssinia by Italy, and German demands for *Lebensraum* in Africa, as well as eastern Europe. The old colonial powers, who had done so well out of the First World War in terms of additions to the acreage and population they controlled or owned, were pressed by public opinion at home and liberation groups abroad to give up some of their privileges. But no one would have believed, in 1937, that in ten years' time India would

---

[3] Though this was no doubt the case with the upper and middle classes who so frequently welcomed the "solutions" of Franco, Mussolini and Hitler, and cared little about the fate of the unemployed, the Jews and the left wing.

have become independent and that after a few years African colonies would have followed suit. Hopes and fears were more centered on Europe than outside; and the rest of the world could be regarded as the arena in which Europe, America and Japan could do battle.

Today, the colonial era is dead, even if there are still colonial powers and colonies, and even though many millions in the world regard the first liberated colony as the leader of the imperialist powers. Just as there was no going back on the French Revolution or the 1832 Reform Bill in Britain, so there is no going back on the revolt against the colonial era. The South with its brown and black skins sees itself as a new world bloc over against the North of the rich white man. The problem of world development has superseded the problems of colonialism. In the West unemployment as an inevitable feature of an advanced industrial society has been replaced by the problems of growth, inflation, and the workers' rat race for middle-class status and prosperity. The welfare state in a society which sets itself targets of twenty-five per cent growth in five years or doubling the standard of living in a quarter of a century is not without tensions, but these are new sociological tensions of status, uncertainty, leisure and abundance, not the acute class divisions of rich and poor. The problem of the motor car has replaced the problem of drink as the major social evil of our times. Exploding populations and crowded leisure facilities are more symptomatic of the industrialized western world than unemployment and poverty. The dream of America and the fantastic achievements of America's Midwest have been realized in Italy, France, Germany and many other countries. There may be wars and revolutions and political instability even in highly mature countries, and the possibility of nuclear war remains, but few believe it to be the imminent threat that hung over Europe in 1937.

Although the industrialized world is divided between the western and eastern blocs, the old issues of socialism and capitalism are dead. There are more similarities between western and eastern Europe than either side would admit, and as the "East" begins to learn how to apply traditional economic theory and modern mathematical tools to its directed planning, the "West" moves in the same direction from laissez-faire to indicative planning and thence on to target planning.[4] The balance between the private and public sectors, the scope of nationalization, the tools to be used in economic planning, the powers to be given to central government, local authorities and private business—these and similar issues are the stuff of politics in many countries. The lines are drawn differently on different sides of the Atlantic and in different countries.[5] The old slogans are repeated, but the crusade has degenerated into a Thirty Years' War of skirmishes.

A year before the Oxford Conference, Keynes' *General Theory* was published, thus undermining much traditional Christian teaching about capitalism. Many Christians have still not awakened to this reality. In a world of economic management and technological expertise, the traditional moralities are not easy to apply, and have not often been applied in detail. The World Council of Churches has, indeed, led the way, from its founding Assembly at Amsterdam through Evanston and the following "Rapid Social Change" studies to New Delhi and now to the study conference of 1966. Stock taking was needed, and this volume is a beginning. Much has been done, notably in the 1960 Conference at Thessaloniki and the two volumes on Rapid Social Change.[6] As Christians we

---

[4] It was British businessmen who pressed Conservative governments in Britain to engage in "planning" and follow the lines already established in France. It was a Czech theologian who whispered at a WCC conference, where a distinguished American Republican layman was extolling the virtues of the American system with its checks and balances between centralization and devolution, that he sounded rather like a communist orator in Prague.

[5] The introduction of American systems of taxation by a Labor Government in Britain is attacked as a radical undermining of business, while the British Government and British shipping industry have to take vigorous action to defend the traditional freedoms of this industry from the incursions of the American Government and its regulatory boards.

[6] E. DE VRIES, *Man in Rapid Social Change,* and PAUL ABRECHT, *The Churches and Rapid Social Change.* S.C.M. Press Ltd., 1961.

22

are beginning to be aware of some of the problems, some of the tools to be used in tackling them and some of the challenges to the churches. But we are still not clear as to the significance in God's perspective of the world in which we live. Rooted in our theological heritage, still shackled by the institutions and habits that developed in the Middle Ages and the Reformation, we have survived the Industrial Revolution without having come to terms with it. "Should we?" ask the theologians. Is it part of "the universe," which, as Carlyle said, "by God, we had better accept"? Or is it the creation of a post-Christian neopagan era which the church can but judge and condemn? Are economic growth and rising standards of living legitimate goals for men who have in God's good time come of age? Or are they idols which hide from us the One True God? The theologians speak with an uncertain voice, and often appear as academic bystanders; and there seems no place for prophesy among laymen, who have to work in a world of rigorous scientific analysis and are concerned with quantities rather than absolute distinctions of quality. It is easy to assert that the laws of Christian marriage are not concerned with whether a man may have two or three wives, either at the same time or one after the other; it is not so easy to assess whether a growth rate of 4 per cent per annum or 5 per cent is a proper target for national endeavor. It is easy to denounce the rich, when an income of £3,000 is compared with one of a few shillings; it is not so easy to assert that the slum dwellers of Glasgow must not be rehoused or provided with university education in order that a few marginal £100 millions may be given to be lost in the depths of Indian poverty.

The problems have changed as our categories have changed, and we have become aware of new ways of handling old problems. The thinking of the ecumenical movement has, necessarily, reflected these changes. The mood of nineteenth-century optimism still reflected at Stockholm gave way to the more somber note of Oxford. The clashes between "capitalism" and "socialism" at Amsterdam reflected the uncertainties of the early days of the cold war, and have now become a rather boring background of the world scene. At Evanston, the importance of Europe began to recede and the "Rapid Social Change" study brought into prominence what was happening, not only in India and the rest of Asia, but also in Latin America and Africa. Thessaloniki witnessed with memorable effect the vital role that Africa was to play in the future in both church and world.

That many of the reports of these conferences reflected the issues of their times, and are today outdated, should not worry us. We should be more worried that they sometimes echoed the struggles of previous years, and settled the Christian "line" on matters no longer of practical relevance. Churches are usually conservative; the World Council of Churches has managed to be less conservative than most, and to be at least aware of the issues of the day. But, although aware of the issues of the day, it has not managed to settle them, nor even to produce a clear Christian framework or perspective in which to view them. And this is not surprising, as Christians are as baffled as others. The issues are complex: they cannot be seen clearly by any one set of experts working in isolation, nor do they throw up the clear moral categories on which theologians or ecclesiastics can pronounce. It is the more remarkable then that the ecumenical movement has managed to clear up some tangles and throw light on some problems for the Christian conscience. Thus, the Oxford Conference in 1937 had a great deal to say on property which has perhaps never been better said.[7] The issues Marxism and Christianity were laid bare at Amsterdam and Evanston, and dividing lines between a proper and an excessive use of state power in economic matters have frequently been made clear. Thessaloniki and the "Rapid Social Change"

---

[7] The implications of this for world economic planning are clearly drawn by the Abbé Houtart and M. Delobelle in their discussion of the "universal destination of wealth," which follows from similar principles. Perhaps I could also refer to my own discussion of this in *God and the Rich Society*.

studies highlighted the challenges of world development. In all this there was no finality. No textbook of moral casuistry for planners, politicians or businessmen has emerged. Indeed, few would wish it to emerge. But the fact remains that the ecumenical movement has been more successful in educating Christians and stating problems than in making a satisfactory theological appraisal of the situation.[8] Hence, the need for new efforts of study and thought in our churches.

The present volume is only one of several. Its major contribution lies, once again, perhaps, in exposing problems rather than in providing solutions. Most of the major economic problems of our time are referred to in these essays. The starting point is growth, the obsession of governments in all parts of the world. The various chapters show the differences between the problems of Africa and western Europe and America, but also the common ground. Behind economic growth lies the development of science and modern technology, sufficiently important to warrant a section to itself. But the context of the whole is a world which is trying to celebrate a "World Development Decade," a world where rich and poor countries have to live together and help each other, and where problems between classes have become problems between nations. Thus a large part of the book is devoted to the relations between countries, between developed and developing, and to the massive dilemmas of international economic policy.

One of the virtues of this book is that it illustrates some of the concrete problems of particular countries and their national perspectives. It is therefore surprising that there are divergences of views, reflecting both differences among experts and differences of national and continental outlook. Thus, some of the problems of Holland, outlined so vividly by Prof. Thijsse, though similar to those of Britain, may seem remote to Africans, and the vivid

---

[8] Even the Roman Catholic Church, with its solidly based theological system of social ethics, has not worked out the full implications of modern trends, as the Abbé Houtart and M. Delobelle make clear.

pictures of South East Asia and the Arab world given by Mr. Espiritu and Mr. Nasir show us some of the peculiar problems of these areas. Not all in the West will agree with Professor Aluko's briefly sketched appraisal of western society. There are differences of emphasis on the role of government in economic planning. Though Professors Aluko and Sumiya stress the necessity for participation by the masses in economic plans, M. Gruson seems to show a rather French belief in economic technocracy, which Professor Cox from across the Atlantic might denounce as falling into the heresy of "Technocratism." Some readers may feel that M. Gruson overstates the possibilities of forecasting the future and limiting uncertainties. The imaginative forecasts of the future by Mr. Theobald, though worthy of consideration, would not by any means be universally accepted. Nor should we be wise to assume that in western Europe hours of work will fall to 20 hours per week in 20 years, as Prof. Thijsse suggests. However much we may disagree with these and other points of emphasis, it is important that Christians should know something of the debate that is going on in the world and, in particular, of the complex problems of world economic planning which various experts expound here so clearly.

It is not all disagreement and difference. Population problems are common to Holland, Britain and India. The proper use of technology is at stake everywhere, and with it the social and political framework that can make the best use of what God offers to men. Everywhere there is social change accompanying economic growth; everywhere there is the problem of the role of the state, the expert and the businessman. Agricultural problems are not a monopoly of the Common Market or of India, and the right balance of industrial investment is not easily achieved anywhere. Above all, everywhere large cities grow and the human environment in which families develop and men and women learn to become sons of God becomes more man-made and divorced from the traditional rhythms of nature. Large-scale organizations replace face-to-face groups; rational timekeeping and regulated leisure are substituted for the disorderly patterns of primitive agricultural societies; status is superseded by contract, custom by regulation or law. And men find new opportunities for wider responsibilities and abuses, as they become healthier, longer-lived, better educated and with more abundant means at their disposal.

These comments have touched on only a few of the issues which are raised in the chapters in this book and have neglected some of the most important, such as those of international economic relations. Readers will find other themes to stir their imaginations. It is to be hoped that the churches will thereby be aroused to deeper understanding and concern, for the issues raised here affect the daily lives of men everywhere. Even if Christians and the churches turn aside from economic growth as no concern of theirs, of one thing we can be sure—that God does not turn aside, because he cares for *all* the details of *all* men's lives.

PART I

ECONOMIC GROWTH
AND THE PROBLEM OF WELFARE

I

ECONOMIC GROWTH
AND WELFARE IN THE
INDUSTRIALIZED WEST

by PIETER KUIN (Netherlands)

Industry and Prosperity

STRICTLY speaking, an "industrial society" and a "prosperous society" are not necessarily the same. An agricultural society may be prosperous (as in parts of France, Denmark and Holland) and an industrial society may be poor (as in some areas of Europe between the two world wars).

Yet industry and prosperity do ultimately go together, because industrial production puts power in the hands of man; thus he can use nature's gifts with less effort and more efficiently. In a prosperous economy fewer and fewer people have to work on the land to produce food for the entire population, because they have at their disposal not only mechanical power but the advantages of scientific developments and modern methods of management. The labor released from the land is absorbed most readily by manufacturing

31

industries and then by service industries. The road to prosperity leads from the land via industry to services.

Statistics on the deployment of people engaged in production bear this out. In the West, countries with a low level of development have a high percentage of workers in agriculture, those with a medium level a high percentage of workers in industry, and those with the highest level a high percentage of workers in services. The last ten or twelve years in particular have seen a rapid fall in the percentage of those engaged in agriculture, and a significant rise in those in the service industries; workers in manufacturing industries show a slight percentage decrease, although their actual number may still be rising slowly. The explanation of this is the same as for agriculture: with more power available, the per-man output of the industrial population and workers is released to supply services; for example, banking, insurance, transport or education and the arts, recreation, sports and travel facilities.

The terms "industrial" and "prosperous" may thus be interchangeable, especially in the early stages of economic growth; later, while industry remains important, services provide more employment. At the same time, the increasingly affluent nation can permit itself the luxury of working less and less: shorter working days, longer weekends, more generous holidays, more people not yet or no longer involved in the labor process. And all this, thanks to the power in the hands of man.

The Stages of Prosperity. Although prosperity might in the last analysis be measured by the number of leisure hours possible with a given level of production, we are accustomed to use the criterion of the average per capita national income. This is a rather rough and ready method. For instance, it disregards the self-suppliers: a nation consisting largely of self-sufficient family units is statistically poor however productive the soil. Nor does it measure such factors as leisure time and the degree of security and mutual aid that a community may offer its members. Nevertheless, it is still the best standard of international comparison, provided the official exchange rates are corrected as in the following comparison based on purchasing power parity.[1]

Estimated Average per Capita National Income in 1964
(£ Sterling)

United States	875	France	445
Sweden	550	Netherlands	410
Great Britain	490	Austria	330
Germany	485		

Obviously the prosperity level varies greatly even among advanced countries. Austria is only half as prosperous as Sweden, and France as the United States. Even countries seemingly as similar as the Netherlands and Britain show an important disparity. Underdeveloped countries such as Trinidad or Uruguay bear the same relation to the Netherlands or Austria as do the latter to the United States or Sweden. How misleading it is to make simple comparisons between the "prosperous" industrialized countries and the "poor" developing countries!

What is more, there is inequality within every nation, and the criterion of the average income makes part of the population seem far better off than they really are. The American government's "War on Poverty" has revealed that one-fifth of the population of the United States lives in poverty—by American standards. Other calculations set the figure at one-third. Some years ago a precise calculation in Holland showed that an average city family of four needed a weekly wage of about 100 Guilders merely to insure the bare necessities. The 1959 taxation statistics disclosed that about one-third of such families had this minimum income or less, though some may have had small untaxed earnings in addition.

---

[1] The official rate of exchange (parity) between the U. S. dollar and sterling is $2.80 to the £. However, $2.80 will buy less in the U. S. A. than £1 in England. If one needed, say, $3.11 to buy in the U. S. A. what £1 would buy in England, then the purchasing power parity would be £1 = $3.11.

Though no absolute distinction can be made between "too little," "sufficient" and "ample," since these vary from nation to nation and from time to time, it may be said that the income structure in most of the "prosperous" countries is more or less as follows:

25 to 30 per cent of the population live at or below the socially acceptable subsistence level;

50 per cent, approximately, have an income accepted as normal and adequate;

20 to 25 per cent are prosperous; the percentage of really wealthy is very low.

Even in the advanced countries prosperity does not increase very fast. Though the gross national product may show substantial annual increases, these are partly offset by (a) inflation which makes growth seem more rapid than it actually is in terms of real income; and (b) the growth in the population which increases the number sharing the product.

This explains, for instance, why it took Holland sixty years (from 1900 to 1960) to double the real per capita income. Progress has been more rapid since 1950, and the income of the working classes has, of course, risen more than the average, but growth is still gradual.

Between 1953 and 1960, Germany's growth was exceptional— about 6 per cent per annum—but in the other industrial European countries the annual increase in the prosperity level was about 3 per cent, and in the United States only 1½ per cent. Since 1960 the rate of growth in Germany has slowed down; in the U. S. A. it has speeded up. At the present time the material standard of living of the average resident of an advanced European or American country is rising by 2 or 3 per cent per annum.

Evaluating the Rise in Prosperity. In the light of all this there seems to be no reason for the Christian churches to be perturbed about increasing affluence in the western world. We are not witnessing a sudden explosion of prosperity; yet, many Christians deplore the ardent pursuit of material wealth, the status seeking, the tendency to take for granted high rewards for little effort, to spend freely and to covet what one cannot (yet) afford.

These views reflect both relevant and irrelevant reasoning. Those concerned often belong to the professional classes whose position in the social structure has declined considerably in the last fifty years. Their salaries have lagged behind, taxes have gone up, domestic help has become unobtainable, tradesmen are no longer helpful and the working classes no longer polite. They see the prosperity of others advancing more quickly than their own, and many have become embittered. Churchmen who write on social subjects cannot always rise above such feelings, and often criticize the prosperity of others or salve their pride with theories of a new asceticism.

Another motivation for such views is the Puritan tradition of some of our churches. They are prone to that austerity, zeal for work and thrift, which are at best secondary Christian virtues, as compared with devotion, charity and purity of heart, and forget that they were cherished by the middle classes because from these virtues they derived their greatness. Neither the aristocracy nor the working class attaches a particular moral or religious value to such qualities.

Other incidental factors also incline people to take a negative view of prosperity. One is historical. Many people unconsciously gauge present conditions by those of the 1930's and are dismayed at the casual way in which the present comparative affluence is taken for granted. They do not realize that in a way this prosperity is more normal than the want and insecurity of the Great Depression. There is also a monetary factor. The decline in the value of money makes all growth seem greater than it is. Dad used to earn four pounds a week; his son now earns sixteen. In terms of real purchasing power this may be one-and-a-half times as much, but it seems like four times. The esthetic factor leads a lot of older people to feel that the very substantial discretionary purchasing power that young workers have in the years during which they are on adult pay and not yet married is not always used with good taste.

From the viewpoint of social ethics all this is totally irrelevant. Those who criticize the prosperity of others (no one thinks his own is very great) should ask themselves whether their judgment is not distorted by these historical, monetary or esthetic factors.

Yet the churches may have some reason for anxiety. The acquisitive instinct, formerly confined to comparatively small groups, has taken hold of the masses, and leaves little room for more spiritual influences. The good life holds greater attractions than eternal life. The hypertrophy of material motives—understandable in the poor and destitute—has not disappeared with the coming of prosperity, but has changed in substance and shape. People are enslaved not only by their income, but by the work they have to do to get it. In the past people toiled for essentials; many now toil for the superfluous, the coveted luxury as yet unattained. Though toil is less arduous than in the past, it takes up no less time and attention.

The churches have long seen the dangers of both poverty and plenty, drawing on the wisdom of the simple, unlettered man whose prayer has been preserved through the ages:

Give me neither poverty nor riches;
Feed me with the bread of my modest allotment [2]

Lest I be full and deny Thee and say, Who is the Lord?
or lest I be poor and steal and take the name of my God in vain
(Proverbs 30:8,9).

Yet the churches have no reason to condemn the gradual rise in prosperity in the more affluent countries as such. Put to good use,

---

[2] This is a literal translation of the words of the Dutch Statenbijbel. The English Authorized Version has "food convenient for me." The essence of the matter is that poverty evokes covetousness and despair, riches arrogance and skepticism. In neither is there room for the life of the soul.

36

such growth can liberate from care and want those who live at or below the acceptable minimum level. They too may then experience at last the joy of having a little more breathing space. Moreover, all governments in this part of the world with any sense of social responsibility have a list of unfulfilled and most commendable aspirations: better provision for widows, orphans, the aged and disabled, the improvement of health care and education, the furtherance of cultural activities, and so on. An increasing national income can make possible their gradual fulfillment. Of course, this can also be achieved by a more radical redistribution of the present income. There is ample room for this in some western countries (though nowhere is inequality so great as in the underdeveloped world); but the countries with the greatest sense of social responsibility (and whose lists of aspirations are the longest) have already made a fairly thorough redistribution of national income: in these countries the most prosperous quarter of the population annually hands over 20 per cent to 50 per cent of its income to the community in direct taxes. The screw could of course be turned a little further, but ultimately this produces social stress and yields much less than the steady growth of the national product which is, moreover, the main, if not the only source of aid to underdeveloped countries.

The Nature of Our Social Problems

Despite our acceptance of the need for economic growth, we cannot say that all is well in the advanced countries. But it is not always possible to indicate the "actual cause" of the difficulties and it is certainly wrong to attribute all ills to economic growth. This would be an outdated Marxist oversimplification. The loss of established moral values, the changed relationships between the generations and the sexes, the growth of a purely pragmatic attitude to life and the paling of ideals and expectations have made their imprint on our times just as have the mechanization of production

37

and the rise in prosperity. The deepest needs and the worst ailments of society are spiritual, not economic or social. Some recent press notices confirm this. It is estimated that in Italy there are a million cases of intentional abortion each year, resulting in the premature death of 40,000 women; in Britain the spread of venereal diseases among young people is becoming alarming, as is the number of suicides in Sweden and of mental patients in the United States (and none of these are limited to the mentioned countries); throughout the western world the sales of tranquilizers and "pep pills" are reaching phenomenal proportions; alcoholism is increasing especially among young people, and crimes of violence continue. These are not "problems of economic growth"—or not primarily so. Aimlessness, boredom, erosion of traditional values and the lack of new ones—in brief, spiritual nihilism which may be seen as the common denominator of these phenomena—have their roots in strata that lie deeper than those of economic or social life.

It may be somewhat forced, therefore, to link the problems of the western society with the phenomenon of economic growth, for secularism and spiritual nihilism play at least an equal part. However, it may be useful to define and examine some of our present-day social problems as side-effects of economic growth.

Changes in Working Life

From Agriculture to Industry. Economic growth involves, in the first place, the migration of people from agriculture to industry. Modernization of agriculture permits this transition to take place without imperiling food supplies. Agriculture is abandoned by small farmers and growers who have to give up the battle, by their sons who lack the funds to start a large and well-equipped farm of their own, and by farm workers made redundant by machinery.

The loss of economic independence and a familiar pattern of life

38

has caused distress, but there are positive effects as well. The modernization of agriculture relieves those who continue farming, from much physical exertion, and makes possible a rapid improvement in both the quantity and quality of their produce. Small farmers and growers, whose struggle for survival in difficult times in the past often ended up in bankruptcy, can now usually get a good price for their land and find a steady job in industry. Farm workers have always been paid badly, suffered from seasonal unemployment and sometimes from the survivals of feudal servitude. The nature of their work does not on the whole create any close bonds between farm workers and the soil; there is nothing very romantic about digging or hoeing someone else's field from six in the morning to six at night. Industrial work is usually lighter and better paid, and provides more security, more social contact and greater freedom.

However, the two problems associated with the release of agricultural labor through modernization require the full attention of the churches and all social workers: the unemployment that arises if industry does not immediately absorb the displaced workers, and the difficulties experienced by the rural family in adjusting to urban life.

Technological unemployment of rural workers is not widespread. In most advanced countries, at least in Europe, the exodus from agriculture receives its main impetus through recruitments of people by industry. But in a period of industrial depression, or one in which industry is introducing labor-saving machinery, the rural unemployed who move to the towns may look for work in vain. Such people should be given help in the form of occupational training or retraining, the opportunity to emigrate or jobs in service industries.

Rural families who migrate to the towns because work is available have a much better start. Even so, the transition may be difficult. They do not know their way around and may suffer because of ignorance or ingenuousness. Many are lonely. The men have opportunities to make new acquaintances in factories and offices, but the women have to sort things out for themselves, often without help from anyone, and their success or failure may be decisive for the adjustment and re-establishment of the entire family. Young men and women who move from country to town alone face the most difficult transition of all. Not only is their loneliness hard to bear; it may have disastrous consequences. Organizations which try to provide for them sometimes put them off by their reputation (merited or unmerited) of being old-fashioned and straight-laced. Many people might find greater help from personal contact or the warmth of a friendly family. Could not the churches in conjunction with employers and social service agencies do more to care for newcomers, both families and individuals? Should there not be some system by which volunteers in the cities could be informed about newcomers so that they could trace them, welcome them and offer them practical assistance?

From Manual Work to Automation. Automation is a catchword of our time. It has not yet had such drastic results as did the introduction of the steam engine or electricity. Fundamentally, the consequences of automation are the same as those of mechanization: more power in the hands of man. But power of a special kind —power to control machines and, should they go wrong, to correct them.

For the factory worker, traditional mechanization means lighter work, higher speed, greater monotony, more noise. Good factory management tries to abate the noise, and the workers themselves make the requisite objections to speeding up. That leaves lighter work and greater monotony: Boredom is substituted for fatigue. There are exceptions to this; for example, men who work with a machine (such as lathe operators, truck drivers and compositors) derive a certain satisfaction from it. Engineers and fitters have little reason to oppose mechanization. It is even recognized that the bad name of the conveyor belt, which has created simple repetitive work, has arisen because intellectuals have projected their own aversion to such work onto others. If the surroundings are pleasant and the pay good, many take the monotony in their stride, while they think and talk about other things. Former farmworkers are used to monotony; they object to the speed and noise. But no factory consists solely of conveyor belts, and workers can, to a certain extent, be assigned to the work that suits them best.

Automation eliminates much routine work, including that of the conveyor belt, and provides employment for various categories of highly skilled workers and managerial employees. The man whose work in an automated department consists largely of dial watching finds himself in a new situation: light, monotonous work that *demands* constant attention. It is for the industrial psychologists to find suitable people for this and to regulate their work so that they do not become bored.

From the social-ethical point of view, mechanization and automation produce certain problems. The first is redundancy. It is said that in the United States some 200,000 workers become redundant every year owing to the introduction of improved machines. This figure must of course be seen in its true perspective: it is less than 0.3 per cent of the total working population of about 70 million. For years, the number of unemployed in the United States has been fairly stable at the high level of about 4 million. Their poverty and bleak existence are a pathetic paradox in a prosperous country and an earnest warning to every responsible person; but it is doubtful whether automation is primarily to blame. Highly developed industrial countries in Europe, such as Sweden, Britain and Germany, also have automation and yet there is a shortage of labor. This may, of course, be a temporary phase, but it is true that the influence of technological change can, to a large extent, be counteracted by changes in economic policy.

If demand is backed by sufficient purchasing power and working hours are adequately reduced, a quantitative equilibrium can always be achieved in spite of automation. The discrepancy in the United States is probably primarily qualitative: Many of the un-

41

employed are unsuitable for vacancies that may exist. Facilities for training and for retraining, improved employment agency services, assisted migration and the systematic development, with government aid, of remote regions lacking capital should be the main remedies. Technological unemployment should not be seen as an essential characteristic of a highly developed industrial society. It is more likely to indicate a fundamental economic disequilibrium (for instance through currency overvaluation) or a lack of government planning and development. Moreover, prosperous nations can now work fewer and fewer hours without lowering their standard of living. In fact, they must do so if they are to avoid unemployment for part of their population.

Another important question involving social ethics is that of the value of human labor in modern industrial enterprises. From ancient times, work has had a dual character: burden and pleasure; punishment and privilege. Work is indispensable, not only for material prosperity but also for man's mental health. As a form of self-expression, as a sport, or as a means of blowing off steam it usually gives satisfaction. But what should be the ethical approach to the boredom that has replaced fatigue for many people in the mechanical age?

Work as a burden, as effort, as achievement, as a source of satisfaction, has a certain dignity. But as a source of boredom it has none. It degenerates into a means to an end, a necessary evil. Even though, of course, the social contacts and rhythm of life it provides are of great value, this is not enough. Something must be done to restore man's pride in his work, for instance by giving him a share in the collective achievement of the unit to which he belongs.

From Workshop to Office. Manual workers no longer form the largest social group in an industrial economy: the white-collar workers are catching up, and even overtaking them. In western Europe before the war, one out of every five employed persons was a white-collar worker; now there are almost one out of three. In the most highly developed countries there are as many, if not more, white-collar than blue-collar workers. The main causes are the expansion of service industries and the civil service, and specialization in management. These have brought an increase in the number of office workers, draughtsmen, supervisors and the like, while mechanization in the factories was reducing the number of manual workers or making possible increased production with the same number.

Human problems in an office are quite different from those in a factory. The factory worker's primary concern is the kind of work he does, his working conditions, his pay and the way he is treated. These are important to the office worker also, but he pays more heed to his position in the chain of command, his status, and especially his prospects. This is because the structure of office organization is infinitely more differentiated, and the ladder has far more steps to climb. Moreover, in offices and marketing services reorganizations are more common than in factories. Objectively, they are attempts to achieve maximum efficiency each time circumstances change. Subjectively, they bring prospects of rapid promotion or acute risks of demotion for those they affect. Lastly, the higher one climbs the greater the element of personal competition. The most coveted positions are few in number, and the candidates more numerous.

In addition to personal competition, there is competition between firms, state enterprises or ministries, or even between departments within an organization. The anxiety over status, promotion, demotion and competition which haunts the white-collar workers and is almost unknown among manual workers, is incompatible with a religious attitude to life. What can the churches do to help relieve this anxiety, and what should they ask of leaders of business firms and large organizations in both the private and the public sphere?

From Home to Job. The employment of married women is not exclusively a feature of the industrial economy. In some primitive

43

communities women work in the fields or as traders. In less primitive ones they work as charwomen or seamstresses in other people's homes. But their mass employment in factories, offices and shops with their rigid routines and regular hours is comparatively new, and varies in extent from country to country. It is estimated that in the Netherlands not more than 15 per cent of married women are employed; in France it is about 50 per cent. As wage levels rise, such work becomes more attractive. The higher the family's material ambitions—and the more attainable they become—the greater the incentive will be. The greater social recognition and better training women receive, the bigger the opportunities become. The tighter the labor market, the greater the employers' demand. This trend has been beneficial for many women who have found fulfillment in interesting work which widened their experience of life. However, there are also less fortunate effects as well, especially on young children who need their mother's loving care and who may suffer if the rhythm of separation and reunion with her is dictated entirely by the harsh demand of employment.

May not the churches demand, in the interests of family life and mental health, that married women be given an opportunity to adapt their outside working hours to the family routine until their children reach adolescence? Even this age limit may be too low.

There is one other danger: that young couples will put off raising a family in order to continue to benefit from their double earnings. They can be heard calmly debating whether to buy a new car or have a baby! Even a church that fully accepts family planning cannot approve this distortion of values. Without being meddlesome, the churches should impress upon their young members and the world that a good family life is a gift from heaven with which no material wealth can compare.

Problems in the Sphere of Consumption

Widening Receding Horizons. We have already defended "industrial man" against the criticism that he is becoming prosperous too quickly. His three per cent more elbowroom a year is not exorbitant, *provided* that it does not cause him—to quote the Bible— to lose his soul. This can happen if affluence gets a hold on him. Anyone who intentionally or unintentionally puts material progress before all else is "losing his soul." In the past the nobility were reproached for their greed; later it was the bourgeois merchants and manufacturers who conquered the world; and now it is the workers' turn. All these reproaches are justifiable: greed seems to be a human characteristic regardless of class. The proletariat of yesterday are the middle classes of today.[3] The prosperous industrial worker now aims at getting a car, a home of his own and better home equipment—all typical aspirations of the lower middle class not so long ago: perfectly respectable aspirations, but of very relative value to one's spiritual life; questionable even, if they turn life into a grim struggle. It is not necessarily the car, the home or the expensive equipment that does this, but the striving for things one cannot afford. The better off the family becomes, the more its perspectives change: winter holidays, a motor launch, a second car and a weekend house join the list. Overtime has to be worked, spare-time earnings sought, and the wife has to go out and get a job. Greed takes over and whips up his steeds to draw every last ounce of effort from them.

What makes so many people live just beyond their means? It is popular among intellectuals to blame advertising or easy payments. Neither is completely blameless, but two deeper causes could be indicated, the first very old, the second more recent. The older is man's need to adjust to his social environment. This is not typical

---

[3] F. Zweig, *The Worker in an Affluent Society.*

only of the industrial society: the strictest social rules and most rigid conformism exist in the old agrarian village communities. When prosperity begins to be evident in a person's environment, he feels a compulsion to show it, too, to avoid being an exception. The newer factor is the competitive nature of our society and the emotional insecurity this causes. It gives many people a conscious or unconscious need to prove to themselves that they have made a success of their lives. In a world where success is measured by external standards, the proof has to be visible. Among officials, the criterion is rank or title; among others it is often obvious prosperity, of which the most common evidence is perhaps living in a "nice" neighborhood. There is also of course the very human consideration that these possessions provide great enjoyment and once they become attainable they exert a fascination. There is nothing wrong with these things nor with the enjoyment of them. It is the hypertrophy of desire and compulsion to acquire possessions to the neglect of helping one's fellowmen and with a disregard for the inner life for which little place is left, against which the church must protest.

It must take a stronger stand against the suggestion of advertisers that more and better consumption is the main object of life and assert emphatically that there are better things that *are* worth living for.

Should our social and economic order be changed to eliminate at least the avoidable causes of greed, rivalry, nervous tension and doubt? The difficulty is that the economic growth, so necessary to eliminate remnants of poverty and permit help to other nations, is partly dependent upon competition and the constant renewal of incentives. A more relaxed approach would be easy in a stagnating economy, but not in an expanding one. Before seeking a way out of this dilemma, we shall look at some of the anomalies in our prosperous society, which prove that all is not well.

Poverty Amid Plenty. A paradox of economic growth in the advanced countries is the persistence of poverty among some groups

46

of the population despite the rise in the general level of prosperity. We have estimated that 20 to 25 per cent of the citizens of the more prosperous countries live at or below the socially acceptable subsistence level. Both "socially acceptable subsistence level" and "poverty" are relative concepts. In the western world even the poor usually eat more than one meal a day and the socially acceptable subsistence usually includes a reasonable home with two or three rooms for a family of four to six. In comparison with many other countries, of course, this is luxury.

Nevertheless, even in the welfare state some people live under wretched conditions. Even though their physical subsistence is practically assured, the lack of money to buy clothes, to heat or furnish their homes properly or to buy anything but bare necessities ought not to be tolerated in a land of comparative affluence. The worst hardship is found in the working or lower middle classes where the breadwinner has become an invalid, or died, or left, and the wife has to provide for herself and the children with an inadequate pension.

Such relative poverty results from flaws in the social welfare system. Basically, the remedy is not difficult to indicate: increase the contributions of the fit and employed in order to raise the benefits especially for families who need prolonged assistance through no fault of their own. Whether the cost is defrayed through social insurance contributions or government grants (borne by the taxpayers) is of secondary importance.

The wage level in a prosperous and developing economy is constantly rising, in terms not only of money but of real purchasing power. This affects the underprivileged in a number of ways. Services become constantly dearer, and the rise is not offset by increased productivity as in the manufacturing industries. For many elderly and invalid people a broken radio or television, or a leak in the plumbing creates an almost insurmountable problem. The well-paid skilled serviceman—after long delay—may turn up with a mate to hand him his tools, but in most cases he leaves a bill

47

which upsets the very modest family budget for months. A nurse, a masseuse or night attendant is quite beyond the reach of this group. Old and disabled people who do not know their way about the social services often just don't bother.

This problem is not automatically solved as economic growth proceeds: on the contrary, the gap between the employed and the no longer employed becomes ever wider. Two kinds of solutions, institutional and personal, are possible, and may have to be used in combination. The welfare state should either: (a) link benefits for the underprivileged and handicapped not only to the cost of living but also to the wage level of skilled workers; or (b) authorize the social services to make special payments to cover such expenditures (this is current practice in various countries). Solution (a) would probably cost more but would be more equitable, because the benefits of (b) would go mainly to the practiced assistance seekers.

The more personal solution puts love of one's fellows into practice. The churches already are doing much through relief work, but the supplementing of state financial assistance is not enough. Greater personal attention and helpfulness should be encouraged. Cannot young people in villages and towns form a voluntary corps to make minor repairs and perform other personal services for those who cannot afford to pay the prevailing prices? As long as there is a shortage of skilled workers, there can hardly be any objection. And, perhaps, some of these workers would join the corps to give expression to their gratitude for their own rising prosperity.

The Plight of the Elderly. In many countries the statutory old-age pensions are not enough to live on, especially if the cost of living is steadily rising as it usually is. A prosperous society should protect its old people from want. They used to be dependent on relatives, which was often resented by both parties. This no longer happens in a society in which the extended family is more and more breaking up. Supplementary company pensions and an ade-

48

quate basic statutory pension based on the cost of living are the most obvious remedies.

Fortunately, not all old people are poor or lonely. Many have built up an adequate pension or other savings during their working years. Many have children, grandchildren and friends who keep them in touch with the world. But their situation in a prosperous society still requires special attention.

In the first place, their numbers are increasing as life expectancy rises. In the least developed western countries, people over 65 represent about 7 per cent of the population. In the most highly developed, the proportion is now 12 per cent and will probably increase to 13 or 14 per cent. Thus a normal west European city of a million inhabitants has over 100,000 people of 65 or older. Recent research has shown that about one-sixth of these, say 17,000, are socially isolated; they lack sufficient contacts to give them an interest in life or to ask for help in case of need. Seventeen thousand in every big city—and so many priests and Levites who pass by on the other side!

It is estimated that 2,000 of the 100,000 in this city need full-time nursing care for chronic physical ailments and 1,500 for mental illness. Many of these 3,500 never receive this full-time nursing, and die before their time. The waiting lists are too long, the facilities too limited. The shortage of houses for the many young people wanting to marry, the demands for factories and offices in a booming economy, the high wage and shorter working hours in industry which drains off nursing staff—these factors explain the shortage but do not justify it.

The new science of geriatrics has helped to bring this burning problem to our attention. If it is to be solved, our concern and sense of responsibility must be translated into concrete terms. The community must simply find the energy to make the necessary sacrifices to create the required facilities. The shortage of nursing staff in some countries has been overcome by a blend of better working conditions and the correct psychological approach. This is a field

in which the greater power in our hands can accomplish something by making faster building possible and providing labor-saving
methods for household chores, but this is still not enough. The
lack of care and human contact cannot be remedied by mechanization. Only love of one's fellows will help, and without it even the
most prosperous economy is worthless. The way in which a civilization provides for its old people is one of the criteria by which
its moral values can be assessed.

Problems Arising from the Social Order

Urbanization. The concentration of millions of people in very
large cities faces the churches—and any group that seeks to reach
human beings as individuals—with very grave problems. Some of
these are of a practical nature. Where do we find the resources to
build churches in all these sprawling new communities, and where
do we find ministers to serve them? Even if village churches are
less full than they used to be—which is not the case in all western countries—they can neither be moved nor abandoned. This
new situation demands tremendous sacrifices and efforts from the
churches in the West. Fortunately, there is a new awareness of
the needs, and in most countries the mistakes and omissions of the
recent past are likely to be avoided.

But there are other problems of a more spiritual nature. New
city dwellers free themselves from old patterns of thought and behavior and, although they find more and better schools for their
children, a greater choice of jobs, more varied and interesting
things to do and enjoyment in leisure, many are lonely, bewildered,
and find it difficult to put down roots. City lights attract the youth
who are bored or disappointed in their work, and they seek the
excitement and companionship of gangs. The native city dwellers
are by tradition skeptical, perhaps even cynical, suspicious of authority, not easily impressed, and most individualistic. All this

50

makes cities—and, in particular, large ones—grounds for spiritual nihilism.

The churches should get in step with all those who are working to decentralize towns, to establish industries outside large cities, to clear slums and to improve recreational facilities. They should seek new ways of attracting people who do not know life in a Christian community, by speaking in contemporary language, and by renewing the meaning of Christian community in the modern city. Thus, they might begin to make inroads in the vast turbulent mass of indifference that is a modern city. St. Paul managed to make himself heard by the Athenians and made his mark in Rome—which was a much tougher proposition than most of our churches are now facing, even in the very large cities of our time.

The Dynamic Economy. Contrary to a common and convenient assumption, economic progress is not automatic. Rising national incomes and personal prosperity levels are the consequence of incessant efforts of expansion and renewal. Governments may plan and steer the economy, but the motive power has to come from enterprises. Whether they are private or state enterprises matters little in this connection—they alone provide, expand and improve the social product. Three kinds of apparatus are available for this: research and development, organization and production methods, and marketing. The first penetrates further and further into the potentialities and uses of matter, the second is constantly seeking to eliminate waste, and the third is continually analyzing present and future demand.

From an economic point of view, there is nothing against the incessant seeking for new ways of using materials and new means of satisfying consumers—on the contrary. But does not this agressive and incessant activity represent a psychological burden for producers and spoil the consumers' peace of mind? To a certain extent it does. But we must be realistic and make a distinction between institutional and personal rivalry.

Institutional rivalry is largely a sport, which provides great satisfaction. To be keyed up is not necessarily unpleasant; players and spectators have discovered this through the ages. In spite of all the bad things said about the tension created by present-day competition, it must be emphasized that, without it, thousands of managers of businesses and other organizations would be far less happy in their work. To deprive them of this happiness by replacing competition with controlled monopolies would be to endanger economic growth. It can, of course, be argued that a slow-down in economic growth is not too high a price to pay for the decrease of tension which a controlled monopolistic society would bring about. The predominant leader in such a society is not the entrepreneur but the technocrat. Overtenseness is not one of his weaknesses, but bureaucracy is, and this causes frustration. From an ethical or psychological viewpoint, one is not much better than the other.

More serious than institutional rivalry is the personal rivalry inside large enterprises and organizations. The results of its use as an incentive to produce maximum effort are, on the whole, outweighed by its detrimental effects on people's minds. It is the responsibility of managers of business enterprises and heads of government services, guided by psychologists and encouraged by religious leaders, to remove the anxiety about possible dismissal or not making the grade and to encourage cooperation and communication.

Modern personnel management is evolving the means for this: effective selection, career planning, timely appraisal, placement according to aptitude, frankness regarding potentialities and limitations, and security of tenure. It is important to take contractual measures against arbitrary treatment and unjustified dismissal, but it is more important still to pervade management from the top with a spirit of respect and consideration for fellowmen. Capacity for teamwork and ability to do a good job without creating an atmosphere of tension should be regarded as among the greatest merits of young managers.

In addition—and this is more difficult—the importance of social success should receive less emphasis by society as a whole. Democratization of society in its widest sense would seem to be the solution. This may mean abolishing social and financial barriers to cultural participation, a struggle against all obsolete forms of homage to wealth and rank and emphasis upon the aristocracy of the soul.

The churches must consider how they can put Christianity's ancient message of freedom, simplicity and joy into such understandable and relevant terms that it will once again appeal to and liberate the agitated, nervous and often unhappy people of this industrial civilization.

Institutional Power and Responsibility. In our age, economic growth receives its main impetus from the research, production and marketing organizations of large enterprises. Though smaller private initiatives are by no means to be underrated, technological progress in particular comes about through organized research and development teams which work with very expensive equipment. Thus, our economic life is becoming increasingly the setting for a contest—sometimes a struggle—between very big businesses.

But concentration is not taking place only in industry and commerce. Groupings are also becoming larger in the social and political sphere. Employers' federations and trade unions largely determine the wage level; farmers' unions try to influence the government's agricultural policy; and there are organizations of retailers and small craftsmen. The professions organize for the purpose of contact with other groupings (the medical profession vis-à-vis health insurance organizations, for instance); newspapers and periodicals merge into bigger and bigger combines; powerful corporations control the mass entertainment and educational media— radio, television and cinema; and even the universities become centers of social power owing to their size and selective procedures.

The man who proves his ability to play a leading part in the life of these large groupings thereby acquires, whether he will act or not, an important measure of power, especially in his own sphere. Without it, he cannot act as an administrator and, without administration, society would become chaotic.

It is clear from this that the idea that all power in society is vested in the government and that parliament is the only decision-making body is a great oversimplification. The same is true of the view that the political parties are the only bodies which mold political opinion or the only legitimate custodians of major social interests.

The defense of interests and convictions by free organizations is an inalienable part of our democratic society. However, it gives rise to several problems. The first is that of pressure groups. This has become a popular term mainly through the influence of American literature, and it suggests improper methods of influencing the public and persons in public office. It cannot be claimed that such methods are never used, but we must guard against blindly accepting the criticism as universally valid. Improper methods are sometimes used because there is no scope for proper ones. The solution is to route consultation between the authorities and the custodians of sectional interests (which may be most respectable) via recognized institutions. Some countries have committees, councils or federations, to channel such consultations. Democracy requires that the light of publicity be shed on this structure. This is the only way to get rid of the unpleasant associations aroused by the term "pressure group."

Another problem concerns the intellectual and moral integrity of all who work in big organizations. There is much popular prejudice about this partly engendered by biased literature. It is certainly not true that all big organizations deliberately mold their members into a standard conformist pattern or undermine their intellectual independence, although systematic recruitment and training methods may tend to create a common outlook and approach. But large organizations also have to prepare those who are to succeed to the top positions, and at that level conformist figures with no independence would fail to stand up to the stresses and problems involved in managing large interests.

The problem goes deeper. A man who has been battling for a cause for many years is liable to put it before everything else. This is true not only of business executives, but of trade union leaders, heads of farmers' organizations, directors of broadcasting companies, people propagating some particular idea, politicians and local officials. Identification with the cause is essential for good leadership, but unquestioning identification is a danger to personal integrity. It is also a danger to society when it involves people possessing great powers as leaders of big organizations or groupings. If they make absolute values of the interests entrusted to them, society becomes a battleground—a jungle—where everyone fights everyone else. The alternative—an all-powerful state as the one power in society—is less attractive. The government may be described as the representative of the public interest, but it still consists of individuals who are no more proof against the moral dangers of absolute power than anyone else. And in an all-controlling state, their power becomes absolute because there is then no democratic control over a supertechnocratic administration.

But the modern, industrially developed society is neither a jungle inhabited by beasts of prey nor an all-powerful state. The power of all the institutional leaders, in both official and private spheres, is kept within certain limits, set not only by the power of other people but also by the law and codes of ethics and decorum. To a certain extent these codes are imposed upon the leaders of society by public opinion, but they also bear them in themselves, molded as they are by the moral traditions of their country's culture.

Nevertheless, Christians and all other responsible people need to be constantly on their guard. Institutional leadership is usually acquired by a combination of skill and zeal. Man has an almost boundless ability to identify his cause with the public interest and to regard the means of achieving it as ethical and proper. Wide publicity should be given to all matters concerning the welfare of the community, and leaders of large group interests—whether business firms or farmers', retailers', employers' or workers' organizations—should be held accountable for their activities.

In the final analysis, however, even this social control is inadequate because the increasing complexity of technical and economic problems requires that institutional managers have such specialized skill that they can be supervised only by people who possess equivalent skill. All the machinery would thus have to be duplicated and, besides, who would supervise the supervisors? Rules can be made regarding publicity and accountability, but it is equally important for leaders of society not to be constantly appealing to their sectional interests as absolute values but to see them in the context of a higher responsibility. Most of them are ready to subordinate their own interests to those of the nation if need be. Praiseworthy as this may be, however, it is hardly the ultimate in ethics; for sometimes the national interest is little better than collective self-interest. A different guiding principle is needed if, as we hope, the nation-state moves into the background in the next fifty years.

The question for the churches is whether—and, if so, how—they can help to build up a system of values that will help the leaders of society properly to safeguard the interests entrusted to them within the frame of a higher loyalty in which opposing interests are reconciled and essentially relative things are not treated as absolute. The churches can do this only by discussion with the leaders of society and by acquainting themselves with their work and problems. Only in this way can the social ethics of Christianity again become relevant for those who bear responsibility for the economic, technical and social leadership of our industrial civilization.

Participation. Not all the problems of our time arise in the rarefied atmosphere of social leadership. One of the problems is that society has become so very complex that it has got beyond millions of people and they feel they are outside it. This is the modern industrial version of Disraeli's "two nations"—no longer the rich and the poor, but the administrators and the administered, the initiated and the laymen, the insiders and the outsiders, the players and the spectators, the subjects and the objects, what have been called "the establishment" and "manipulated man." This division occurs equally in the collectivist and in the individualist society; and the manipulated mentality is not—as some industrial sociologists assume—confined to industrial workers. In the advanced countries, the social problem of our time is no longer poverty, nor even inequality (though this has not ended), but the lack of mass participation. It is reflected in apathy or irresponsible rebellion in organizations (including the trade union movement), a concentration on using one's own leisure time for one's own profit, profound skepticism about politics, distrust of the motives of the leaders of the economy and society, and withdrawal into the circle of one's own private life. The feeling of the masses that there is an unbridgeable gap between "them" and "us" is a threat to civilization. It leads readily to a spiritual nihilism, of which hooliganism is only one of the mildest forms.

Some racial reformers and part of the trade union movement in western Europe seek the solution of this problem in giving the workers more say in management. There is a case for this as an outward recognition of the emancipation of the working class. But there is also a danger of high-pitched expectations being shattered. Management has two aspects—external and internal. On external policy—market operations, introduction of new products, relations with suppliers and customers, competition, new capital issues— management consultation with joint committees or work councils can hardly be expected to have any helpful, or even psychologically valuable, result. Elected representative bodies of this kind lack the requisite skill. The management does not, of course, make all these decisions alone; but it consults only employees who can be expected to have specialized knowledge of the particular subject under consideration. However, on internal questions concerned with the regulation of work and working conditions, much can be gained by consultation between management and joint committees or works councils. Consultation with these bodies on important internal steps such as reorganizations helps to make the employees feel that their opinions count in matters that closely concern them. Some people expect little of this consultation, for they believe the workers are coming to look upon their jobs more and more as a means of subsistence, a necessary sacrifice to be made as painlessly, and as profitably, as possible. These people forget that nearly everyone is interested in the work he does and likes to be consulted about it. However, formal consultation in a joint committee is not enough: it is too remote from the individual employee. There is need to reform the mode of management at the working level. Instead of simply handing out orders, management from top to bottom should draw upon the employee's interest and sympathy to the full.

This does not solve the big problem of social indifference. Jointly with psychologists and educationists the churches must seek means whereby this great threat to the unity of our culture can be removed. These means are not to be found in working life alone—in the next century when the working week has been reduced to twenty-four hours, during the remaining 144 hours, there will have to be enough cohesion between the members of society to enable them to share the responsibilities they will then be called upon to bear.

There is a danger that in a prosperous world where most social problems have been solved people will live as strangers, each in his own private sphere, using the community as a means to an end—satisfied with his own health and prosperity and forgetting Agur's warning: "Lest I be full and deny thee and say, Who is the Lord?"

The future generations will still have much to do in helping the world's poorer nations. But within their own prosperous spheres the challenge may be just as great. They will have to "meet their fellowmen" on the spiritual level, give not of their money but of themselves; from their smooth-running society they will have to build a real community where no man need be lonely, tense or bewildered because his fundamental responsibility for others matches his own spiritual progress.

2

THE DYNAMICS OF ECONOMIC GROWTH IN THE DEVELOPING COUNTRIES

by S. A. ALUKO (Nigeria)

Income as a Measure of Economic Growth

ECONOMICS is the study of the production, consumption, distribution and exchange of goods and services which are desired by man. It deals essentially with why goods and services are produced, which ones are produced, with what techniques, by what economic organization, in what quantities, in what places, with what regularity and for whose eventual use.

Today most people in the world are poor and have not enough to eat. Many live in bad huts and houses, which are not large enough for their families. Others are poorly clad or have little or no clothing. There are not enough schools, hospitals, roads, factories and equipment to provide the goods and services they need. The question of how to produce more of these things for human use is called the problem of economic growth, and the rate at which the people are able and prepared to produce these things determines the dynamics of economic growth.

Economic growth is measured in terms both of the absolute aggregate supply of goods and services and also of the increase per capita in productivity.

If within five years, for instance, a worker doubles the quantity of yams, potatoes or rice which he produces in the same unit of time, the rate of growth in his productivity, whatever the cause, is appreciable. But it is not easy to compare the rate of growth between two or more countries, in terms of output in goods and services. Production possibilities vary from country to country as a result of climate, tastes, customs and natural resources. A ton of yams is not worth the same amount as a ton of potatoes or a ton of rice. Nor is a barrel of petroleum comparable with a hundredweight of gold or tin.

Such comparisons can be meaningful only when the values of the different commodities are expressed in money terms. A country may not find it easy to exchange its tin for the oil of another country, and such an exchange is usually made through the medium of money. So economic growth is usually calculated in units of money income per capita rather than in terms of goods and services.[1] The level of a country's income reflects its volume of production. It determines the purchasing power, the level of wages, and the general standard of living of the people, the number and the quality of houses and hospitals, the length of the roads and the volume of capital equipment that can be built.

Differences in Levels of Economic Growth

Though most people in the world are poor, underfed and badly housed, a few countries are rich. Table 1, showing the per capita

---

[1] There is no unanimity among economists as to the value of money-measurement of economic growth, in view of the wide variations in the purchasing power of money in different countries, or in the same country at different periods. In spite of its shortcomings, money-income measurement is gaining increased acceptance.

61

TABLE 1

Per Capita National Income of Selected Countries: 1961

Income	English Speaking and European Countries	Communist Countries	Latin American Countries	Middle East Countries	Asian Countries	African Countries
Over £300 or $840 High-Income Countries	United States £650 ($1820) Canada £595 ($1750) Sweden £450 ($1260) Switzerland £450 ($1260) Australia £430 ($1200) New Zealand £430 ($1200) Belgium £370 ($1040) Gt. Britain £370 ($1040) Norway £355 ($1000) W. Germany £350 ($980) France £350 ($980)	Nil	Nil	Nil	Nil	Nil
£100-299 $280-837 Inter-mediate Income Countries	Netherlands £285 ($800) Finland £270 ($760) Austria £250 ($700) Eire £200 ($560) Italy £175 ($490) S. Africa £130 ($364) Greece £120 ($336) Spain £105 ($295)	U.S.S.R. £240 ($675) E. Germany £200 ($560) Czechoslovakia £180 ($505) Poland £170 ($460) Hungary £140 ($395) Bulgaria £120 ($336) Poland £120 ($336) Roumania £120 ($336) Yugoslavia £110 ($310)	Venezuela £175 ($490) Puerto Rico £175 ($490) Argentina £140 ($395) Uruguay £125 ($350) Cuba £120 ($336) Jamaica £105 ($296) Chile £105 ($296) Mexico £102 ($290) Colombia £100 ($280) Panama £100 ($280) Brazil £100 ($280)	Israel £205 ($575) Lebanon £102 ($290)	Japan £150 ($425) Hongkong £110 ($310) Malaya £105 ($296)	Nil

62

TABLE 1 (continued)

Income	English Speaking and European Countries	Communist Countries	Latin American Countries	Middle East Countries	Asian Countries	African Countries
Below £100 or $280	Portugal £80 ($225)	Albania £80 ($225) N. Korea £30 ($84) N. Vietnam £30 ($84) China £25 ($70)	Ecuador £75 ($210) Dominican Republic £75 ($210) El Salvador £75 ($210) Guatemala £60 ($168) Nicaragua £60 ($168) Honduras £50 ($140) Peru £50 ($140) Paraguay £36 ($100) Haiti £32 ($90) Bolivia £31 ($87)	Turkey £65 ($186) Syria £50 ($140) Saudi Arabia £50 ($140) Iraq £45 ($126) Jordan £35 ($95) Iran £30 ($84)	Philippines £75 ($210) Ceylon £40 ($112) Formosa £40 ($112) S. Vietnam £35 ($95) S. Korea £35 ($95) Thailand £32 ($90) Indonesia £32 ($90) Cambodia £25 ($90) India £25 ($70) Pakistan £22 ($63) Burma £21 ($60) Afghanistan £20 ($58) Laos £18 ($52) Nepal £16 ($45)	Algeria £75 ($210) Rhodesia £55 ($155) Tunisia £50 ($140) Morocco £48 ($135) Ghana £48 ($135) Congo £35 ($95) Kenya £32 ($90) Liberia £30 ($84) Nigeria £30 ($84) Ethiopia £25 ($70) Sudan £25 ($70) Tanganyika £25 ($70) Uganda £22 ($62) Libya £22 ($62) Togoland £22 ($62) Dahomey £22 ($62) Ivory Coast £22 ($62) Nyasaland £20 ($56) Zanzibar £18 ($50)
Low-Income Countries						

Sources: United Nations Statistical Year Book 1962, Table 162, and other available statistics from individual countries.

income of one hundred independent countries, reveals the enormity of the income differentials. The ratio of the income of the richest country (United States) to that of the poorest country (Zanzibar), for instance, is more than thirty-two to one. When allowance is made for differences in the purchasing power of money within the different countries, and assuming that the general price level in the poorest countries is about a third of that in the richest countries, the ratio in real terms between the per capita income in the United States and Zanzibar is about ten to one.[2] It is also obvious from the table that the high-income countries, those with annual per capita incomes of over £300 or $840 per annum, are in western Europe, Australasia and North America, and that the poorest are found mainly in Latin America, Asia and Africa. Not a single country in Africa (with the exception of South Africa) is in the high- or intermediate-income range. The economies of the high-income countries have grown, and their problem is to sustain the economy rather than to make it grow. The economies of the intermediate-income countries are growing, and their problem is to discover how to accelerate the pace of growth so that they will gradually catch up with the high-income countries rather than sink back into poverty. The problem of the poor countries, with stagnant or declining economies, is how to "take off" on the road to growth, to overcome the resistance to steady development and to control the fluctuation of their modern economic sectors and the enclaves of enterprise so that they will proceed to the intermediate- and finally to the high-income stage.

Our main concern in this chapter is to discover what determines the dynamics of economic growth in the low-income countries of the world. The experiences and the problems of the intermediate- and high-income countries will be useful in this analysis.

---

[2] This ratio has no scientific basis. See, however, "Movement of Wholesale and Consumer Prices in Selected Countries," *U. N. Statistical Year Book*, 1962, Tables 160 and 161.

The Determinants of Economic Growth

What determines the rate at which a country is capable of building its economy? The first factor is the willingness and determination of the people or/and their leaders to discern and eliminate those conditions which hinder the proper functioning of their economies, and which are absent in those of the rich economies. These conditions are: a social and/or political structure that is incompatible with rapid economic and social change; a high proportion of the employed population engaged in primitive agriculture instead of in productive industry and trade; exports consisting mainly of foodstuffs and raw materials; very little money and real capital per head of the employed population; almost no savings by the large mass of the people and poor credit facilities to mobilize any available savings; high birth- and death-rates; low life expectancy; rudimentary education and a high degree of illiteracy; inadequate and crude communication and transportation facilities to assist trade and commerce; crude technology; little entrepreneurship and weak political and economic leadership.

Table 2 shows the supply of some of the measurable prerequisites for rapid growth in selected high-, intermediate- and low-income countries. It is obvious that the more developed, and therefore the richer, a country becomes, the lower the percentage of the working population that is employed in agriculture and the higher the percentage that is employed in industry and commerce; the higher the percentage of total national income that is saved and can, therefore, be invested in the production of further goods and services, the greater the provision for the mobilization of savings for further investment; the longer the life-span and, therefore, the productive period of the workers, the higher the level of literacy and technical competence, and the greater the provision of capital equipment to assist in further production of goods and services. When an economy is ill provided with all these factors of production, it remains poor. This is why economists say that "a country is poor because it is poor."

How can this vicious chain of poverty be broken, and a dynamic process created? Under what impulses can an essentially agricultural society begin the process of modernization? What social and political forces drive the process of growth forward along a straight path and sustain it once the process has begun?

The Indigenous Basis of Growth

Economic advance depends upon the willingness of large numbers of men, industrious, thrifty and shrewd men, to devote their time and energies to the acquisition of material things for themselves and their societies.

The idea that people should improve their social and economic status, and that in given circumstances, they can do it through their own efforts, must be spread among the leaders of society and, through them, to a large section of the population.

Far too little attention is devoted today to mobilizing indigenous forces behind the efforts to bring about economic growth. Large sections of the population in many nations which have multiyear Economic Development Plans, are not aware of their existence and purposes. In some cases, the plans result from the calculations and prognostications of foreign technical advisers, United Nations Agencies or foreign governments, cooperating with a few overworked and well-equipped local civil servants, and are presented to the leaders of the countries as what is thought to be good for them. There is no popular participation in their formulation and execution, and most of the economic and noneconomic activities of the people negate the very purposes of the plans. The projected rate of growth is never achieved, because of the lack of domestic cooperation. A good deal of time and effort is therefore wasted in activities which make little or no contribution to economic growth, because they are undertaken in an environment which is incompatible with advance or because they are imposed on people who have not been organized and conditioned for growth.[3]

In many of the underdeveloped countries, both political power and their meager wealth are a monopoly of a small minority. The masses are excluded from all incentives and means to improve themselves. Where they believe that the taxes they pay are spent for the comfort of a few, any public drive for local capital accumulation is defeated by massive tax evasion. Where the landlord takes most of the farm yield and lives indolently and luxuriously at the expense of his tenants, it is difficult to persuade them to work harder and to use more modern production techniques, so that two crops can be grown where one grew before, since they know that improved yields will increase the earnings of the landlord disproportionately to their own.

Also it is idle to imagine that good economic plans can be formulated or executed without a strong, efficient and determined indigenous leadership. Rapid growth did not occur in Britain until Parliament curtailed the absolutism of the monarch. It did not come about rapidly in the United States until an American continental government supplanted the British Colonial Administration. The rapid growth of the economies of Japan, U. S. S. R. and modern China is largely attributed to the strength of the local leadership and public administration, which are able to mobilize the support of the people. It is only when the people are prepared for growth that all the other factors of growth—labor, capital and entrepreneurship—can become effective tools. The first prerequisite for growth, therefore, is for a nation to discover itself, to alert its people, to remove most of the social, political or economic handi-

---

[3] Even where attempts are made to associate the masses of the people with the Plan it is hardly ever during the time of its formulation. The few feverish attempts to "sell the plan to the people" are usually made at short conferences with farmers' organizations and other professional bodies. A Plan that took months to prepare can hardly be intelligently made familiar to nonexpert planners at such conferences. Popular participation must include participation at the levels of formulation, approval and execution of the Plan.

TABLE 2

Indicators of Economic Growth in Selected Countries: 1961

Country	Percentage of workers employed in agriculture	Percentage of total national income invested in the economy	Savings institutions per million of population	Birthrate per 1,000 of population
	1	2	3	4
High-Income Countries				
U.S.A.	13	18.0	800	23.3
Canada	19	33.0	1100	26.0
Australia	20	25.5	1600	22.8
New Zealand	19	20.0	1000	27.1
Denmark	25	19.0	1100	16.6
U.K.	8	16.0	800	17.9
Intermediate-Income Countries				
Brazil	48	15.0	120	26.5
U.S.S.R.	38	36.0	1200	23.9
Union of S. Africa	45	17.0	80	40.2
Japan	42	31.0	950	17.0
Israel	35	29.0	1000	25.2
Italy	35	22.0	900	18.8
Low-Income Countries				
Nigeria	65	12.5	15	56.5
Egypt	55	22.0	35	50.5
Ghana	60	20.0	30	55.8
Sudan	65	10.0	30	45.8
Ceylon	50	13.0	90	50.4
India	60	13.0	30	42.5
Pakistan	63	11.0	30	43.5
Republic of China	55	26.5	40	40.0

Sources: United Nations Statistical Year Book, 1962; U.N. Demographic Year Book, 1962; Statesman Year Book, 1962; International Year Book,

Deathrate per 1,000 of population	Life expectations from birth	Percentage of literacy above 15 years old	Road & Rail mileage per 10,000 sq. miles	Number of motor vehicles per 10,000 of population	Energy consumption per capita per annum (kilograms)	Consumption of agricultural fertilizer per farmer (lbs.)
5	6	7	8	9	10	11
9.3	54	98.5	11.5	4,060	8,010	840
7.7	55	98.0	3.3	3,040	5,679	270
8.5	53	98.0	3.6	2,500	3,902	640
9.0	54	98.0	8.5	2,200	2,982	950
8.2	55	99.0	6.5	1,500	2,821	1100
12.0	54	98.6	5.5		4,920	550
14.5	35	55	1.0	140	372	4
7.2	50	89.5	2.5	280	850	180
18.5	35	40.8	3.5	640	1,410	13
7.4	50	94.8	8.5	350	2,164	150
5.8	53	95.1	5.5	470	1,266	250
10.6	50	95.0	5.6	450	1,150	160
25.0	25	18.0	1.5	22	39	1.5
18.6	20	38.0	4.0	35	231	37
23.0	27	30.0	1.6	58	98	2.5
20.5	20	18.5	1.1	25	50	1.5
18.3	40	25.0	2.8	130	105	4.5
20.0	25	23.0	3.5	15	140	6.0
20.5	25	25.0	3.0	13	67	6.0
19.5	35	30.0	2.8	15	75	7.0

Year Book, 1962; F.A.O. State of Food and Agriculture and Production 1962.

caps and to be determined to push ahead. An economy dominated by tradition-bound citizens, manorial lords, the belief in witchcraft and mystiques is not ready for growth. Also, the nation must believe that its available natural resources, particularly labor and capital, can and should be so organized as to yield goods and services in greater quantities and improved quality. In this regard labor plays an immensely important role.

The Roles of Labor, Capital, Entrepreneurship and Governments

The Role of Labor. The majority of the poor economies are amply provided with natural resources in land, forests, water, minerals and favorable climate. For instance, few countries are better endowed with natural resources of all kinds than Brazil, yet she has made remarkably little use of them. Nine-tenths of Nigeria's large land area is habitable and suitable for human activities; she has a large population and rich agricultural and mineral resources, yet she is one of the poorest countries. The African continent as a whole has a large reserve of potential hydroelectric power; it is amply provided with agricultural, mineral and fishery resources, but it has remained the poorest continent on earth. On the other hand, there are few countries more poorly endowed with natural resources than Denmark and Switzerland. P. T. Ellsworth says that Chile possesses more arable land and more land per capita than California, Sweden, Switzerland or New Zealand; it has good soil and a favorable climate, yet its per capita production of agricultural commodities is less than half that of Sweden and Switzerland, one-third that of California and less than one-seventh that of New Zealand.[5] The differences in the rate of development in various countries are traceable to differences in labor productivity. A na-

---

[5] P. T. ELLSWORTH: *Chile: An Economy in Transition,* London; 1944, Ch. VII. See HENRY W. SPIEGEL: *The Brazilian Economy: Chronic Inflation and Sporadic Industrialization.* Philadelphia; 1949, Ch. 1. K. M. BUCHANAN & J. C. PUGH: *Land and People of Nigeria.* London: 1956, Ch. 1.

tion has no greater asset than its people. If they refuse to work, or work negligently, the economy is doomed to poverty, whatever its natural resources.

At present, the popular belief in the poor countries is that their poverty is due to the predominance of agriculture in their economies. Though there is some truth in this, agriculture itself has not played the major role which it should in the transition from stagnant to growing economies. Agriculture should supply more food to meet the needs of the rising population and create a surplus for export to finance purchases of the capital equipment required to modernize both agriculture and industry. It should provide a rising income to the farmers, out of which they could pay taxes to governments and buy the products of industry and commerce, thus providing a solid foundation for stable economic growth. Almost all the developed economies have, as a precondition of growth, developed an efficient agricultural sector.

But, in several of the poor countries of Asia and Africa, large quantities of food have to be imported to feed the population because domestic agriculture is inefficient and farm productivity low. For instance, a United Nations Report states that "in general, production per head of population in Oceania (Australia and New Zealand, mostly), North America and North-West Europe appears to be 10 to 20 times greater than in the Far East, Near East, Latin America or Africa. It is true that estimates of production per acre tell a different story . . . but this situation usually reflects rural over-population in the poor countries." [6] Again, the average size of the farm cultivated per farmer in Nigeria is about 3 acres, compared with about 16 acres per farmer in eastern Europe, 25 acres in northwestern Europe and 28 acres in North America.[7]

---

[6] Proceedings of the World Population Conference in Rome, 1954. United Nations Department of Economic and Social Affairs, New York, July 1955, p. 107.
[7] Economic Survey of Europe, 1960, Ch. 3, p. 5. F. A. O. Production Year Book, 1960, Ch. IV, Table 4, p. 12.

In Africa, wherever Europeans and Africans work side by side, the productivity of the African worker is markedly inferior. For instance, in Algeria, the European farmer produces 11.1 quintals [8] per hectare (2.47 acres); the African produces 5.1 quintals. In Morocco, the relationship is 10.8 quintals per European per hectare to 6.3 quintals per African. In Tunisia it is 8.3 to 2.8; in South Africa it is 8.2 to 2.3, and in East and Central Africa it is 9.2 to 2.9.

Productivity per worker in industry and commerce in the poor countries is also low, about a sixth of that in the rich countries.[9] Although there are other nonpersonal factors that account for this low productivity, there is no doubt that most of the workers in the poor countries are badly equipped for work. They lack adequate supervision and they are badly organized for productive activities.

The first essential of economic progress, therefore, is to organize domestic labor—both agricultural and industrial—in such a way as to increase its productivity per man so that it can contribute its maximum to the rate of economic growth. A more determined attempt must be made to discover the most appropriate farm manures, tools and rotation systems that can be employed, and the most economical type of industrial and commercial organization that the local people can usefully operate, and to evolve a more effective and efficient system of communication between the farmer, the business man, the industrialist and the national leaders and governments.

The Role of Capital. Capital is a factor produced for further production. Whatever the number of workers in field or factory, and whatever their determination to work hard, if they work with outmoded and primitive tools, their productivity will necessarily be lower than that of their counterparts who work with modern tools.

---

[8] A quintal is the equivalent of 220.46 lbs., that is, about 2 cwts. or 100 kilos.

[9] See COLIN CLARK: *Conditions of Economic Progress.* 3rd edition, 1960, Ch. X.

Maurice Dobb says that "we may take it that the largest single factor governing productivity in a country is its richness in capital instruments of production . . . available as mechanical aids to living labour, and I think we shall not go too far wrong if we treat capital accumulation in the sense of growth in the stock of capital instruments . . . as the crux of the process of economic growth and development." [10] The rate of economic growth in the poor countries will also depend largely upon the amount of money and capital equipment that the people can accumulate.

How can a poor country accumulate capital? In many poor countries wealth is concentrated in the hands of kings, queens, princes, politicians, oligarchies, who do not spend it to create additional capital equipment, but waste it on conspicuous consumption. If economic growth is to come about, such wealth must be shifted into the hands of those who will spend it on roads and railways, schools and factories, rather than on houses, personal ornaments, palaces and temples. The social investment and the other physical capital equipment needed can be created only when profits of businesses are ploughed back into the economy, and when every effort is made to accumulate savings by minimizing consumption expenditure and by maximizing the rate of capital formation. As Adam Smith rightly proclaimed at a time when the economy of Britain was as underdeveloped as those of the poor countries today, "Capitals are increased by parsimony and diminished by prodigality and misconduct. . . . As the capital of an individual can be increased in like manner . . . parsimony, by increasing the fund which is destined for the maintenance of productive hands, tends to increase the number of those hands whose labour adds to the value of the subject upon which it is bestowed . . . it puts into

---

[10] MAURICE DOBB: *Some Aspects of Economic Development* (three lectures). New Delhi: 1951, p. 7. Cf. W. W. ROSTOW: *The Stages of Economic Growth*, Cambridge University Press, 1960, p. 55. See ADAM SMITH: *Wealth of Nations*, Everyman's Library Edition. London: J. M. Dent & Sons, 1957, Vol. I, Book II, p. 301.

motion an additional quantity of industry, which gives an additional value to the annual produce." [11]

Table 2 shows that a large proportion of the national income in the richer countries is invested in those countries than is the case in the poor countries. Consequently social investment—roads, hospitals, schools and the like—and physical capital equipment are more abundant in the rich countries than in the poor.

The Role of Entrepreneurship. Even if a country has ample natural resources, an adequate labor supply, technological knowledge and capital equipment, a high rate of economic growth cannot be achieved and sustained unless there are entrepreneurs who have the ability to organize labor and capital to work on the natural resources for the production of economic goods and services. The whole history of economic development in Europe, North America, Australasia and Japan is the history of enterprise.

The successful take-off of an economy is dependent upon the continued activity of people who are prepared to innovate and experiment, to break from the past, to rebel against tradition and against stereotyped ways of life. A new elite, a new leadership must emerge, determined to build a modern progressive economy. Gradually such a spirit of enterprise and adventure must spread, first to the urban and later to the rural areas. Most of the employed population must be prepared to participate in the new drive for modernization, if appreciable and sustained economic growth is to be achieved.

It is often claimed that the strong family or communal loyalties that exist in most of the underdeveloped economies act as an obstacle to economic development, since they prevent individual entrepreneurship, reduce capital accumulation and impede the growth process. There is some truth in this, but their deleterious effect on growth must not be overemphasized. The fact that people act together and that the advance of isolated individuals is not desired,

---

[11] Adam Smith, *op. cit.,* pp. 301-302.

could be utilized for economic advance, where there is good indigenous leadership.

Most initial development projects in the poor countries should be of the community project type: the building of rural health centers, malaria control, improvement in local water supply, agricultural extension services, the building of schools, the construction of new roads or the widening of existing ones and the setting-up of rudimentary systems of local administration. These activities are perfectly compatible with, and should indeed be based on, the idea that their benefits accrue equally to members of the community, rather than to individuals or groups of individuals within it, and that therefore the combined labor of the community should be utilized to provide these services. Where strong local loyalty prevails, communal labor can usually be employed for this purpose with a good chance of success. The more successful the schemes, the more rapidly the community is introduced into modern ways of living and expectations, the more it is freed from the bonds of tradition and the more easily it can be guided along the path of further growth.

In Nigeria, most of the early motor roads, schools and colleges were built with communal labor. The first Ten-Year Development Plan (1946–55) was based essentially on the need to utilize local patriotism and community concerns. The result was encouraging. The success of the missionaries in Nigeria was based on the mobilization of local group enthusiasm for the provision of churches, schools and colleges. Similar experiences are common throughout Africa. The task of the nation builder is to discover the strength, rather than the weakness, in the communal spirit, and to utilize and direct it for national development.

The strong family and communal loyalties have been used to provide education for most of the African leaders of today. Families and communities have raised money to educate their sons and daughters at home and abroad. Without this type of contribution to educational and social development, the African continent might

75

well be a quarter of a century behind in political and economic development. Thus, even when the community or family expects its more privileged members to help the less privileged, such contributions constitute some form of repayment of the capital invested in their training by the family or the community.

In many cases the family commitments act as a check to extravagant living by the privileged. Many of those in the underdeveloped countries who indulge in conspicuous consumption are free from these extra extended-family or communal responsibilities. Many others, including the writer, who have to contribute to the education of two or three brothers and sisters in secondary schools and universities, must limit their expenditures on nonessentials. Few of us would save all or most of the money that we spend on the education of our relations, nor would we invest it in capital projects.[12]

Furthermore, the social controls and group action which are supposed to be inimical to individual entrepreneurship serve to ameliorate the harsh effects of economic advance and provide some form of welfare services in countries where governments are not able to provide for the needy, the unemployed and the unfortunate. Japan and China have demonstrated that a society does not need to be socially atomistic before it can achieve rapid economic growth. Foreign welfare officers visiting in Nigeria have often recommended that some form of Nigeria's family system be used to solve some of the welfare problems of advanced countries. The task of the nation builders is to discover what is good in social and communal systems and to utilize them not only as instruments of social control but also as mechanisms for economic advancement.

The Role of Governments. In most of the poor economies, the government sector attracts and retains most of the educated and experienced workers who might otherwise be private entrepreneurs, local leaders and captains of industry. Since the mass of the people

---

[12] See Chapter XV, by Charles Elliott, for a rather different approach to this. (Ed.)

are poor, they can save very little for individual and corporate investment. Only the governments have the ability to mobilize savings out of a mass of small incomes, by the judicious use of their public financial operations, and to generate the flow of investment funds into new forms of economic enterprise. External capital also is increasingly made available only through government channels; and even private investors are more and more seeking government partnership as a safeguard against possible nationalization. No economy, therefore, that is saddled with an inefficient, backward or corrupt government can achieve a dynamic rate of growth. But a government with political leaders who are devoted to the achievement of rapid economic growth can mobilize not only material but also human resources for a dynamic economic leap forward. It can plan the economy and lead in the execution of the plans as governments have done in Russia, China and India, for example.

If governments are to make their maximum contribution to economic growth they not only must have political and administrative stability, but also must make a determined attempt to set up an educational system that will influence the supply and deployment of the country's manpower by providing the necessary technical know-how and will also modernize the social and economic orientation of the people. No illiterate community has ever been progressive. Few literate communities are backward. Therefore, the government should give priority to the creation of literate citizens.

The governments of underdeveloped countries should also undertake two other basic educational tasks. Since most of these countries are predominantly agricultural, their governments should provide agricultural extension services to show farmers who are too old or too busy to go to school how to increase their yields by adopting improved methods and better tools. Increased agricultural productivity can thus be achieved without any substantial increase in capital investment. Only a very few developing countries assist their farmers in this way, and as a result the agricultural sections of their various development plans are out of touch

77

with the needs and practices of the farmers. The agricultural sector of their economies (except in the export sector) are either static or going backward.

The second task is to provide training of all kinds for those who will actually undertake the economic planning, supervision and execution. Most of the developing economies today emphasize the high-level training of manpower, particularly in the scientific field. But they soon discover that they have spent much of their scarce resources to train first-class engineers, scientists and administrators, only to lose them to Europe and America, because the trainees find no comparable opportunities to use their specialized training at home. Even if they do return, they discover that there are no intermediate and junior assistants for them to work with, so that the specialist engineer, doctor or administrator spends too much of his time on menial or routine duties.

The developing countries must gear their educational plans to the needs of their economies. J. K. Galbraith, after he had spent a few months in India as the U. S. A. Ambassador, said:

As an economist I look with considerable discontent on much of the economics that is taught in the new countries. It is not clinically concerned with the problems of these countries nor pragmatically with their solutions. Rather, it is often a fashionable elucidation of the sophisticated models and systems which are currently in fashion at Cambridge, the London School, or even at Harvard. As a layman I have often wondered if medical education has been really adapted to the situation of the poor countries. . . . [13]

The missionaries must bear some blame for this, since it was they who introduced the foreign system of education now being operated by governments in Asia and Africa. Rapid economic and social change demands drastic "nationalization" of the educational curriculum if it is to contribute to the rapid transformation of the community.

---

[13] J. K. Galbraith: *Economic Development in Perspective.* Harvard University Press, 1963, p. 56.

Governments in developing countries must also be able to determine wisely orders of priority in planning their economies. Far too many of them waste scarce resources on prestige projects like the building of expensive dams, steel mills and atomic power stations, and the needs of the people for clothing, food, and shelter are ignored. They import unduly costly foreign technical equipment and personnel to run the projects and yet do not have enough money to establish or maintain simple industries and improve agriculture, transport and communications which would provide work for a large number of the unemployed and bring about a more rational development process and a more rapid rate of growth.

J. K. Galbraith describes with exasperation his experience in an Asian country where there was much unemployment, but which had just installed expensive imported automatic gates at its railway crossings, instead of employing gatemen at less cost.[14] Nigeria bought diesel railway engines and then had to import diesel oil and engine operators, leaving its coal unused and throwing coal miners and railway firemen out of jobs.

External Factors

The essential ingredients of economic growth must be supplied from inside the country. But these can be supplemented by technically qualified personnel, capital funds in aid and loans, and capital equipment imported from abroad. However, in view of the fact that over four-fifths of the world population depend for aid on only one-fifth, it must be made clear to the leaders in the poor countries that if the rich countries wish to maintain their own rates of growth, the resources available are inadequate to finance the anticipated rate of growth in the poor countries.

External impetus for economic growth can also come through trade relations. Favorable prices for the exports of developing

---

[14] *Ibid.*, p. 25.

countries can create the necessary funds for capital investment. However, the competition among the many poor countries to sell their products in the few rich countries leads to falls in the prices of exports and to reduced economic activity in the poor economies, where not only the level of domestic activity, but also the ability to import capital equipment for further production and to pay taxes depend upon exports. This decrease in the prices of export products cannot be avoided unless there is a determined effort to develop greater internal demand for the goods produced through increased industrialization.

The United Nations Organization is an important external factor in the acceleration of economic growth in the developing countries. But its agencies are so many and varied and so lacking in coordination in the developing countries that their effectiveness is considerably reduced through duplication of effort and of organization, with consequent waste of human and financial resources.[15] In addition to the many U. N. Agencies, numerous foreign governmental bodies and organizations operate in various forms in many of the developing countries.

All these external agencies would contribute more effectively to the economic growth of the poor countries if their assistance could be channeled either through the national governments or through the International Development Association of the United Nations which should act in close collaboration with the national governments. Suspicion of external aid arises in the developing countries because most of the activities of the foreign agencies and

---

[15] The United Nations Technical Assistance Board (UNTAB) and the United Nations Special Fund (UNSF) tend to bring some order into the chaotic operations of the United Nations agencies. But each of the other agencies is autonomous and is expected to employ the UNTAB and the UNSF only as a clearinghouse, which in most cases they never use. The UNTAB and the UNSF have no overriding authority. Such a lack of authority constitutes a lacuna in the U. N. operations. [This was written before the decision to merge the work of the UNTAB and the UNSF into one body now called the United Nations Development Program (UNDP).—EDITOR]

governments are outside the control or surveillance of the local administration.

Population Control

Finally, the rate of economic growth will be slow if every dynamic effort to increase the material well-being of the community is offset by a constant increase in the population. The tendency to have large families, which is usually dominant in the poor countries, must change, until ultimately there is a decline in the birthrate.

Most of the poor countries are relatively poorer now than they were half a century ago, in spite of some urban centers dotted here and there. The urban areas are peopled with families of many children, who are uneducated, badly nourished, living in slums and in crowded surroundings. Comprehensive free education, or free medical services, as the first step toward economic development, is almost impossible, both because of the cost and because, unless accompanied by a reduced birthrate, measures to improve health and social services will lead to population explosions as the death-rates are reduced.

Table 3, showing rates of population increase and of economic growth in selected countries, reveals that although in both the high- and the intermediate-income countries the economic growth rate is about double the rate of population growth, in the low-income countries population increase almost cancels out the use in income, and that four countries have higher rates of population growth than of economic growth.[16]

---

[16] The solution to the population pressure in developing countries poses social, moral and political problems. Even when the birthrate falls, improved health facilities reduce the deathrate and so increase the population growth rate or keep it constant. Since most of the people are religious, birth-control measures are regarded as immoral. These countries revel in large populations as a measure of political prestige. Many of them, particularly in Africa, have unused space and could support larger populations by stepping up their productive efforts.

81

TABLE 3

Annual Population Growth and Annual Rates of Economic Growth in
Selected Countries in 1961

Country	Annual Percentage Rates of Population Growth	Average Annual Percentage Rates of Growth in Gross National Product in the 1950's
	1 *	2 *
High-Income Countries		
United States	1.7	3.3
Canada	2.2	3.9
Australia	2.2	3.6
New Zealand	2.0	3.2
Denmark	0.7	2.4
United Kingdom	0.7	2.1
Intermediate-Income Countries		
Brazil	2.4	5.0
U.S.S.R.	1.8	7.0
Union of S. Africa	2.6	4.5
Japan	0.9	9.3
Israel	3.0	7.0
Italy	0.5	5.9
Low-Income Countries		
Nigeria	4.5	4.0
Egypt	2.5	2.1
Ghana	6.2	5.6
Sudan	2.8	3.2
Ceylon	2.7	4.0
India	2.2	3.5
Pakistan	2.1	2.0
Republic of China	2.4	8.0

* Sources: 1. United Nations Statistical Year Book 1962, Table 1.
 2. United Nations Year Book of National Accounts 1962, and other sources.

Is Economic Growth Desirable?

Throughout the world the poor countries have made economic development a major political-economic ideal. They have associated it with the symbols of real political independence, as part of their sense of sovereignty and as a means of redressing the long-standing feelings of inferiority and resentment vis-à-vis the rich countries. They see economic growth not only as a source of prestige but as the most effective means of overcoming the hunger, disease, misery and premature death which are prevalent in their countries.

As Christians we cannot approve a course of action primarily motivated by pride, a desire for personal pleasure, or political aggrandizement. Many high- and intermediate-income countries of the world want to possess atomic warheads, rockets, and the like, claiming that they will use them to defend humanity or to save civilization from annihilation. But the Christian should question the urge to accumulate these military weapons. Does the same apply to the incessant urge, apparent in all countries, to achieve material well-being and to the measures taken to meet the urge?

There is much greater evidence of mental disturbance, crime and suicide in the rich countries of Europe and America than in the poor countries. Economic growth breeds undue individualism and selfishness, as men become absorbed in their own interests, forgetting that they are their brothers' keepers. The social system becomes eroded, tribal bonds are severed, acute poverty exists side by side with extreme wealth as the struggle for more wealth leads to the exploitation of one man, group, or nation by another. Above all, economic growth leads to reliance on technology and human ingenuity, and tends to undermine belief in God. As a result Christianity today often seems more vital in the poor than in the rich countries. We are told that "love of money is the root of all evil." Why then is the church so keen on finding ways and means of assisting the economic growth of nations?

The Christian should be engaged in the search to increase the volume of goods and services available for human consumption because, as a leading economist has said, "unless a steady stream of money comes into the family's hands every week, every month, and every year, even though it be made up of saints, the family is sick. Not only its materialistic activities, but its non-materialistic activities—the things that convert existence into living—must suffer: education, travel, health, recreation and charity to say nothing of food, warmth and shelter." [17]

Not only does economic growth give man greater control over his environment and thereby increase his freedom; it also reduces the deathrate, increases life-expectancy and diminishes famine, plague and pestilence. A greater supply of goods permits society to help those who cannot help themselves, and thus increases the range of human happiness.

But, clearly, economic growth is not an unmixed blessing. It has its advantages and its obvious dangers. It is the duty of those who are guiding its dynamics to maximize its social advantages while minimizing its disadvantages. This raises the problem of the form of economic organization and role of the church and of other people who are interested in minimizing the harsh effects of economic change.

The Problem of Economic Organization

One of the main problems of economic growth concerns the organization of economic activities. Labor, natural resources, capital and entrepreneurship must be efficiently organized to produce economic growth at the desirable rate. But how are these forces to be organized? The communist way? The way of other dictatorships—for example, fascism, nazism? The capitalist way of eighteenth- and nineteenth-century Europe, Australasia and North

---

[17] PAUL A. SAMUELSON: *Economics: An Introductory Analysis.* London: McGraw-Hill Publishing Co., 1951, p. 61.

America? Or through a more humanitarian, liberal, democratic process? What is the role of Christians in the choice of economic organization? Christianity is by nature inconsistent with communism, nazism, fascism or doctrinaire capitalism.[18]

Christianity and economic advancement have long been partners. Professor Hagen, for instance, claims that "industry and innovation are directly associated with religious dogma." [19] The Protestant ethic was closely linked with the rise of capitalism and the industrial revolution of the eighteenth and nineteenth centuries. The religious independents—the Congregationalists, Baptists, Quakers and Anglicans—were the leading entrepreneurs and business executives in Europe after the Reformation. It was their acquisitiveness, combined with asceticism, that created the increased volume of savings and investment without which capitalism and the accompanying rapid economic growth would have been impossible.[20] Even where a direct relationship between Christian ethics and economic progress has been denied, it has not been denied that individual Christians played prominent roles in the course of economic progress, for instance, in western Europe, Australasia and North America.[21]

Today, many of the leaders of the poor countries are Christians. Their Christian ethic can be utilized to bring about dynamic economic growth and to guide its course. They must be reminded that those who wish to eat must do their fair share of work, and contribute their quota to the achievement of rapid economic growth, through saving and investment, through abstinence and hard work, as did Christians of earlier generations.

But Christians must go further. Max Weber has argued that the

[18] See S. A. ALUKO: *Christianity and Communism.* Ibadan: Christian Council of Nigeria, 1964, Chs. 1 and 2.

[19] EVERETT E. HAGEN: *The Theory of Social Change.* Homewood, Ill., U. S. A.: 1962, p. 289.

[20] See MAX WEBER: *The Protestant Ethic and the Spirit of Capitalism.* 1958, p. 85.

[21] See NILES M. HANSEN: "The Protestant Ethic as a General Pre-Condition for Economic Development," *The Canadian Journal of Economics and Political Science,* November, 1963, p. 468.

religious root of economic humanism is dead, that the economic ethic has been stripped of its religious import.[22] In the poor countries today the church must discover how the Christian economic ethic can be reinterpreted so that the strains and stresses which give rise to human frustration and social tension may be reduced and checked.

Therefore, we must be concerned not only with economic growth: we must have Christian standards for assessing the performance of any economy. The people need material comforts; and so the economy should produce an increasing quantity of goods and services. The widest possible range of individual liberty should be insured; and so the economy should be structured to permit individual or community choices. There is need to ensure personal security; and so the economy should protect the individual from the adversities of unemployment, old age, sickness and other unfortunate social and economic contingencies. Economic justice is essential. Therefore, the economy should afford equality of opportunity. Above all, economic benefits should not go only to a very small group in society, whether a religious body or the members of a political party or a social class. A wide distribution of purchasing power and freedom of economic action have the effect of sustaining demand and accelerating economic growth and expansion.[23]

It may not be possible to achieve all these goals at once. We may have to choose between justice and plenty, between plenty and personal security, between personal security and freedom, and between freedom and growth. The Christian choice must depend upon Christian values which regard human beings not as tools of economic growth but rather as its controller. Increased goods and services should bring about the increased human welfare and happiness without which economic growth has no meaning.

---

[22] MAX WEBER: *op. cit.*, pp. 58-67; 178-182.
[23] See C. HOLLIS: *The Church and Economics*, A Faith and Fact book. London: Burns & Oates, 1961, pp. 53-54.

3

SOCIAL AND POLITICAL FACTORS IN DEVELOPING SOCIETIES

by MIKIO SUMIYA (Japan)

BEFORE the Second World War, the countries of Asia and Africa had been defined by social scientists as backward or stagnant societies. Such a broad definition was of course not always adequate to cover all countries in the Afro-Asian world. However, it was a workable concept to indicate the fundamental common character of their social setting.

The situation of these countries has changed drastically since the postwar period. They have been emancipated from their former colonial or semicolonial status and have been experiencing a rapid social and political transformation. Today, they are called "developing countries." This new definition implies not only that they have been experiencing changes within the established social framework, but also that the social framework itself has been altered.

87

The over-all development of their societies has brought new hopes and opportunities to these young nations. But, it has also created difficulties and complications. The primary objective of this chapter is to discuss the dilemmas involved in such social change.

All the young countries of Asia and Africa embarked on programs for economic growth after the war. Their common goal is industrialization, but their socioeconomic backgrounds vary widely. It is inevitable therefore that the process and means of their development also vary. I shall analyze three types of development and then turn to three specific social problems of national and international development which have to be solved in implementing an economic development program: (1) nationalism as an integrating ideal and its implications for development, (2) the problems involved in the changing value systems, (3) the problem of poverty.

The change of social framework or structure necessitated by economic development has affected inevitably the value systems of the Afro-Asian and Latin American societies. In this situation the integrating ideal is nationalism.

Capital Formation in Developing Societies

There are many possible criteria for classifying developing countries. One criterion is the composition of the elite who constitute the nation's leadership.[1] Political institutions would be another criterion.[2] However, as we are concerned with economic growth it is natural to use a fundamental socioeconomic requirement of economic development—capital formation—as the criterion.

Using this criterion, we can distinguish three types of development:

---

[1] See C. KERR, J. T. DUNLOP, F. HARBISON & C. A. MYERS: *Industrialism and Industrial Man.* Harvard University Press, 1960.

[2] B. F. HOSELITZ and W. E. MOORE, eds.: *Industrialization and Society,* 1963. See esp. an article by DAVID E. APTER.

1. Where there is a certain measure of capital formation by big landlords and merchants operating in the indigenous economy.

2. Where settler colonialism is predominant, and considerable capital is accumulated, with the settler as the central figure.

3. Where the indigenous economy under colonialism is still underdeveloped and there is little capital formation.

Asian countries are often characterized by the *first type* of development. Some Arab countries may be included here also. Private ownership of large tracts of land has developed in such societies. This has its roots in the indigenous society, although the impact of old colonial policy must be recognized in some cases.

Though large ownership of land may provide only a luxurious life for the landlords, it can also provide financial resources for industrialization. At least the economic activities of landowners may develop a money economy, which in turn produces a group of rich merchants. Together they may initiate economic development, but in most cases they represent the conservative forces in society because they depend on vested interests. The economy of such societies is based on agriculture; and the traditional attributes of an agrarian culture, such as the village community and extended family system, persist. These traditional social institutions tend to overpopulation through communal solidarity. Poverty and overpopulation are the serious problems in such societies causing frustration among people who are striving for economic development.

Societies of *type two* are frequently found in Latin America, and the Philippines offer an Asian example. Europeans emigrated to such countries a few hundred years ago, intermarried with the local people, particularly the elite, and settled down permanently. Today their descendants are the landlords and merchants who form the upper classes of society; the "pure" natives and some sections of the hybrid peoples—the great majority—come from the lower social classes as farmers and manual laborers.

A considerable amount of capital has been formed by the rich who constitute a small group in society. They make efforts to develop industries, and these nations as a whole have a high annual rate of economic growth. But the rich are at the same time trying to hold on to their vested interests. In many cases, Catholicism functions as the integrating factor. The poor naturally tend to be critical and oppose the existing ruling system, with consequent class conflicts. In addition, the ruling classes are frequently involved in political struggles among themselves. Therefore, societies of this type are often politically unstable.

The societies of Africa south of the Sahara are of the *third type,* as is Indonesia. Colonial policy had long prevented, or at least had not prompted, changes in these countries, and they have remained almost static for several hundred years. The private ownership of land has failed to develop, and the village community and patriarchal extended-family system have remained as an inviolable tradition. Class differentiation has not yet developed.

A money economy does not develop easily in such societies, and native merchants cannot emerge. Commercial activities are largely controlled by Arabs, Indians, and Chinese. The amount of capital formed by the local people is negligible, and under such circumstances leadership in economic development must be taken by the government. Most of the people are poor peasants, and in undertaking development programs the government is politically and economically dependent upon them. This is why economic programs in developing countries often follow a socialist pattern regardless of the ideological background.

The three cases of developing societies described above are simply models. Actual societies are not so simple, and we might describe many other cases. But individual societies have some of the characteristics of these three cases, and they are today carrying out their economic development programs on the foundation of their respective social settings. It is instructive to look at the basic problems of economic growth in the light of these different types of capital formation.

Basic Social Problems of Economic Growth

Agriculture is the economic basis of the developing countries, and the fundamental problem of agrarian societies is landownership. Societies of the third type often experience confusion and social unrest at the onset of economic development because the system of private ownership is suddenly introduced as necessary for economic development. The vested rights of the native peoples are often neglected, and even their possessory rights are negated by the authorized goal of economic development.

The impact of economic development is more severe on societies of the first and second type. In these, many peasants do not own their land; and the rent is usually 50 per cent or more of the year's harvest. Their high rent and traditional social relationships bind peasants to poverty and subordination. Poor peasants have no funds to invest, and this impedes the improvement of agricultural productivity. Land reform, therefore, becomes the most urgent problem in these societies.

However, land reform and a reduction in rent are not enough to solve the agricultural problems, as is clearly demonstrated by the experiences of those countries which introduced land reform after the last war. Some recent surveys indicate that poor peasants in these societies have begun to sell their land, resulting in the accumulation of large holdings by landlords. To be effective, land reform, like any other, must be coordinated with other economic programs.

The fundamental problem in the changing economic relationships in developing countries is the market mechanism. The underlying assumption of every plan for economic development is that the supply and demand of capital, commodities and labor, as well as the adjustment of prices are controlled through the market mechanism. In other words, it is assumed that the market mechanism functions as it does in advanced countries. But this is not so, because in general a commodity economy has not yet developed.

91

Therefore, the government has to play the central role in economic development. It designs the economic program and raises funds by taxation, issuing bonds and borrowing through foreign loans. It may promote the development of private industry by giving subsidies. Sometimes it takes part directly in the operation of industrial enterprises. A well-designed program and strong leadership are essential to economic development, and the government has to take charge of the entire process, beginning with the procurement of capital and ending with the management of business enterprises. Consequently, a certain type of "guided economy" is usually necessary in developing countries.

Economic development cannot, however, be attained by government planning and guidance alone. The general public must be ready to cooperate. The motivation for cooperation with government planning has to be created among the people. Nationalism provided the motivation, at least in the initial stage of development, but it has proved insufficient as economic development progressed. Thus, as more planning has been necessary, nationalism has been replaced by a socialist goal for economic life. The "socialist pattern of society" in India is an example of this.

The young nations of Africa do not reject communism outright, partly because communism condemns colonialism. But, it should not be overlooked that this attitude is also an outcome of the national aim for a "planned and guided economy." The developing countries are now facing a serious difficulty—lack of the socio-economic data necessary for economic planning. Most of these data are available only through market structure. One of the ways to overcome such a difficulty will be a powerful leadership by the government, and the other way will be the utilization of the backlog of theoretical and empirical studies made by the different social sciences.

Economic Development and International Relations

In addition to the national problems described, the programs of economic development in developing countries encounter a variety of problems arising from international relations. After the war when the developing countries began to grapple with economic development a great gulf existed between them and the developed countries in terms of industrial productivity and national income. Of course, developing countries need not follow the course of the developed countries: they can take a shortcut; that is, they can raise industrial productivity quickly by adopting advanced techniques developed by the industrialized nations. But, there is no shortcut to the establishment of public service facilities such as power plants, roads and housing. Nor is there any shortcut to increased national income and purchasing power.

In order to promote economic growth, developing countries have to export some of their products to developed countries in exchange for industrial techniques. Since they cannot compete with advanced countries in the international market for manufactured goods they export mainly primary products. But here they face two difficult problems. One is that the market for primary products is threatened by the influx of substitutes produced by the rapidly developing synthetic industry, sometimes even forcing a change in the economic structure of the developing countries. Another is the great fluctuation in the market prices for primary products, due to the variation in the level of production caused by weather and other natural conditions, which makes them the object of speculation. Sometimes, when market prices decline sharply, production cost cannot be met, and a severe blow is inflicted upon small-scale producers who in many cases cannot recover. Such a market situation impedes economic growth because it results in instability of national income.

One of the big problems of the international economy, therefore,

93

is to stabilize market prices and to secure an international market for the primary products of developing countries.

Economic aid from developed countries is also a factor in the economics of developing countries. Although they often refuse to accept foreign economic aid because of anticolonialist sentiments, it is nevertheless clear that it is indispensable for their economic growth; and, once it has been accepted, the amount of foreign aid tends to snowball.

In many cases, the payment of interest on foreign loans is a heavy financial burden on developing countries, hinders their economic growth and makes them dependent on their creditors. Quite naturally, developing countries with a long colonial history are especially sensitive to the implications of foreign aid; and such international financial organizations as the World Bank are a more acceptable means through which financial aid could be offered.

The more unstable the economic situation of the developing countries, the greater is their need of foreign aid. However, such a situation does not attract foreign private investments, and most of the foreign aid must come as government financial assistance or loans. The tragedy is that much of this government assistance has been given as military aid, and linked with the East-West cold war.

Thus, foreign aid has had two unfortunate consequences in developing countries. First, the military aid, which was aimed at strengthening the defensive power of the receiving countries, has forced them to make additional military appropriations which have been a heavy financial burden upon their national economies, seriously impeding their development. Second, the aid from developed countries has, in some cases, had an adverse effect upon the national economy of the developing countries because it has been given in the light of the military and political, rather than economic situation. For example, the surplus farm products offered by developed countries may menace the local production of food and raw materials.

Nationalism and National Vision

Nationalism has provided the motivation for economic growth among peoples of developing countries that are in a difficult internal and international situation. In Asia it played an important role in maintaining the people's integrity during the period of social and political chaos following the gaining of their independence after the Second World War. But today this initial enthusiasm is waning. Economic development cannot be achieved simply by enthusiasm. Leaders of the newly independent nations came to realize the necessity of economic planning soon after the initial period of social chaos, and tried to implement their nationalist ideals in concrete programs for economic development. The young African nations that are still experiencing the initial social chaos of independence will sooner or later come to this second stage.

In some developing countries, various conflicts which were latent in nationalism came to the fore soon after the initial period of "Sturm and Drang" was over. These conflicts appeared in the struggle for leadership in the construction of the nation-state. In most of the societies of types one and two the conservative forces have been strong and have assumed the leadership. But, Communists or Socialists have succeeded in gaining power in some countries by organizing the dissatisfied masses. In the former group, the traditional social relationships have been maintained, and nationalism has taken on an authoritarian character. Among the societies of the latter group, nationalism has often become democentric.

In the societies of the third type ethnic groups were not really unified as a single nationality. Therefore, intertribal conflicts have often come to the fore. Most of the young African states are "multitribal" nations, and these tribes have different languages and customs. In this situation, the crucial issue is how to maintain the national unity.

These young African nations have already reached the stage of preparing for a national vision of development, after experiencing the stage of nationalism based on the hatred of colonialism. The evolution of such a national vision is unusually difficult. In developed countries, economic planning is done with the aid of estimates on investment, employment and the distribution of national income. Such a sophisticated method is of no avail in developing countries, not only because the market mechanism does not work but also because the value system necessary to support a market mechanism is alien to developing societies.

Economic growth can be defined as a function of national income per capita. An economic development program is aimed at increasing this income and must be based on a value system which accepts this increase as valuable. Such a value system is foreign to the traditions of developing countries. The idea that human society should develop is part of the value system of developed societies. The agrarian and patriarchal society of developing countries has a different set of values for money, labor, consumption, socioeconomic and technical changes and social classes. When economic growth takes place in such a society, the changing socioeconomic institutions come into conflict with traditional values. Those nations which have been able to acquire a new system of values suitable to the new economic situation have been successful in socioeconomic development. Thus, the traditional values, particularly those related to economic life, are being lost in developing societies. However, it must be remembered that the collapse of an old value system does not always produce a new set of values.

A developing country must have a value system which can be accepted by its members as a fundamental consensus, if it is to develop as an integral society. The graver the difficulties faced the more urgent the need for such a system. When the enthusiasm of nationalism wanes, severe internal conflicts, concerned not only with political and economic interests but also with the old and the new value system are bound to emerge. This is why the early realization of a national vision is necessary. However, this vision

96

tends often to be hostile to developed countries and sometimes leads to the suppression of opposition in a society where internal tension is serious.

Economic Development and Personal Relations

About 100 years ago Sir Henry Maine wrote in his *Ancient Law* that human relations in society were shifting from patterns based on status to those based on contract. In modern society the contract itself has been institutionalized and depersonalized. It is depersonalized institutions such as the market mechanism and its components—that is, corporations and exchanges—that sustain the economic growth of developed societies.

Human relations in the developing countries are based on personal contact between individuals. The basic organization of traditional societies is the patriarchal extended family and village community. Solidarity among members of the family and community varies from country to country. Generally speaking, it is the weakest in societies of type one, and strongest in those of type three.

The institution of the family is not always detrimental to the economic growth of developing countries. When a traditional society collapses as a result of economic development, it often suffers from unemployment and overpopulation. The family institution then acts as a safety valve and provides for destitute members of the society. Personal contact is the primary type of social relationship in a closed society. But although a particular ethical code based on confidence and responsibility can hold good in a closed society, it is not adapted to any other. In other societies, an ethical code may work for a particular social class, but not for other classes.

Economic activities in a family-based community are usually subject to a double limitation. First, the abilities of people outside the community cannot be used, as is often the case in family-

97

managed enterprises. Some people do not have an opportunity to develop their abilities due to the handicaps of conventional family relationships or status. An increase in the number of such discontented people makes for social instability. A high social mobility is desirable or even necessary for socioeconomic development.

Another limitation, more significant than the first, is that as economic development progresses, it is difficult to maintain the traditional personal relations through the traditional values. Economic activities have to be regulated in accordance with the market mechanism, and a rational type of human relationship that is suitable to the economic mechanism has to be created if there is to be economic development.

The market mechanism must be accompanied by the individuation of economic activities that will bring about the collapse of family-type institutions. Socialism does not rely upon the market mechanism as an important means to economic growth, but the family-type social institution is an impediment even in the socialist setting, and efforts are made to replace it with more functional human relations.

All the problems of developing countries are focused in the disintegration of the family-based community. The collapse of family-based institutions necessarily entails the collapse of traditional values. The collapse of the family-type commmunity as a result of economic development means that the family gradually loses its function as a social security agency. The depersonalized cities develop, and slums, as an embodiment of all social problems, mushroom. A money economy prevails in the cities, and men have to make money to live. Such opportunities are not easily found, and so the worker has to take whatever work he can find. Unfortunately he is usually unskilled and there are many like him! Hence his conditions are miserable. Moreover, he has usually left his rural family, and finds himself alone and lonely. As conventional morals do not carry over into city life, new evils such as drunkenness and prostitution are the natural consequences.

The Poverty of the Masses

One of the biggest problems faced by the developing countries today is the poverty of the mass of the people. Although it is not true that the national income per capita in developing societies has been declining since the last war or since the early years of this century, nevertheless, the poverty in these societies is a crucial problem. This is because it is related to the changing value system in these societies.

In the traditional society, where the money economy was not extensive, prestige in the community was not measured by simple economic criteria. Therefore, poverty was not conceived of as a big problem. The fact that economic development has become the primary goal in developing countries has a revolutionary significance in that the social evaluation of people is now based on economic criteria and poverty has become conspicuous. The influx of attractive consumer goods from developed countries increased people's consumption. The demonstration effect of consumer goods is particularly large in the developing societies where the traditional pattern of consumption has lost influence. The destructive impact of the commodity economy upon people's consumption has been large particularly in type three societies where a commodity economy had least prevailed.

The mass of poor people in developing countries who have come to realize their miserable economic condition have begun to demand a larger share of wealth. One of the most important causes of hostility to colonialism was the general belief that it had prevented improvement in the living standard of the people. Thus, an increase of national income became the primary goal of government efforts after the attainment of political independence. However, this is not so easily achieved. In many cases, the results of economic development programs have not been appreciably large; in some, national economic power and national income per capita have even declined. When the economic goal cannot be attained or

99

the possibility of realizing it is not apparent, people experience unbearable frustration, and social unrest is inevitable. Then, internal conflicts come to the fore.

The rapid increase in population, especially since the last war, has been a new factor contributing to the poverty of the masses. Where any increase in the gross national product is offset by the population increase, the national income per capita cannot rise. Family planning must be considered seriously as the only available means to meet this difficult situation.

In the developing countries, where the great majority of the people are poor, one of the most challenging tasks is to organize these impoverished masses and stimulate them to participate in the building of the new nation-state.

4

CHRISTIANS AND ECONOMIC GROWTH

by RONALD H. PRESTON (United Kingdom)

IN the last ten years the Ecumenical Movement has given a great deal of effort to unraveling the problems arising from economic growth, especially in its inquiry into areas of rapid social change. The results of this are summarized in the very important booklet *Dilemmas and Opportunities* with its subtitle "Christian action in rapid social change." [1] It is the report of an International Ecumenical Study Conference held at Thessaloniki in 1959, when the results of the inquiry were presented. The conclusions were published in a fuller form in two volumes, *Man in Rapid Social Change* by E. de Vries, and *The Church and Rapid Social Change* by P. Abrecht. It is doubtful if the churches realize the debt they owe to this valuable project. Anyone who studies the history of

---

[1] Published by the Dept. on Church and Society. Geneva: World Council of Churches, 1959.

Christian social thought will realize that for centuries it has suffered from the grave defect of irrelevance. There was a time in the high Middle Ages when Christian thought had more or less come to terms with the current social order, understood it and spoke relevantly to it. But soon the empirical situation shifted, and Catholic thought became increasingly out of touch with it by working within *a priori* categories. It intended to deal with particular situations, but it did not allow sufficiently for the autonomy of "secular" studies and in consequence misunderstood much of the secular world. Protestant thought has been little more relevant, chiefly because it has been particularly prone to an individualistic pietism which has simply bypassed the problem of social ethics. In practice this has resulted in an uncritical acceptance of the status quo. In Britain at the time of the first industrial revolution (where it originated) this lack of a Christian critique of the social order had disastrous consequences. Now, however, when the West is beginning a second industrial revolution, and other parts of the world are at last on the threshold of their first, we have through the Ecumenical Movement a theological basis for Christian social ethics which pays attention to the facts of economic and social and industrial life, and has gone a long way to securing them.

The survey of areas of rapid social change mainly covers Africa, Asia and Latin America. It does not cover the already industrialized countries which are beginning their second industrial revolution, based this time not on coal and steel but on atomic energy and electronics. A good deal of empirical investigation of these latter countries has in fact been undertaken, as the chapters of this book show, but they have not been focused in one document or book as the problems of Asia, Africa and Latin America have been. Meanwhile, for the areas covered, the fact remains that for the first time for centuries (in fact, the first time ever as far as the church in those lands is concerned) Christians have up-to-date knowledge of what is happening and a diagnosis of significant changes. They need no longer be a generation or more out of date, rushing—as so often in the past—to lock the stable door long after the horse has bolted. All church policy, all missionary society policy, all Christian witness by ministers or lay folk in the field of Christian social ethics in those areas must begin from the facts of the situation as uncovered by the inquiry.

Behind that inquiry was a considerable theological impetus which had been built up through the work of the Ecumenical Movement since the Stockholm Conference on Social Problems in 1925. For instance, the Oxford Conference of 1937 broke through the individualistic thinking which had characterized so much Protestant social theology by emphasizing the significance of the economic, social and political *structures* of life, and the need for changing them, not merely of converting individuals to Christ. That conference was dominated by two background factors, the political menace of nazism and other totalitarian systems, and the economic menace of mass unemployment in western democracies. At Amsterdam the first Assembly of the World Council of Churches in 1948 gave some criteria for changing these structures when it spoke of "the Responsible Society" which it described as one "where freedom is the freedom of men who acknowledge responsibility to justice and public order, and where those who hold political authority and economic power are responsible for its exercise to God and the people whose welfare is affected by it." The background of the Assembly was postwar reconstruction, and this concept gave some principle of criticism to apply to contemporary social orders, whether communist, capitalist or the modified welfare capitalism of western Europe, while refusing to absolutize any one of them. All continually need scrutiny in the name of God and all are reminded that they are ordained by God for the good of mankind and not mankind for their good. The second Assembly of Evanston in 1954 showed itself particularly sensitive to the situation of "little men in big societies." It met against the background of the "cold war" and tried to get beyond the crude simplifications of either side of it.

103

Christ the Transformer of Culture

As we have mentioned, there is underlying this whole ecumenical development of Christian social thinking a stress on the necessity of paying attention to *facts*. It is of course true that there are a number of subtle questions which can be raised both as regards what exactly is a fact and how it can be evaluated. Sufficient to say here that the stress is a corrective to all theologies which proceed in a deductive *a priori* way. Beyond that, there are various possible theological frameworks which could serve as the pattern for Christian thinking in social ethics; and it would be idle to pretend that there is unanimity about them in ecumenical circles. But, if one takes, for example, the late Richard Niebuhr's well-known analysis, in his book *Christ and Culture,* of five different theological positions which have persisted in Christian history (an important corrective to Troeltsch's classical delimitation of only three positions), it is clear that there is something of value in the five or they would not have persisted through the centuries. It is also clear that Niebuhr thinks that the fifth (Christ the transformer of culture) is more adequate than the others. [2]

It is within this fifth position that the theological basis for dealing with the dynamic problems of economic growth will be found. The reason is that it is the only one which is specifically geared to a dynamic and changing society. This is what all the world is now living in. For most of recorded history social change has been very slow. But it is now clear that what gained momentum in Britain during the course of the eighteenth century has now become a permanent and worldwide movement and one that proceeds at an

---

[2] The others are (1) Christ against culture, (2) the Christ of culture (i.e. the accommodation of Christianity to culture), (3) Christ above culture, (4) Christ and culture in paradox. They are not of course found in Christian history in distinct separation from one another, but in varying proportions in different theologians. But in a very broad way it could be said that the first is particularly characteristic of pietist Protestantism, the second of liberal Protestantism, the third of Thomism, the fourth of Lutheranism, and the fifth of St. Augustine and Calvinism.

increasing speed. Rapid and continuous social change is the great new fact of our time. The theology associated in Niebuhr's fifth position, whose ancestry is traced back through F. D. Maurice via Calvin to St. Augustine, is best fitted to deal with endemic rapid social change, and it is a true interpretation for such a situation of the New Testament whose time scale was so foreshortened that it does not deal with social change. Traditional Catholic theology will need to have a more empirical concern (and there are growing signs of discontent with traditional moral theology in Roman Catholic circles about this), and traditional Lutheran theology will need a more dynamic outlook (and we can see in someone like Bonhoeffer the struggle to arrive at one). Neither Catholic natural law theology nor Lutheran order of creation theology is precluded, but they need developing in a new way. (It is not clear what position Orthodoxy takes on these matters or whether it has ever had much opportunity to think about them.)

The Evanston Assembly adopted a flexible and pragmatic attitude to the social order within the broad criterion of the responsible society. It did not succumb to any "cold war" attitude. It refused to become simply anticommunist or simply to extol the virtues of "laissez-faire." It uttered warnings about inequality, injustice and inhumanity, and raised a query about the development of a society based upon the stimulation of unlimited wants. A study conference at Arnoldsheim in Germany in 1956 took up the theme in more detail, but it is the Thessaloniki Conference of 1959 which is the most significant one for us. The conference analyzed the problem of rapid social and cultural change, and then discussed the Christian responsibility for political action, for economic development, and for the promotion of community life in both rural and urban areas. Recognizing the social dislocation and moral confusion caused by rapid social change and the danger which affluence can bring, it elaborated the Christian attitude toward the development of the world's resources. It said that "providentially it provides opportunities for the development of each person, for

the enrichment of the equality of human living, and for the sub-
duing of the earth and exercising dominion over it of which the
Bible speaks." It affirmed that "it is right and Christian, however, to insist on the need for a reasonable level" (that is, standard
of living), and that "in discovering and making use of the wealth
of the earth and of the human mind we have some of our greatest
opportunities to give God the worship due to him," calling in the
parable of the talents to support it. But it emphasized that these
resources must be used for the benefit of all men "for God looks
on the whole human family as one." "No man, or country, therefore, has the absolute right to enjoy by themselves either the fruits
of material riches they happen to inherit, or the fruits of ability
or effort. God does not draw boundaries of responsibility at national frontiers, nor can we." These theological positions were
stated rather than argued. The report went on to say that the
ultimate aim is to abolish unnecessary poverty among nations, and
to this end those with the greater resources and abilities have the
greater obligations. Not least must the rich countries be aware
of the impact of what they do on the poorer ones. An ideal of an
international division of labor is realizable (a curious echo of
laissez-faire theory in view of the unequal distribution of natural
resources in the world and the consequent poverty this would mean
in some areas).

The report discussed some of the ethical issues involved in the
methods of economic growth. Here again it adopted a flexible approach. For instance, in the question of capital formation, many
western readers may be surprised to find the Chinese Government
commended for its use of the labor force as a method of indigenous
capital formation. The report is realistic about the inescapable
problems involved in developing a competent and socially responsible industrial leadership, and what this means in terms both of
management training and the development of trade unions. It
urged Christians to help with both these tasks and with the achievement of the increased productivity that is the urgent need of most

countries. It remarked how few examples there are of Christians doing this, and indeed how isolated the church is from the life and needs of the industrial workers. It faced the problem of strikes. All this is far removed from the ethical outlook that is customary in the churches of the underdeveloped countries. The report stressed the need for the churches to understand both the real costs of economic development in terms of human values and at the same time the human cost of inaction. Within this general awareness "Christian responsibility involves decisions as to whether a particular economic choice is really a moral or merely a technical choice. In the former case responsible Christian action is required. In the latter, Christians should help to divert the choice of moral and theological overtones."

Every problem is connected with everything else. Problems of economic growth are related to problems of population, which were briefly touched on. It pointed out, for instance, that if the Indian birthrate continues at its present level and assuming the five-year plans achieve their goal (a big assumption), in thirty years the standard of living will rise only by 14 per cent; if the birthrate were halved it would improve by 75 per cent. Again, social and industrial change produces profound changes in both village and urban life; and these were dealt with in the closing pages of the report. Vast problems of community life, town planning, "commuting" and the like are involved.

On the question of the spiritual dangers of economic development the report mentioned five points:

1. Men do not necessarily know how to consume responsibly.
2. Men become absorbed in the means and techniques that make for an affluent society.
3. When men get richer they worship riches and forget God.
4. Society may become marked by new forms of social stratification, conspicuous consumption, and status seeking, as people look for marks and symbols of personal prestige and success.

107

5. Men may become slaves of the production machine and victims of the vast and elaborate apparatus upon which they have come to depend for material abundance.

In addition to ecumenical thought in Christian social ethics, there has been a good deal of miscellaneous material covering similar ground from various church sources. One of the most exhaustive was the six-volume inquiry for the Federal Council of Churches in the U.S.A., *The Ethics and Economics of Society,* edited by Dudley Ward. Another was a small report on behalf of the Congregational Church of England on *"Technology, Community and Church,"* edited by H. Cunliffe-Jones. These, and many more, have contributed to the wide ecumenical discussion.

In this discussion there has been a notable change in the theological mood in the past few years. This is something that grows out of what has gone before but that would have been difficult to foresee. It has taken the form of a new theological humanism. It is not that the Christian faith has been abandoned for a secular humanist one, but that the concern in the Christian gospel for the truly human in life has been emphasized, and with it a sense of the solidarity of the Christian with all men. This involves the desire to fight for the human in the dynamic social changes we are experiencing and, where possible, to find a "common ground" ethic with men of any faith or none who at a particular point will fight for the same end. Jacques Maritains' book *True Humanism* (which originally dates from 1934 and comes from a Thomist background) in a sense foreshadows this development, and is one indication among many of the extent to which Roman Catholic thought and that of the Ecumenical Movement are arriving by different routes at similar positions. John XXIII's encyclical *Mater et Magistra* is another.

Ethical Problems of Economic Growth

Since the Thessaloniki conference the emphasis of ecumenical studies has shifted slightly to a study of the processes and methods of economic growth which underlie rapid social change. This time the economically developed areas of the world have also been included. The results of the inquiries are presented in these volumes of essays. It is obvious that every part of social life is affected. A society that learns to be flexible, to make rational forecasts and take calculated risks and long-range decisions, that requires a high level of literary and sophisticated techniques of administration, is obviously very different from most societies in human history. The human consequences in the breakup of the traditional family structure and the necessity of social mobility and technical adaptability are immense. The political consequences are equally great, for the laissez-faire attitude of western government to economic problems (which had been their chief characteristic from the beginning of the industrial revolution until recent decades and is by no means a spent force yet) is completely irrelevant in less-developed countries.

In the more-developed countries we have a very high production of goods and services; the pressure is to consume more as former luxuries come to be considered necessities. The basic question for Christians to consider is how far we can baptize economic growth and affluence in the name of Christ. The question is acute because of the warnings in the Gospels about the danger of riches and of covetousness. Indeed, Jesus explicitly reversed the current belief, shared by his disciples, that riches were a sign of God's favor. He clearly regarded them as a main cause of anxiety, and anxiety as a key symptom of lack of trust in God. It would be true to say that the church has never found it easy to come to terms with this note in the Gospels. Its radical note has sometimes been held to apply to the few who are called to the "religious" life, following the counsels of perfection as distinct from the

109

precepts binding on all. But the voluntary poverty of those who answered this call has nearly always been accompanied by the enormous wealth of the order to which they belonged. The more usual position has been to urge on the rich the duty of being charitable to the poor without challenging the basic distribution of riches. An obvious position would have been to stress the need for greater common ownership of wealth, but on the whole it has been left to secular socialist critics to develop this criticism. Certainly any Christian justification of private property that has been worked out would presuppose the widest possible diffusion of it, though this has seldom been remembered by Christian teachers and preachers. It would perhaps be ironical if Christians began to take exception to economic growth only when for the first time in the world's history it appeared that there might be the possibility of removing the crippling poverty, squalor and disease from the backs of the majority of humanity who have hitherto always suffered them. Christians in the West have hardly as yet got used to their own relative mass affluence, and if they have seen no reason to query it they can hardly query the desire of other countries to share in it. In Great Britain, for instance, only fifty years ago 96 per cent of the average family income went on food, rent, fuel and clothing. Now, since the last war, only 60 per cent does. This is what the relative affluence amounts to, and this is the relative newness. Christians have for the most part accepted it without comment. Those who have thought about it have welcomed it as a gift from God; they have not just accepted what has happened uncritically on the "Whatever is, is right" principle, but have seen this economic growth as a means of more human beings being better fed, clothed and housed; as a challenge to use new skills; as an opportunity to pursue other interests than merely keeping oneself alive; and as a possible solvent for some of the tensions in political life. Underprivileged nations and races can behave irresponsibly if they have nothing to lose; the rise in the standard of living in the U.S.S.R. has, for instance, been welcomed as a stabilizing factor in international relations. These Christians have not found anything in the Gospels which require human beings to be kept in conditions of abject poverty if it can be prevented.

Poverty and riches are terms relevant to their situation. The task of Christians would appear to be, first of all, to admit that the church has far too easily accepted worldly standards of wealth, and to regard this a challenge to deal more effectively with the new problems of economic growh and affluence. This means being suitably wary of the pressures of the affluent society to ever greater consumption, and translating the Gospel warnings on riches from their *Sitz im Leben* in first-century Palestine to the entirely different economic circumstances of today. This will involve a right use of individual and corporate wealth within one country and between richer and poorer countries; it will also mean thinking out afresh the relation of work and leisure. We shall then see that economic growth may well be accepted as one of the most signal examples of man's mastery over nature which he is given by divine command in the Genesis parable of creation. We shall realize that although economic growth, properly controlled, can remove terrible privations from the majority of the human race, this may not in itself make them any happier. Human life will always present human beings with pain, loss, disappointment and frustrations, no matter what level of economic growth we may achieve. The Christian challenge comes in the way these inevitable deprivations are met and in the quality of our relationships with others in the bundle of life in which we are tied up with others. Here the Gospel warnings against the deceitfulness of riches and the call to a responsibly corporate use of wealth will always have their place.

The question may still arise as to whether the Christian can sanction indefinite social accumulation. There has been talk in Britain of doubling the standard of living by 1984. It is quite feasible. And what after that? But the U. S. A. is already much farther advanced on that road than Britain. Do we look to an economic system which requires an even greater proliferation of

wants in order to keep going? Does it mean that we must establish
a deliberate system of built-in obsolescence, scrapping things long
before they are worn out in order to keep the system going with
new production? In that case the whole economy would be run on
the principle on which women's fashions are already run. Would
it be possible to give a Christian sanction to such a system? Clearly
it would not. There are various factors which may make this prospect less immediate than might appear. One is the growth in population. Another is the vast amount of resources that are needed
if anything like a satisfactory urban environment and town development is to be secured. A third is the scope there is for helping
consumers to be much more exacting in their requirements, much
less satisfied with the careless and the shoddy. But, beyond that,
Christians cannot be content to toil for the superfluous or permit
men to be evaluated by external standards of conspicuous consumption. They will want a wholly new attitude toward leisure.
In most of the world this is a system hardly over the horizon as
yet, one which our successors may in due time have to solve.

Need for New Social and Human Attitudes

Perhaps the underlying Christian concern is to insist that "economic growth is made for man and not man for economic growth,"
a conviction that springs directly from the Christian belief in the
status of man, made in God's image, remade in Jesus Christ, and
destined for an eternal fellowship with God and with his fellowmen in God. The roots of this belief are at the center of Christian
theology and in the light of it the church and the Christian must
stand for what helps man to be truly human and oppose all that
tends to dehumanize him. From these beliefs the Christian has a
permanent concern for such values as justice, freedom, security
and equality, which act as criteria for evaluating the status quo,
none of them being able to be pursued without reference to the
others. They also make the Christian sensitive to the use and abuse

112

of power. It is with these considerations in mind that the Christian approaches the opportunities and dangers of economic growth and rapid social change. They are old criteria rooted in the fundamentals of the Christian faith, but brought to bear on the new situation of affluence and potential affluence.

One would expect, for instance, the church to be sensitive to the underdog, to those who get a raw deal in life. It was the scandal of the first industrial revolution that it was so callous to those who suffered in the process. That is why one set of historians can point to the general rise in the standard of living and to the benefits it brought, while others can stress the appalling conditions of work and housing and the long agony of the superseded trades like the handloom weavers. (It was from Manchester that Engels got most of the evidence for his *Condition of the Working Classes* in 1844.) There will always be the old, the lonely, the neurotic, the mentally handicapped, the unskilled, those burdened with large families, for whom "ambulance work" is needed and for whom the Christian conscience should be alert.

Rapid and continuous social change, however, brings strains which affect much of the population. Pursuit of productivity regardless of its social effects may have serious effects on the power of adjustment of individuals and families. A skill learned at 20 may be valueless at 40. It is hard then to learn a new skill. Yet the shock of becoming unskilled is great. The experience of the father becomes irrelevant to the son, and this is dangerous because parents should always have something to give to their children. How many times in a working life can a man stand the strain of becoming redundant and having to adapt himself to a new occupation? Anxieties of this kind arise in white-collar as well as manual jobs. Clearly, much greater public policy in the way of severance pay, assisted retraining and resettlement is needed; it cannot be left to chance. Perhaps a more versatile basic training rather than a single craft training will be needed. The church needs also to be much more alert to ministering to people on the move; in many

113

countries the parochial structure is far too static. Mental illness can easily arise, and so can crime. The crime rate is much greater in a continuously mobile and urban society than it is in a comparatively static and rural one. Loneliness is also much greater, especially among women at home with young children, and new arrivals. (On all this there is much of value in Professor Titmuss' chapter on "Industrialisation and the Family" in *Essays on The Welfare State*.) [4]

A further point one has to query is whether in the pursuit of productivity enough thought is given to the using up of non-renewable resources like fossil fuels. There are many technical and imponderable factors here, not least the possibility of the discovery of new resources, and the invention of substitutes, but it is clear that politicians and technologists and the general public are very conscious of their own wants and deprivations and apt not to think of those of their grandchildren. These are not articulate and they do not possess votes. There are limits to the extent to which it is a moral duty to consider an unknown future, but Christians ought to help society to look beyond the end of its nose.

We need to look further at the problem of directing the ever-increasing productivity to socially desirable ends. Here the influence of advertising has to be critically examined. It is easy to exaggerate the scale of the problem and to succumb to the exaggerations with which the industry surrounds itself. For example, only 2 per cent of the British national income is spent on advertising, and at least a third of it is essential expenditure. Disquiet arises about the remainder because much of it does not respect the dignity of the human person. It is designed to produce impulse buying rather than considered behavior, it is inclined to appeal to social status and snobbery; or to profit by human weakness, fears and anxieties; or to exploit fundamental human traits

---

[4] By RICHARD M. TITMUSS. New Haven, Conn., U. S. A.: Yale University Press, 1964.

like the concern for one's children or the need for security, status, and love. That is why the consumers' movement in many countries is a welcome counterbalance to aspects of modern advertising and salesmanship techniques.

Equally important is the question of collective expenditure. J. K. Galbraith hit this off in his well-known book, *The Affluent Society*, where he contrasted the growth of private affluence in the West with the poor standard of collective provision and the resulting public squalor. There is the wanton ugliness of much industrial environment, the mean housing, the out-of-date hospitals, schools and prisons. What is lacking is sufficient concern for the common good and awareness of the corporate nature of society.

Galbraith also raises the question of leisure (which has already been mentioned) when productivity reaches the scale it is approaching in the U. S. A. People need help in wanting to work less, accumulate less, and enjoy more. In most industrialized countries it is still the stage where the mass of wage earners find their relative affluence so new that when statutory hours of work are reduced, they are eager for more overtime in order to accumulate more goods and enjoy more services. In the U. S. A. there are said to be four million people doing two jobs. In fact the prospect of leisure presents a challenge. Before the century is out, a three- or four-day working week should be possible in many economically developed countries, but most people at the moment do not know what to do with such resulting leisure and are frightened of it.

New social attitudes and new social disciplines are needed. This applies to the car. Affluence in western Europe is making the car available to ordinary citizens, and it is no longer the luxury of a few. The motorcar is so convenient that western communities are simply shutting their eyes to its social cost in the disruption of urban life and in the frightful toll of deaths and injuries on the road. This amounts to a continuous raging epidemic that would not be tolerated for any other form of disease or cruelty. We are putting personal convenience before social good, and the necessary expenditure and social discipline needed to reduce the human cost of the motorcar.

This discussion has so far been mainly about economically developed countries. But whatever Christian justification we advance for economic growth it must be one that applies to all countries, and to whatever extent we can accept affluence as a divine gift it must mean that those who enjoy it have a great responsibility for those who do not. This will remain a permanent feature of the world. For just as men are not empirically equal, yet in varying ways we ignore their natural inequality and treat them as equal (and the varying proportions in which this is done is one of the key points of political difference), so different areas of the world—and therefore different nations—are unequal in resources and so will have markedly different standards of living, which it must be the aim of those with higher standards to make less unequal. One corollary of this is that those who fortunately live in developed countries have to accept the privilege. It would do no good to level down. Indeed, the prosperity of the West, rightly used, is a help to the rest. But it is very necessary to remember that economic strength is no indication of moral virtue; this thought should lead to a proper humility in economically privileged countries.

It is difficult to believe that the resources of the West are being properly used when we realize that the gap in living standards between them and the rest is growing greater rather than less. Do the British people, for instance, realize that any economic aid they have given since the war has been outpaced by the fall in prices of primary products from which they have benefited? It is salutary to note that at the United Nations Trade and Development Conference at Geneva in 1964, 77 underdeveloped countries made common ground against the economically privileged ones. It is also interesting to note that from the point of view of the poorer countries some of the richer ones, who think that they fall into different camps, appear in the same group. The U.S.A., Great Britain, and western Europe, the U.S.S.R. and Japan from this angle belong together. It seemed that the developed countries were not very receptive listeners. Because the U.S.S.R. had not much to offer, the West did not rise to the occasion.

There seems an undeniable loss of vision in the West compared with a few years ago. The underdeveloped countries need aid, but they need trade as well. They need a more certain income through more stable prices for primary products, perhaps by compensation for losses if the terms of trade turn against them, and they also need free entry for their manufactured goods in the markets of the "West." This in turn means a willingness of the West to modify its internal economics to this end, and this means, further, the willingness to make the social adjustments necessary. A larger vision and a vigorous public policy are called for. Neither is as yet readily secured because people in the relatively affluent West do not want to be disturbed in their ways. Cotton textiles are always a good instance of this, because their manufacture is always one of the first that newly industrializing countries turn to and can produce relatively cheaply. The cry in the West is usually to keep such imports out, or severely to restrict them, thus making the gigantic problem of a place like overcrowded Hong Kong even more difficult.

Help for developing countries needs increasing if the growing disparity in standards of living is to be checked. The West should consider whether some of the money it is spending on military and space research and development could not be better spent. It should also consider whether it does not need a higher annual rate of economic growth to fulfill these obligations to others. At the moment a growth of 4 per cent per annum is the most that it is usual to aim at, and it is far from being achieved because of built-in resistance to change from management, workers, sales executives and government officials alike. It is probable that 7 per cent is the annual rate of growth that should be aimed at. But this would require still greater flexibility, and the necessary social policies to help individuals to make the necessary adjustments. And

117

this would be in order to discharge responsibilities to the less wealthy rather than to get rich still more quickly at home. Merely to state this is to realize how far the West is from grasping it. Yet can the moral responsibility of those who have riches such as the West possesses be any less? Has any western government ever begun to plan how to lead its citizens in this direction? One of the most striking features of the economic affairs of states is that their domestic decisions affect other states far beyond their frontiers. Consultation and planning need to extend beyond the bounds of a state just because of the repercussions of economic policies on other countries. The less strong countries economically are particularly vulnerable to those with developed economies. Here again the sense of the common good is only rudimentarily developed, and the moral responsibility of the wealthy countries correspondingly great.

One of the central problems for both poor and wealthy nations to pay attention to is urban renewal. The movement of people into cities is one of the chief features of our time. Even in the West an immense effort of urban investment is needed if anything like a suitably human city life is to be achieved. But in Asia towns are growing 400 per cent faster than in Europe. In Latin America 60 per cent of the population of Caracas consists of squatters who have come in from the countryside within the last ten years. The human misery from the dirt and overcrowding is extreme. Housing would appear one of the chief things to which economic aid from wealthy to less wealthy countries should be given. It is a useful economic spur in providing jobs, stimulating ancillary industries and providing a basic security for a family. Yet on the whole housing has been much neglected by government and private agencies as compared with the attraction of investment in factories and machines. These countries lack the expert skills to plan and carry through big housing programs, but this is an instance of the fact that aid from the West must be in technical and professional skills, and not only in goods and loans and grants.

118

The Moral Dynamics of Change

It is evident from this inquiry into economic growth that much depends on the actions and attitudes of the underdeveloped countries themselves, including the development of what are sometimes called the "Protestant virtues" of thought, efficiency and the avoidance of waste. These are not traditional attitudes in such countries, but have become established in industrial societies. The precise role of Protestantism in this is an issue much discussed. But without going into this question it is clear that any religious motivation suitable to a country beginning to develop must have a dynamic element and not merely provide a sanction of the status quo, as religion has so often done in human history.

This discussion has presupposed that there is a real struggle to achieve the economic growth which both the West and the rest now presuppose. There are some who so emphasize the productive power of technology, with the new achievements of automation and cybernetics as to suggest that this whole discussion is beside the point. Automation takes over labor, memory and logical choice. The machine has only to be fed with the right program. Repetitive jobs for human beings will go. The distinction between work and leisure will go. There is no prospect of providing jobs for most of the inhabitants of the developing countries. The problem will be boredom not fatigue. They should be encouraged to retain the old tribal virtues to cultivate the more passive and contemplative ones. Men should be issued with a basic income by right without working for it. It would be foolish to rule this out as a possibility in the future, but it is unlikely to be within the future that we have to adjust ourselves to now. Future generations must deal with it if and when it comes. But it could well be that by the turn of the century a 20-hour working week would be the usual stint in the West, and this would give rise to the beginnings of many problems of work and leisure to which we have already re-

119

ferred. In the immediate future, however, there is no doubt that big efforts must be made by the underdeveloped countries.

How best to help the poor countries to achieve a "take off" is in fact a difficult question. The phrase was coined by W. W. Rostow, the economist, in his book *Stages of Economic Growth*.[5] He distinguished five stages: (1) a traditional society, (2) when 10 per cent of national income is invested, and there is the beginning of an elite, (3) the "take off," (4) an economically mature society after sixty years, (5) when a level of high consumption is reached. It is not necessary to accept every detail of this analysis to see that the problem is how to get from the first to the third stage. There are many technical problems here, and it is a hard fact that much of the effort can come only from within the country concerned. Nevertheless, imaginative trade, aid, cultural, educational and administrative policies pursued by developed countries can immensely help or hinder. In all countries the control and use of power is a major matter of concern to the Christian conscience, and the shifts of power in the process of economic growth give rise to many problems, not least those of the growing scale of operation. If power is centralized in the state, it may easily be overweening, especially in a one-party state where the citizen has in effect no status outside the party. There are particular temptations to the abuse of power in the small elites in new nations who are pressing ahead with economic and political development. There is a tremendous need for firm and stable government in new and developing countries, and for Christians to play their full part in them. Too many have been brought up in pietist forms of a Christianity that is politically irresponsible and regards participation in political activities as worldly and wrong. Power centered in private hands can easily become anonymous in giant corporations, and it becomes very hard to ensure that the private power is responsibly

---

[5] Cambridge University Press, 1960.

used, and indeed is not more powerful than the government. It has been calculated that some 500 people in the U.S.A., through inter-locking directorships, control the greatest concentration of eco-nomic power in private hands ever known. It does not follow that it is used irresponsibly. Indeed, it may be so great as to be removed from some of the pressures to irresponsibility affecting those less powerful. But it is extremely hard to know whether it is or not. Similarly the development of power in trade unions can have a tyrannous effect. In some cases a member can find little redress against abuse of power by officials of his own union, which can in effect keep him out of employment. In addition, the freedom of each union to bargain independently in the wages market, when it is unrestrained in a period of practically full employment, can result in recurrent inflation, which produces its own social imbal-ance and is persistently unfair to those with fixed incomes, and in particular the retired and the old.

When we consider power at the level of the shop floor, issues of industrial management loom that are of profound importance to the lives of those involved. One wonders, for instance, how far those engaged on work study pay enough attention to the signifi-cance of work and the relations of a work group in a factory. Many of the resistances to change, which can be shown to be of economic benefit to the workers involved, are due to the disruption of established relationships at work, and to the feeling that a bit of one's life which was to some extent within one's own control has been taken out of it and put under the impersonal thrall of the stop watch. Indeed, it is problems of organization rather than ownership that are usually the key ones in industry. Questions of nationalization may well be a side issue. Granted that much must remain in the hands of management—for instance, problems of prices and investment—and that much can be controlled by gov-ernment policy and affected by organized consumers (whether in public or private industry) at the grass roots the perennial problem remains, that of giving a sense of freedom and responsibility in daily work. There is always the struggle to set men free so that they are not the servants but the masters of machines.

If the implications of this are that the traditional socialist economic criticisms of capitalism are too simple (and that capitalism itself is changing rapidly), what of the traditional socialist criticism of inequality? There still seems much force in this. It was given an added sting by the arbitrariness of the inequalities in capitalist society and the way in which they were inflated by inherited wealth. But we can imagine a society that has pruned away the artificial inequalities derived from this factor and that has achieved a career open to the talents and promotion by merit only. In fact, the pressure for economic growth may work toward this. We should then have what has been called a meritocracy. It could merely mean an opportunity to get on, with the gap between the classes widening, leaving a *lumpenproletariat* at the bottom with no way of escape from the knowledge of its own lack of talent. Where would human solidarity be then? Indeed, one of the problems of advanced economies in the future will be to find jobs for those of low intelligence and mental handicap. And there is nothing worse than the feeling that one has no status and is not wanted.

Somewhere in this realm of a crusade for the human, with all that this means in terms of the criteria of justice, freedom and equality, may lie the springs of social enthusiasm, which is badly needed, now that the furious ideologies of the earlier years of the century are no longer what they were. In the more economically developed countries there is a certain disillusionment with past causes, a vacuum of enthusiasm. The poor countries are at the moment fired by "the revolution of rising expectations," which is associated with a heady nationalism and finds a convenient bogey in neo-colonialism. It is not easy for those who have had their share of nationalist fervor, and are only slowly growing out of it into supranational (for example, regional) conceptions, to be

122

believed if they point to the dangers of nationalism. And it is of course a necessary advance in building new nations from tribalism. But the facts are that the poorer countries have a long and difficult struggle ahead, even if the rich ones behave in the most far-sighted way toward them, and that they may easily become disillusioned in their turn when this becomes evident, and it is seen that the enthusiasms of new-found independence are not enough. A crusade for the human, for making economic growth the servant of man is needed. Christians have the strongest reasons for wanting this, but it is something that they can share with those who lack the profound Christian grounds for wanting it. Christians should be able to demonstrate a distinctive style of life and an obedience to the call of Christ in the world that can have profound, if indirect, results in the struggle to work with God to make and to keep human life human under the stresses and opportunities of economic growth.

PART II

TECHNOLOGY AND THE CONTROL
OF ENVIRONMENT

5

FUTURE SOCIAL PROBLEMS
OF AN "ADVANCED COUNTRY"

by J. P. THIJSSE (Netherlands)

COUNTRIES that have a low standard of living and countries that recently have won their independence are generally called "developing countries." All are eager to fulfill their development in the shortest possible time, and they have therefore great problems to overcome. It is a situation characterized by labor pains.

But the expression "developing countries" is misleading. It could imply that countries which have reached a higher standard of living and are called "advanced," have completed their development process and reached the stage of *homme arrivé*. This would mean that these countries now have a static economy and that planning is no longer necessary.

In the present conditions, it would mean that such countries are going backward, compared with those which are raising their economic and social level. But competition requires the "advanced countries" also to run hard in order not to be left behind in the economic race.

The "advanced countries" are, like the poor and young countries, "developing countries," though at quite a different stage of development; their problems are different, but just as difficult to solve, and they require constant and urgent planning. It is remarkable that in contrast to the developing countries where the problems result from great poverty, the problems of the "advanced countries" are the consequence of their greater wealth.

History has shown repeatedly that dynasties and states have collapsed through excessive wealth, and in many of the "advanced countries" it is essential that measures be taken to ensure that the increase in national income is constructively used and not wasted in worthless activities. A higher economic standard means more personal income, more free time, and the danger of wasting these is great. For that reason, it is essential to develop comprehensive planning for the use of resources.

There are many types of social problems facing the so-called advanced countries, and, as a case study, we shall look at those problems which the Netherlands will have to face in the near future.

The Social Consequences of Continuing Urbanization

We have too long underestimated the problem of growing concentration of people and activities in one part of the country. In fact, this is *the* problem of the "primate city," the metropolis which attracts population to the extent that it depletes the rest of the country. This problem occurs in all areas of the world; we see it in Tokyo, Calcutta, Paris, Athens, Cairo, and elsewhere. In the Netherlands, we encounter it in the "Randstad Holland" (Conurbation Holland), which is an unusual metropolitan area, stretching in a horseshoe shape from Utrecht through Amsterdam to Rotterdam.

Its effect on the rest of the country is the same as that of other centrifugally developed metropolitan areas of the world.

The Randstad Holland owes much of its importance to the fact of its location at the point where the Rhine, which has always been the principal traffic artery in western Europe, flows into the sea. It is a meeting point for sea and inland navigation, rail and road traffic; and for this reason large industries have established themselves in the west of the Netherlands, along the two rivers which reach the sea at that point. Consequently, two urban centers have sprung up, consisting in a row of towns, which have been there ever since the Middle Ages, and which together form the two arms of the horseshoe. Between the two arms is a space which has not yet been urbanized and where, in addition to milk and dairy products, horticulture is developed; the airport is located here also and there is a network of roads allowing for easy communication between the different parts of the Randstad.

The growth of activities, the settlement of new industries, the increase of "clerical staff" in the government offices as well as in private companies, have increased the percentage of population in the three western provinces constituting the Randstad. Today it is estimated that well over half of the population of Holland lives in these three provinces.

There have been considerable migration streams from all parts of the country toward the Randstad. If this trend continues, we shall be faced by the dangers, first, of a too great congestion in the Randstad and, second, of a gradual depopulation of the "outer provinces." In order to solve these problems, the central authorities have adopted measures to make the privileges of settlement in the outer provinces so attractive that over the last few years, most of the new industries have settled of their own free will outside the Randstad, thus arresting the immigration stream. During the past year it has been observed that the migration tendency has been centrifugal, so that the population in the Randstad showed only a small increase, resulting from natural growth.

129

The land still available within the Randstad territory, insofar as it is located along the deep waterways, is to remain reserved for those specific industries which depend exclusively or indirectly on such waterways. Thus, it will be necessary to exercise a clear selection before new industries are allowed to settle in the Randstad; and even then the land that fulfills these requirements and is located along the two means of communication will in due course be sold out. Other possibilities of making land available along deep waterways will have to be examined. For this purpose, two locations along the coast, outside the Randstad, are favored. Their development will prevent an increased congestion of the Randstad, but they must be connected with the Rhine.

Population Trends in the Netherlands

There is also in the Netherlands the problem of the high density of population. With the exception of Monaco, the Netherlands has the heaviest population density in the world and, compared with other western European countries, the rate of population increase is extremely rapid (1.4 per cent).

Between 1850 and 1900, and again between 1900 and 1950, the population doubled; and, according to the latest forecast, it can be expected to increase even further by the year 2000.

The population now totals over 12 million with the likelihood, by the year 2000, of a further 8 million. In addition to feeding this large population, providing them with work and shelter, we shall be faced with the problem of how and where to settle them.

In a country already densely populated, where land is such a scarce commodity, we shall have to deal with it as sparingly as possible, concentrating the population to a maximum in order to prevent splitting up the land. In view of the need to avoid congestion in large cities and to distribute the people, for social and cultural reasons, harmoniously over the country, the solution will lie in decentralization through regional concentration. In other words, a number of urban centers will have to be developed outside the Randstad, all of them surrounded by rural territory.

In order to determine the number of people who should be living in these cities, another factor must be considered.

In 1900, 30 per cent of the working people were employed in the primary sector (agriculture and cattle breeding). This percentage has sharply decreased, first as a result of larger opportunities for work in industry, services and free professions, but also because of modernization and mechanization in agriculture and cattle breeding. Now only 9 per cent of the working forces are active in the primary sector, and it is expected that in the year 2000 this will fall to 2½ per cent. Assuming that as many people will be needed to serve the former group (such as bakers, butchers, clergymen, teachers, doctors), only 5 per cent of the population will have to live in the country. Thus in forty years only one million people will live in rural areas; the other 19 million would potentially be urban and *could* live in cities. If this is achieved, it would be possible to keep the territories between the cities strictly rural, and thus suitable for modernized agriculture, cattle breeding and horticulture and also for recreation, of which there will be a greater need. Urban centers, which should all acquire an industrial and cultural function, must offer their inhabitants as favorable living conditions as possible; and the density in the cities should therefore be kept down to a maximum of fifty inhabitants per hectare "gross." This will allow for doubling the density of population in the residential areas.

To illustrate the manner in which the population of the Netherlands could be distributed in the year 2000, we give here a few examples of possible spacing. In each instance, we have proceeded from the development of existing towns, with the exception of Lelystad which (since the center of the Zuiderzee polders area is in the process of being claimed) will have to rise, so to speak, from nothing, as the only "new town." If existing towns are very close to one another, two or three have been merged, in conformity, in fact, with the scale enlargement of the urban-rural pattern which is taking shape everywhere.

The first solution calls for concentration nuclei varying from 400,000 to one million inhabitants, distributed over the country as harmoniously as possible and with never more than 50 kilometers between them. Thanks to this limitation, it is possible to serve the whole national territory, economically and socially speaking. But, in reality, conditions for development are not equally favorable everywhere; and we shall have to adopt measures to stimulate the development of the northwest region, which lies outside the international traffic streams, if this pattern is to materialize.

The second solution would allow the greater development to be concentrated in the territories that offered the most favorable conditions.

A third solution, again, offers a more harmonious population spread, still not in isolated centers, but in the shape of a ribbon, grouped along the existing domestic means of communication.

A fourth solution, which could result from a situation where government leadership was absent or misdirected, shows the filling-up of the open spaces of the Randstad, seriously harming the living conditions because of a shortage of open recreation areas. This solution should be avoided at all costs.

Shape of the Future Society

There are, no doubt, many other solutions. What the real solution will be depends largely on government initiative with regard to physical planning. Action is urgent. When the state authorities know that the number of inhabitants will double, triple or even be multiplied by five in a period of 35 years, they should without doubt plan and develop a program with the greatest diligence. Business enterprises that propose to set up a new industry will want to know whether they are coming into a town with a quick expansion potential, or into one that has not been included in the

132

scheme for regional concentration. Thus, the government is faced with important decisions that they should reach without delay.

There are other problems, connected with the increased welfare, some of which may be mentioned here, though none of them are peculiar to the Netherlands.

The economic situation in the Netherlands is propitious. The income per capita has risen very much since the Second World War, and economists expect this trend to maintain itself. The increase is itself not so big as that of Japan where it is expected that between 1960 and 1970 the national income will have doubled. But our economists anticipate that in 25 years the buying power of the per capita income of the Dutch population will double, and all will be able to afford a more luxurious life.

At present, we live in a period of full employment and of great pressure on the labor market. Minimum wages have gone up, and poverty has virtually disappeared. Social laws ensure the individual's protection against many of the risks to which he was formerly exposed. For over a year now the five-day working week has been in operation, and free time has very much increased. We may expect the four-day working week to be introduced within twenty years. The proportion between work time and free time, which at present, in government administrative offices, stands at 42 hours against 38 hours (after deduction of sleeping and eating time), could well become 20 hours against 60 hours. In other words, we shall have more and more time available and less work. This is a good symptom, if we compare it with the conditions before the industrial revolution, when the working classes had to work long hours, with no free time for recreation and hardly enough for adequate rest. But the new situation also conceals some dangers already apparent. Our people have been taught and trained to do their work well, but they have been inadequately educated and guided in how to spend their leisure in a worthy and enriching manner. Our educational system will have to be revised fundamentally if we are to solve these problems constructively. We shall have to set up a curriculum, cultural in character, in which the exercise of an art, the love and study of nature and of voluntary scientific activities will receive new life. This cannot be done without purposeful leadership from the authorities.

In a shorter working week industries will have a lower employment occupancy. This can be brought about without inconvenience because, thanks to the increased use of automation, the industrial manufacturing sector will demand fewer employees. With work in several shifts we should no longer expect so large a regression of work possibilities as Fourastie predicted. An increase of the existing percentage is not to be expected, and a gradual or spasmodic decrease is obviously likely.

Though the primary (agricultural) sector will show a large decrease of work possibilities, the tertiary (service) sector will increase considerably. This will be absorbed largely in services for recreational activities, the demands of which will rise (transport and catering, for example).

In connection with this greater need for recreation, it is important to preserve land areas and to foster new nature-recreation areas on land that is now being set aside as marginal agricultural land. The problems involved here are obvious.

In agricultural policy the influence of the European Economic Community plays an important role. Only in favorable circumstances can the modern enterprises and the large agricultural initiatives compete successfully with the other EEC countries. It looks as if farms of 30 hectares will have a very tough task. With the exception of intensive and perfectioned horticulture, it will be necessary to do away with the smaller enterprises and especially with "fragmented farm ownership." This can be done through planned land consolidation of large territories or by the conversion of agrarian into recreational land. (A combination thereof will probably be most lucrative.) Here, attention should be given to reforestation. With regard to the problem of fragmentation there has been fairly successful work in the Netherlands since the end of the Second World War. Rational forms of exploitation have been used in the large territories, with much attention to better drainage and to the accessibility of the agricultural and cattle-breeding lots. The application of these principles has totally changed the landscape and has not rendered it more attractive. Large areas, scattered over the whole country, still await similar treatment. We should, however, question whether the land, which is becoming so scarce, could not be utilized for another purpose, more profitable to the community. The answer depends closely on the competitive position of the Netherlands in the EEC. Greater concentration on intensive horticulture will perhaps produce better results, with the advantage that more land would remain available for other purposes, such as recreation.

Reclamation of new land is a method long used by the Dutch who started to drain lakes and ponds and to build dikes in strips along the seashore as far back as the twelfth century. Large-scale reclamation, such as that of the Haarlem polder, for example, in the middle of the last century and that of the former Zuiderzee by an enclosing dike, has added much to the territorial area of the Netherlands. But the future possibilities of this process are limited. We could still turn the Wadden Lake into a polder, but this is practically the end to the country's expansion possibilities. This point will probably be reached in the year 2000.

There is also the problem of the *salinization of the surface water*. About one-sixth of the Netherlands is water, in the form of lakes, rivers, canals or ditches, which together make up a complicated system providing irrigation and draining wherever it is needed. This whole network is threatened in many places by salinization. The danger has two origins: first, from the sea which finds its way through the estuaries into our delta zone and ship canals, and by filtration into the low polders where the water level is much below the average sea level (up to 7 meters). With the

135

completion of the so-called "Deltaplan" which involves closing in a great portion of the estuaries, this threat will be to some extent removed.

But the danger threatens from other sources as well. For its industrial and "domestic" water supply the Netherlands uses the Rhine, which rises in Switzerland, flows through a part of France and through Germany and finally reaches the Dutch border. This "water source" of the Netherlands is at the same time the main sewer for the Swiss, French and German industries which dump much of their industrial waste into the Rhine. As a result, when the Rhine water reaches the Netherlands, it often has a high saline content and is polluted by undesirable chemicals. International agreements have fixed the acceptable level of saline concentration. This hampers the French and German industries in their disposal of industrial waste, especially whenever the Rhine "discharge" is small. In the future these factors will greatly increase the difficulties, and we shall have to resort to desalinization of sea water for "domestic and industrial" water supply, an expensive procedure, which we cannot, however, avoid.

Urban Congestion and Its Problems

The Netherlands is exposed to other causes of pollution, many of them the result of greater wealth. There is, for example, the effect of *greater automobile ownership*. In 1948 it was assumed that the number of cars in the Netherlands would never exceed the ceiling of 151,000, but over the last few years the number has increased beyond all expectations (in four years from 500,000 to one million). The relation between population and the number of cars is now 12 to 1, and our automobile density is one of the highest in the world. There is no sign of any slowing down, and we may expect that in 1970 there will be over two million cars, over three million in 1980, and possibly seven million in the year 2000. We refer here to car *ownership*. We should not necessarily assume that the *use* of cars will follow the same trend, though in any event the road traffic is likely to increase rapidly, and we may expect the intensity of traffic to go up by about 50 per cent in five years. The road system will have to be expanded, involving large investments.

This automobile invasion also congests the traffic in city centers. Expensive measures are necessary to alleviate this situation, probably by means of an improved and more frequent public transport system and the limitation of parking possibilities in the "downtown areas." Moreover, car parking already presents immense difficulties, not only in the town centers, but near the car owners' residences as well. The paradoxical proposition according to which the more private cars there are, the greater is the need for more, better and more frequent public transport, seems to hold true.

Then there is the problem of disposing of the cars as waste after they have become useless, an obvious problem which also applies to many other consumer goods—wrappings and containers and all industrial "waste products." The greater the economic development and the higher the standard of living, the larger the amount of waste products. Their quality is also changing, which makes their destruction more difficult still. A banana leaf, which is used as wrapping material in many developing countries, raises no destruction problem, but a plastic bag is a hopeless matter.

The pollution of the earth, water and air constantly creates problems, and their solution will demand important financial sacrifices, especially in the most congested areas. In heavily populated countries, "disposal of the dead" constitutes a problem. Where there is little room for the fast-growing population, room for the dead will have to be restricted to the minimum. In fact, it looks as if cremation will have to become the rule.

Housing also brings problems. Because of greater longevity, the average family has regressed from 4 to 3.25, with the result, also because of stagnation in construction during and after the Second World War, that a housing shortage has occurred which has not yet been overcome. If we add the fast population growth (1.4 per cent) and take into account that the old and substandard houses have to be replaced, the Dutch government has a heavy and difficult task if they are to solve this housing shortage within a measurable period of time.

To this we must add the comment that the houses which were built after the war do not, qualitatively speaking, come up to present standards, offering insufficient space and unsatisfactory sound-proofing. With the higher standard of living people will no longer be satisfied with these houses once the present shortage has been overcome.

In all these respects the Netherlands is in the midst of great problems, all demanding accelerated action and heavy investments.

6

GROWTH, TECHNOLOGY AND MODERN ECONOMIC PLANNING TECHNIQUES

by CLAUDE GRUSON (France)

ECONOMIC development is a phenomenon associated with technological progress and is characterized by the constant growth in the volume of goods and services produced in comparison with the number of people directly employed in producing and marketing them. It is measured in terms of annual rates of expansion, based on national balance sheets.

Technological progress manifests itself in constant changes in the nature and use of the goods and services produced. Hence, it is always difficult to establish a comparison between the total goods and services produced during a certain period in a country and those produced during an earlier period, or in another country. In a single country the standard of measurement may be arbitrary, but it remains more or less the same over a period of time; the

139

calculated rates of growth in successive periods can thus be compared with each other. On the other hand, the figures showing the rates of growth in different countries are obtained by methods which may not be exactly identical, and therefore not strictly comparable. This observation is very important when it comes to comparing the figures showing the rates of expansion in the developing countries with those for highly industrialized countries and even those for rates of expansion of two industrialized countries whose economies are similar.

Economic expansion is always related, directly or indirectly, to demographic phenomena:

(1) an increase in the total population, and changes in the age-group pyramid, especially in the proportion of the population who are of working age;

(2) the not necessarily parallel changes in the population of working age and in the active population directly employed in the production and marketing of goods and services. Divergences in these two may be due to three causes: changes in the behavior of the population of working age—for instance, raising of the school-leaving age or fall in the number of women working in certain socioeconomic groups, increase of women working in other groups; employment in administration (consequently not directly related to production and marketing of goods and services), which may affect a variable percentage of the total active population; the possibility of more or less extensive unemployment cannot be excluded.

When economic growth is superimposed upon these demographic phenomena, the result is often that the volume of goods and services per *consumer* grows less quickly than the volume of goods and services per *producer*. This is what happens if the school-leaving age is raised, if fewer women are at work, or if employment in the administration increases rapidly. In these cases the production and marketing of goods and services depends on a rapidly decreasing

140

proportion of the total population. Such phenomena are exceptional: in general, and certainly in western countries, they occur only when the standard of life is rising all round, and especially when the volume of goods and services available per consumer is growing. Yet it is not impossible that economic development may take such a form.

On the other hand, in a situation where unemployment causes an unhealthy reduction in the number of persons employed in the production and marketing of goods and services, production per person employed may increase while the volume of goods and services produced per unit of the total population decreases.

Can Economic Development Start and Continue Spontaneously?

The basic phenomenon of growth, that is, *the technical invention* (small or great), has always been connected with the development of scientific thought itself. In this respect, the new fact (which originated during the Second World War and which is growing in importance) is the role of systematic technological research. In the nineteenth century technical invention was usually the work of an isolated inventor. It was therefore slow, and its application in the countries engaged in the industrial revolution was haphazard.

Today technical progress depends primarily upon the adaption of a scientific attitude to the processes of production by the trained technical staff in large and small enterprises—an attitude that implies the will to understand and to draw the practical conclusions from a rational analysis. Furthermore, today technical improvement is systematically sought in laboratories and research departments within the enterprises themselves. Sometimes these research centers go so far as to do what could be called "pure research"— that is, research whose future economic application is not clear and may be far distant. This is especially true of large-scale enterprises with considerable capital. Thus, the forces that bring about technological development are very unevenly divided between coun-

141

tries, between different branches of production, and between different enterprises within a single branch, since the financial power of the units of production is itself unevenly distributed.

The political consequences of these methods of technical progress are significant. The forces that bring about this progress tend to concentrate in those countries where they can depend upon considerable financial resources: the United States, the Soviet Union, and to a lesser extent the European Economic Community and other industrialized countries of the western world. The effort needed to apply the results of this research can be produced mainly under the economic conditions peculiar to highly industrialized countries. It is directed toward supplying the principal markets of those countries, and is designed to use as cheaply as possible fairly highly skilled workers, whose wages are based on a relatively high standard of living. In other words, technical progress tends spontaneously to benefit those populations which have a high standard of living. In the developing countries, the financial resources available for technological research are inadequate. Progress is therefore necessarily much slower, inasmuch as it cannot be achieved by simply transposing the progress already achieved in highly industrialized countries.

The economic application of technical progress comes about spontaneously whenever it produces financial rewards sufficient to cover the cost of putting it into operation. When a firm has a reasonably safe future market, when it is able to put into production a technical improvement that will enable it for a foreseeable period to manufacture more cheaply than its competitors, when, in fact, it estimates that the profit during a period for which it can make reasonable forecasts will repay the expense of research and investment involved, then the elmentary machinery of economic development functions effectively.

Technical progress therefore depends on the ability of enterprises to forecast the future. From the beginning of the industrial revolution up to the great depression of 1929, forecasting took various forms, approximating more or less to the following extreme types: on the one hand, a forecast based on the assumption that the market would remain relatively stable, or at least change very slowly; on the other hand, the imaginative view expressing itself in more or less bold gambles. Long-range initiatives were undertaken by gamblers who, when they won, were rewarded for the accuracy of their forecasts with enormous speculative profits, and who, when they lost, disappeared from the business world altogether.

At the present stage, however, enterprises tend to be too large to be controlled by individuals. Decisions are no longer made by intuition and are no longer in the nature of a gamble. They are based on systematic study of data that are collected and considered more and more systematically, and this makes increasingly important the methods whereby economic developments can be systematically forecast. The question of how economic development starts and continues therefore raises the question of how this development can be forecast.

The Problem of Forecasting in Expanding Economies

An expanding economy is marked by changes: in the nature of the needs which economic life tries to satisfy; in the relative importance of the goods and services that correspond with these needs; and lastly in the relative importance of the various branches of production and in the technical and commercial links that unite them.

Technical progress and rising standards of living introduce constant changes in the nature of needs and methods of satisfying them. Once the elementary physiological and social needs are met, ever greater resources can be assigned to needs that only a privileged few could formerly satisfy. And new products appear that create needs never before imagined.

143

The change in the methods of satisfying needs is reflected in two types of phenomena:

1. Changes occur in the proportion of the needs that can be met by purchasing goods and services in the open market and those which entail the intervention of government; for example, the needs relating to health and hygiene. In some countries these needs are met largely through the purchase of goods and services in the open market. In countries where a system of social security is being developed an increasing proportion of such needs is provided for by public medical equipment and public health services. Other needs, such as those for education, which figure among the most pressing in prosperous economies, cannot be met except by the public administration.

2. The methods required to satisfy both those needs which can be met on the open market and those which can be met only through public services change constantly as time goes on. For example, the proportion of money allotted to personal consumption shows a relative decrease. At the same time, expenditures on culture, amusement and health are increasing much faster than consumption as a whole. Among the needs which can be met only through the agency of public services, those pertaining to the traditional sphere of the public authorities take second place (excluding the expenditures on national defense, which are increasing rapidly).

These changes in needs and in the methods for satisfying them succeed each other very rapidly. Moreover, their consequences continue to develop independently while remaining interwoven with each other, as a result of the general interdependence of economic processes. These phenomena of interdependence may be grasped and explained whenever they occur in limited sectors of production. For example, we can explain and predict the phenomena related to the new methods for the production of energy by comparing the cost of research, extraction and transport in the different energy-producing industries, and also the cost and the ways of using the different forms of energy. But economic interdependence is much more difficult to describe and explain when it is the outcome of world economic influences and market mechanisms. Whenever the explanation involves these worldwide phenomena it eludes the experience of the individual. The only people who are capable of explaining them, and consequently of predicting, are the specialized bodies which can take a comprehensive view of economic activities and trace a complete picture of them.

The Interaction Between Forecasting and Action in Economic Growth

Forecasting should shed light on decisions of widely differing range. The majority of economic decisions are of short range and can be taken in the light of market trends; this applies to the decisions that enable commercial firms to supply their distributors; or the decisions of industrial firms in fixing the level of current production. But certain economic decisions cannot be made rationally without a precise idea of their consequences over a long period.

These long-range decisions may be classified under seven broad categories:

1. *Decisions relating to agricultural production.* For a whole series of reasons, both technical and social, the methods of agricultural production, the proportion of the working population that must be engaged in it, and their distribution between categories of products, can only be altered slowly. Equilibrium can be maintained only if the needs can be forecast over several years.

2. *Capital investment in industry.* Industrialists tend naturally to reduce the volume of investments that will yield profit only over a long period. It is very clear, however, that certain equipment in the energy-producing, steel, chemical and engineering industries

can be set up only where there is a reasonable certainty that it can be used for several years, perhaps as much as ten or twelve years. Capital investment in industry must include not only the equipment properly so called, but all that can be described as capital technical research, that is, research calling for expensive machinery and the cooperation of big teams of research workers and engineers, which are difficult to assemble and to train.

3. *Decisions that affect international specialization.* A branch of production that works for external markets is just as likely as other branches to be involved in heavy investment. In addition, the fact that it works for a worldwide market, whose reactions may be difficult to assess, and where competition is normally intense and disconcerting, tends to create costly commercial systems and—in the field of production-organization as well as in research into technical improvements—tends to develop means of resisting all forms of competition. International specialization therefore corresponds to heavy investment with objectives that can be clearly defined only over a long period.

4. *Long-range decisions in the field of public services.* For the most part, the equipment used by the public services cannot be adapted at frequent intervals. This applies to systems of communication, town-planning equipment, medical equipment, educational equipment, and so on. They must therefore be planned over a long period in situations that are constantly changing because of traffic developments, the process of urbanization, revolutions in medical techniques, rising standards of culture. Among the long-range decisions that concern the public services, emphasis must be given to those which fall into the sphere of *education.* On a purely economic level, the systems of education and training should be capable of equipping an active population of working age with the qualifications required by the various sectors of the economy, now and in the future. This implies, first of all, a precise view of economic and technological developments. And since long-range forecasting is uncertain, intellectual and technical training should make

those who receive it adaptable, capable of acquiring, as the need arises, the new qualifications called for by changing techniques.

5. *Financial machinery.* The foregoing considerations show that the mission and consequently the responsibilities of the state may vary greatly according to the stage of economic development. The financial machinery of the state must therefore also be adaptable. In a general way, the various private and public sectors of a developing economy may have to bear financial responsibilities that vary considerably from one stage of development to another. The financial machinery, therefore, cannot adapt itself to continuous development unless it is very flexible. However, financial institutions and methods are generally associated with very strong traditions. Flexibility can be obtained only by means of long-range forecasting of the special kinds of financial problems that will arise over a long period in different sectors of the economy.

6. *The major trends of consumption.* The evolution of consumption patterns is generally observed and described as the empirical result of a certain number of market forces. But a deeper examination reveals the following:

- The role of psychological and sociological phenomena that are today the result of uncontrolled publicity, but that could be controlled by deliberate collective decisions;

- The role of certain collective associations, especially cultural ones. Their creation is today decided (or retarded) by governmental or administrative authorities on the strength of political intuitions and financial considerations. These associations may help to determine ways of life.

- More generally, the problems posed by stability and the adaptation of ways of life and of biological, psychological and sociological balances in rapidly changing milieus. These problems, which are extremely serious and which are likely to become still more so in the future, can be studied systematically.

147

7. *The rational attitude toward uncertainty.* Finally, we must emphasize that long-term forecasting is bound to be uncertain. Even when the bases of information are extended and strengthened, and when the techniques of forecasting have become more reliable, the data upon which future evolution depends can never be completely definite. In these conditions, the best forecast can only restrict the field in which it is possible to predict; it cannot reduce it to a single view in which all the elements, predictional and decisional, would be completely related.

A rational attitude to uncertainty consists in setting long-range decisions in such a way that they remain coherent in relation to each other and compatible with a balanced economic development within the perspectives that can be envisaged. Such a policy is obviously costly: a long-range decision, compatible with a whole *group* of objectives, is bound to be less well adapted, and consequently less profitable than a similar decision wholly designed to fit a clearly defined objective. Even when the techniques of economic development have been perfected, we shall still have to choose between the cost of complete insurance against uncertainty and the search for a rise in standards of living that could not be completely guaranteed against all conceivable risks. In practice, and in view of the incomplete development policies in force today, this cost of uncertainty is reckoned with (although always more or less obscurely) in certain fundamental decisions, especially in capital investment.[1]

---

[1] The mere enumeration of these long-range decisions shows that they are very varied and of fundamental importance. This explains why the techniques of long-range forecasting are developing and are coming to rely upon a basis of information that is as vast and varied as possible. All the centers of decision must be provided with common perspectives of economic development, which each can take as its starting point—finding therein the general indications needed to build its own views of the future in the form suited to itself.

This explains why several countries of the western world centralize their long-term forecasting at the governmental level. This is the case in France,

The Political Problem of Economic Growth

From the foregoing analyses it follows that control of the mechanism of economic growth cannot be assured unless all long-range decisions are so conceived as to be coherent with one another and compatible with steady development. Today there is no country, even in eastern Europe, where certain long-range decisions (including some of the most important ones) are not left to chance. The economic development of the whole world therefore runs grave risks of confusion at the present time. If the present situation were to continue for long, these risks would certainly become realities sooner or later. This means that economic progress would no longer be under the clear control of the decision centers. Progress would stop, or else collapse in disorder, because it was not based on well-informed decisions.

This risk is considerable today, especially because the vast zones of free exchange complicate long-term forecasting for all the countries that are trying to plan their development. Progress in national planning can indeed be challenged by the increasing difficulties which that planning encounters owing to the setting up of the Common Market in Europe and the vast zone of free exchange in the whole western world.

This is the main technical conclusion that must form the starting point for all who are reflecting about the political and social equilibrium of the world at the end of the twentieth century. The second conclusion is that the dynamics of economic growth can be controlled only by a great collective effort, which takes full account not only of the mechanism of this growth, but also of the decisions that determine it and the objectives to be pursued by

---

the Netherlands, the Scandinavian countries, Great Britain and Italy. The European Economic Community is just embarking on a project of long-term forecasting. A government which undertakes long-term forecasting finds itself increasingly able to make well-thought-out decisions in fields formerly completed controlled by technological determinism or social psychology.

means of it. A technical necessity is thus bringing about a profound revolution in the collective view, which clearly cannot put its trust any longer either in blind determinism, in the strength of traditions, or in the spontaneous harmonies of liberal societies.

This revolution is possible; at any rate one cannot see any reason why it is not. The necessity for it appears on the plane of the technique of economic organization. The strictly technical problems that must be solved are, as far as we can see, soluble.

The first task is to describe the mechanism of economic change properly and to explain how it worked in the past. Explanation of the past may then be extended to a forecast of the future, in a form that clarifies the different centers of decision.

These different points must be developed rapidly:

a. *Description of the mechanism of economic change.* The instrument for undertaking this description will be the techniques of national accounting. They will enable us to classify the main agents of economic activity in a country or area and the operations effected by them. By using the same principles and the same methods of classification, the national accounts would describe clearly the activities of the different economic agents, by showing:

- the proper role of each category of economic agents (in production, distribution and use of revenue, and the formation and use of savings);

- the relations of each category of agents to all the others.

The national accounts are the basic instrument for all economic information. In order to assess the different elements that they link together, and to describe their evolution and to explain them, an adequate system is needed for observing the economic and demographic trends. All the statistical systems today are being perfected under the pressure of the need for information revealed by the national accounts. The series of accounts drawn up for each year (sometimes for each quarter) give a picture of the economic trends that is becoming increasingly accurate.

b. *Explanation of economic trends.* The purpose is to describe the relations existing between the different elements in the national accounts. Ultimately such methods of explanation culminate in working out econometric models using adequate mathematical instruments, and enabling them to show correctly that the past trend is the result of the interplay of certain laws. Some of these laws appear as a pure result of experience; others as the manifestation of deeper phenomena of a technological, sociological, psychological, or even biological nature.

Conceived of in this way, the explanation would demand nothing except careful observation—carried out (as in the study of nature) by an observer who remains as much as possible outside the phenomena that he observes. But the explanation must clearly go a stage further. Economic life cannot usually be explained by the phenomena which directly characterize it, namely the phenomena of production and exchange directed toward the satisfaction of needs. Economic life is usually connected with phenomena that arise from other branches of human science. The explanation never attains perfection unless the observer enters into communication with the agents of the phenomena studied, in order to understand more of the attitudes and the desires by which their behavior is determined. That is why the economic explanation cannot be restricted to the phenomena of scientific and technical change. The different economic agents must also contribute by showing the observer their projects, preferences and reactions to the necessities that tend to be imposed upon them. Ultimately, no explanation is possible without a dialogue between them and those responsible for the explanation.

c. *Supplying decision centers with an effective forecast as the basis for further decisions.* The analysis above enables us to understand the change which in different forms and under different names is gradually taking place in the management techniques of our economies. As we saw at the beginning, certain decisions (the important ones that determine the long-run policies in economic life) cannot be taken without an effort to predict the future. It is impossible to make predictions before giving explanations. On the other hand, economic life cannot be explained unless we try to predict how it will develop, taking into account not only the objective facts that determine it, but also the plans of the different economic agents and their attitude toward the future. Effectively helping the decision centers therefore means committing the whole community of interests to a course of action in which it realizes what it is doing. This realization is not merely explicative and passive; it is active, it announces plans, criticizes their compatibility, and makes possible finally a collective decision about points that hitherto have been under the domination of obscure economic machinery.

The achievement of this by the economic community poses entirely new ethical problems. For the liberal economies the problem that arises is whether to accept or to reject the facilities offered by technical progress. There are also the problems of personal adaptation to the changes in economic and social life; these changes are sometimes very distressing because they involve complete uncertainty about the future; this uncertainty is felt increasingly as the technical change speeds up. Finally, there are the difficulties arising from the growth of technical urban society, which are dwelt upon in other chapters.

An economy that is aware of where it is going can solve these problems and overcome these difficulties. It can reduce the uncertainty that accompanies economic expansion by organizing that expansion so that it adapts itself without a crisis to the technological machinery to which it is due. Correct programing extending over a sufficiently long period can take advantage of the benefits of automation for economic progress and at the same time control the threat of technological unemployment. And such analysis with adequate planning should enable us to find solutions for the biological, psychological and social risks of living in modern organized urban societies.

Most of these ethical problems confront the individual only insofar as he participates in the life of the whole economic community. The first problem, therefore, is to adjust the political organs so that the participation of the individual may be effective, and not limited to a discussion ending in a decision by the majority, which is in danger of oppressing the minority. The individual cannot really participate in social life unless the social collectivity is pluralistically organized.

This is not the only condition that must be fulfilled in order to solve the ethical problems of economic life. The individual who participates actively in the collective life is not really using his freedom unless he understands the nature of the decisions that he must take, and the scope of the instruments in whose use he is participating. He must be capable of taking long-range decisions, because it is through long-range decisions that the collectivity can free itself from the blind forces that control it today. This means that the individual must commit himself in the present about a decision that will not take effect for some time. In short, the right use of the liberties that may appear when rapidly changing societies are rationally organized presupposes a grasp of political and social problems and a knowledge of economic machinery that very few people possess today.

In spite of the difficulties, these are lines along which societies must advance, whether they belong to the industrialized countries of the western world, to the East, or to the underdeveloped countries. If they do not make an effort to understand economic developments and to organize them, they all will experience a confusion that will bring about their collapse (like the confusion of the 1930's). Or they will subsist, as Germany did under Hitler, only

153

by means of haphazard attempts to prevent future insecurity by adopting the simple aims of totalitarianism and applying those aims to economic growth.

On the other hand, if economic growth is properly organized, the effects can be positive. Economic progress can be harnessed to equalize the conditions of life so that progress is not limited to small groups of privileged people. And it will mean progress in knowledge—knowledge of the physical world and knowledge (and love) of the world of men.

7

NEW POSSIBILITIES IN MODERN TECHNOLOGY

by ROBERT THEOBALD (United States)

THERE are two fundamental approaches to the impact of modern technology on the economy and society. One approach argues that today's technological progress is greater in degree but not essentially different in kind from that of the past.[1] The second states that today's technological progress is setting up totally new dynamic forces that demand major modifications in socioeconomic systems throughout the world.

I believe that we are entering a new socioeconomic order, the drives and requirements of which are as different from those of the industrial age as those of the industrial age were different from the agricultural era. In the agricultural era, human skill combined with

---

[1] Though this is still the dominant viewpoint, it is being increasingly challenged by representatives of a wide range of disciplines and interest groups.

animal power in a system which provided a minimal standard of living for the vast majority of the people and a leisured existence for a small elite. In the industrial age, which we are now leaving, human skills were combined with machine power to provide great wealth for a few, a reasonable standard of living for most and abject poverty for those unable to find a place within the productive system. Today, the cybernated productive system is emerging—a new innovation in productive techniques and organization, based on machine power and machine skill: that is, on automated machinery and the computer.

There is unfortunately a growing gap between the technological realities of computers and public understanding of their potential and of the speed at which developments are occurring.

Speaking before the 1964 American Joint Computer Conference, David Sarnoff, chairman of the board of the Radio Corporation of America, one of the United States' leading computer producers, outlined the way in which a universally compatible computer symbol-system will emerge and the unifying and systematizing effect that it will have. Implicit in Sarnoff's remarks is the startling revelation that computer systems, not men, will finally realize humanity's age-old dream of a universal language and that the subtleties and nuances of human thought will be mediated through the restricted and standardized symbols of computer communication.

Sarnoff illustrates the "technological Tower of Babel" in which, in this field of communication, we function today from the fact that there are now in use "more than one thousand programing languages, eight computer word lengths, (and) hundreds of character codes in being, at the ratio of one code for every two machines marketed . . . at least fifty different tape tracks and codes." But he sees a day approaching, once compatibility and standardization have been achieved, when the computer's vocabulary "will extend to thousands of basic words in the language of its country of residence, and machines will automatically translate the speech of one country into the spoken words of another." He anticipates, as this pattern emerges, the release of forces of change that will "affect man's way of thinking, his means of education, his relationships to his physical and social environment," and "alter ways of living." [2]

Richard Bellman, of the American Rand Corporation, seeing industrial automation at the point of no return, expects the pace to "increase astronomically in the next decade," with "the scientific know-how to automate American industry almost completely" already available. He anticipates the eventuality of large-scale staff reductions—banks, for example, by half. Steel and automatic industries can increase their use of automation by a hundredfold. There will be the displacement of whole grades of workers, especially lower and middle management and production workers, as the need for "decision making at that level" disappears. He recognizes "that industries are holding back . . . to avoid increasing the severity of the problem," but that they will have to come to terms with the likelihood that "two per cent of the population . . . will in the discernible future be able to produce all the food and services needed to feed, clothe and run our society with the aid of machines." [3]

The Research Institute of America, a management advisory firm, considers the United States almost totally unprepared for the approaching "moment of truth on automation." It anticipates "a great deal of anguish and dislocation as emergency adjustments

---

[2] Paper given at the Joint Computer Conference, San Francisco, Oct., 1964.
[3] Reprinted in the *Chicago Daily News*.
Terminology in this new field is still confused: for example, automation is used in this and the following quotation to cover the same range of phenomena as is covered in the rest of this paper by the word "cybernation." I believe that the most satisfactory, and increasingly common usage, is as follows: "Automation" is used to cover any advanced technological development in production that does not involve the computer. "Cybernation" is used to cover the combination of advanced machinery with the computer in systems allowing for both production and control; this involves the combination of both machine skill and machine power.

are made . . ." to contend with a crisis situation, as the major systems of automation, already complete, spread in such a way that "the effect will be revolutionary on everything from office and plant to society itself." [4]

Although the process of cybernation is most advanced in America, it will spread rapidly in Europe during the rest of the decade and will also have major effects on the economies of the poor countries.

The Drives Produced by Computer Applications

There are four fundamental drives that arise from the application of computer systems: the drive toward unlimited destructive power, the drive toward unlimited productive power, the drive to eliminate the human mind from repetitive activities, and the inherent organizational drive of computer systems.[5] The drive toward unlimited destructive power results from the combination of nuclear energy with the control and communication system of the computer and the activities of those involved in research and development. It is now generally accepted that there are already sufficient nuclear explosives, as well as bacteriological and chemical weapons, available to destroy civilization, if not all life.

The drive toward unlimited productive power also results from the combination of effectively unlimited energy with the control and communication system of the computer and the activities of those involved in research and development. This drive is still denied by the conventional economist, but it is fully accepted by

---

[4] Research Institute of America Recommendations, Dec. 27, 1963.

[5] One other drive not directly related to computers but very directly caused by increasing knowledge should be mentioned here: the drive toward unlimited population. This follows from the availability of ever-improving medical care: it is a result of providing increasingly effective death control without birth control. For an analysis of the effect of this, see ROBERT THEOBALD: *The Rich and the Poor*, New American Library, 1961, Ch. 6; and ROBERT THEOBALD: *The Challenge of Abundance*, New American Library, 1961, Ch. 11.

those most closely associated with production—the manufacturer and the farmer.

There is no longer any effective limit to our productive abilities: we have passed beyond the dismal science of traditional economics. U Thant has expressed this reality in the following words:

> The truth, the central stupendous truth, about developed countries today is that they can have—in anything but the shortest run—the kind and scale of resources they decide to have. . . . It is no longer resources that limit decisions. It is the decision that makes the resources. This is the fundamental revolutionary change—perhaps the most revolutionary mankind has ever known.[6]

This is the true meaning of abundance: not that goods and services are already available and waiting to be used, but that we possess the potential to call forth enough goods and services to meet our needs—not only within the rich countries but also internationally.

The drive to eliminate the human mind from repetitive activities results from the fact that the computer is a far more efficient worker than the human being. Already we know that the production worker can be replaced by the cybernated system, that the computer controls inventory more effectively than the manager, that the computer handles bank accounts far more cheaply than the clerk. These, however, are primitive developments: in the near future we shall see that the computer can take over *any* structured task, any task where the decision-making rules can be set out in advance. Thus, for example, the computer will take over the process of granting most types of bank loan, the analysis of stock portfolios and the process of odd-lot trading on Wall Street. The last application is particularly noteworthy, for it will replace a group of people whose median income is around $50,000 a year.

The computer will force man's mind out of the repetitive productive system just as surely as industrial machinery forced out

---

[6] Speech in connection with the launching of the Development Decade, May, 1962.

man's muscle. Gerard Piel, publisher of the *Scientific American,* has stated this truth in the following words:

> The new development in our technology is the replacement of the human nervous system by automatic controls and by the computer that ultimately integrates the functions of the automatic control units at each point in the production process. The human muscles began to be disengaged from the productive process at least a hundred years ago. Now the human nervous system is being disengaged.[7]

Lastly, there is the inherent organizational drive of the computer. The initial setting up of computer systems is a response to a need to increase economic efficiency or to rationalize operations, but as computer systems become fully operative, a drive emerges toward the reorganization, for purposes of computability, of interacting systems and institutions. The greater the number of areas of computer application, the greater the force behind this drive. There is now quite clearly a trend toward the emergence of a total computer system organized for maximum efficiency in terms of the immediate tasks.

Changes resulting from these four drives have already begun. The transformation that is taking place around us should not, therefore, be regarded as a process involving the occurrence of random, isolated, nonpredictable events, but rather be urgently studied to determine what trends are developing. In addition, we must always keep in mind the anthropological insight on culture change: that change brought about in one part of the system will be accompanied by other changes, both predictable and unpredictable, in many parts of the existing socioeconomic system and culture.

It is now clear that the impact of the computer is destroying the industrial-age balance between the economy and the society. We continue, however, to assume that after a period of apparent disorganization, a new, favorable socioeconomic balance will become

---

[7] GERARD PIEL: *Jobs, Machines and People.* Center for the Study of Democratic Institutions.

evident; we have further assumed that if it becomes clear that a sat-isfactory balance is not emerging, we shall be able to intervene at the last moment to correct unfavorable trends. These kinds of assumptions would appear analogous to the precybernetics in-dustrial-age economic theories of laissez-faire and, later, of pre-crisis intervention in the economy. But these theories were based on the impossibility of prediction and resulted in the establishment of a policy of remedial, not preventive, action.

Today, the availability of the computer enables us to spot trends long before they would otherwise be visible, to carry out the necessary discussion and to prepare any required programs before the need for action develops. We can thus use these systems to control their own effects. Using information provided by computer systems, we can speed up the observation-discussion-action process so that we can keep up with the developments in our own tech-nology. We can recruit technological drives to aid us in our effort to achieve our fundamental goals. Already, information obtained through the use of computers can enable us to perceive more rapidly both problems and opportunities.

The remainder of this chapter contains three sections. First, it suggests some necessary policy steps in the rich countries. These policies are most immediately required within the United States, but they have relevance for all the rich countries. Second, it dis-cusses the relationships which should be developed between the rich and the poor countries. Finally, it touches briefly on the special role that the churches should play.

Policy Changes in the Rich Countries

The drive toward unlimited productive power destroys the valid-ity of the mechanism at present employed to distribute the right to resources. So long as we preserve our present socioeconomic system, internal economic stability is possible *only* if the amount that people and institutions are willing and able to buy rises as fast as the amount that we are able to produce. Effective demand must keep up with potential supply. This necessity follows from the fact that the viability of our present scarcity socioeconomic system is based on a very simple relationship: it is assumed that it is possible for the overwhelming proportion of those seeking jobs to find them and that the income received from these jobs will enable the job holder to act as an adequate consumer. The successful functioning of the present socioeconomic system is therefore completely dependent on an ability to provide enough jobs to go around; a continuing failure to achieve this invalidates our present mechanism for income distribution, which operates only so long as scarcity persists.

It is for this reason that businesses of all sizes, economists of almost all persuasions and politicians of all parties agree that it is necessary to keep effective demand growing as fast as potential supply: that those who are still able to act as adequate consumers, because they are still obtaining sufficient incomes from their jobs, be encouraged to consume more and more of the kind of products that the economic system is at present organized to produce. The economy is dependent on "compulsive consumption," in the words of Professor Gomberg, and manufacturers spend ever-increasing sums on consumer seduction to persuade the consumer that he "needs" an ever-wider variety of products.

We can eliminate the need for demand to keep up with supply only by breaking the job-income link. We must provide every individual with an absolute constitutional right to an income adequate to allow him to live with dignity. No governmental agency, judicial body or other organization whatsoever should have the power to suspend or limit any payments assured by these guarantees.[8]

---

[8] The reasoning behind this proposal and its consequences are set out at length in ROBERT THEOBALD: *Free Men and Free Markets,* Part 2. Clarkson N. Potter, 1963; Doubleday, 1965. This book also sets out a scheme for income maintenance for those with middle-income levels who will also lose their jobs in large numbers in the coming years as a result of the development of the computer.

Such an absolute constitutional right to an income will recognize that in an economy where many jobs already represent make-work in any social sense and where the need for workers will decrease in coming years, it is ludicrous to base the right to an income on an ability to find a job.

Many people will reject this proposal because they fear that it would prevent us from supplying all the needed resources to the poor countries of the world. This objection is unjustified: it is increasingly used as a last-ditch stand by those who would deny the reality of abundance. The rich countries should take an unlimited commitment to provide the poor countries with all the resources they can effectively absorb, but it is now quite certain that the poor countries could not effectively use more than ten to twenty per cent of the annual *increase* in the production of the rich countries. If development is to be satisfactorily achieved, we must recognize that the main problem in the process of development is social and not economic: that the basic need is to develop patterns of society that will be viable in the second half of the twentieth century.

A right to an income would not alone be sufficient to guarantee human rights: society must also make an unlimited commitment to produce the conditions in which every individual can develop his full intellectual potential. The acceptance of this principle would make one highly optimistic for the long run. We have so far developed only a tiny proportion of the potential of the majority of human beings. Acceptance of an absolute right to an income and complete education would allow a flowering of the spirit and mind the dimensions of which we cannot even guess today.

If we are to achieve the complete education of every individual, we must recognize that the student is "working" at least as relevantly as the man in the factory. The time has come when we must introduce the concept of a student salary, starting possibly at fourteen and increasing with age, payable to all students attending school or university. This salary would be tangible proof of the recognition by society of the value of this young individual, and its acceptance by the child would be a recognition by him of his obligation to the society which has accorded him this right.[9]

Society must be concerned not only with the individual's mental abilities but with his physical health. We must develop a system that will ensure that everybody can obtain the best medical care—both preventive and curative. Income levels should be seen as totally irrelevant to rights to health and life.

Absolute rights to enough resources to enable an individual to live with dignity and to the full development of his capacities would allow him to achieve his own patterns of meaningful activity. However, recognition of the validity of new patterns of meaningful activity would require a cybernation-era reinterpretation of the values of work and leisure. The nineteenth-century concept of a man's life as a mere division between toil and respite from toil should be allowed to disappear along with the production-oriented factory organization which gave rise to such a curiously twisted version of the relationship between an individual and his society.

In the future, work will no longer be essentially a labor payment to society, but rather the full use of an individual's potential for the material benefit of his fellows and his own self-fulfillment. In the same way, leisure will no longer be simply time not spent in toiling, but rather the full use of an individual's potential for the psychical benefit of his fellows and his own recreation.

The toiling machines which will produce the bulk of all goods and services need no income rights. Nontoiling men cannot now, and will not in the future, continue their creative progress without a guaranteed income for their physical support and for their lifelong process of education and training.

---

[9] The techniques that could be used to introduce a "student salary" and to guarantee an income are set out in the Appendix to *Free Men and Free Markets* and in *Income Provision in a Cybernated Era.* Quoted there from *Congressional Record,* July 8, 1964, and *Vital Speeches,* August 1, 1964.

The long-run potential is immensely challenging. But we shall not reach this desirable future state unless we recognize that the upbringing and education of much of the present population has limited their horizons so severely that they cannot fully benefit from the potential abundance which their own work has created. Society crippled these people in order to get them to produce efficiently and suitably. Since their productive efforts are no longer required, society must not only provide them with rights to adequate incomes but must also provide new types of activity that will give them a sense of satisfaction from their lives.

This can be done only through new types of organization. The provision of a guaranteed income sufficient to allow everybody to live with dignity will greatly simplify this necessary task, for workers will not have to be paid wages. We can anticipate the organization of what I have called "consentives": productive groups formed by individuals who will come together on a voluntary basis simply because they wish to do so. The goods usually produced by these consentives will not compete with mass-produced products available from cybernated firms: the consentive will produce the "custom-designed" goods which have been vanishing within the present economy.

This type of productive unit will continue far into the future, for using his hands is one of the most satisfying ways for a man to use his time. Nevertheless, the proportion of the population who spend most of their time in production will decline as the right to education takes full effect and other activities seem more challenging.

Relations Between the Rich and the Poor Countries

Perhaps the most acute problem raised by exploding technology is the ever-widening gap between the rich countries and the poor. The expressed policy of the western powers is to aid the poor

165

countries to catch up to the rich within an acceptable period of time. It has been generally argued, most articulately in W. W. Rostow's *Stages of Economic Growth,* [10] that the way by which the poor countries can attain this goal is to heed the lessons of history, to pass through the western stages of growth, although hopefully at a faster pace.

This seems to me to be pure cynicism or pure stupidity. It is now almost twenty years since the end of the Second World War, and almost fifteen years since the rich countries committed themselves to help the poor countries achieve an adequate pace of development. The general condition of most of the poor countries has not improved significantly during this period, and there appears to be no real prospect that major progress will be made in the coming years unless a dramatic shift in approach and in philosophy occurs.

Most economists would reject such a pessimistic view, using evidence derived from national income figures: these can be shown to have increased steadily, if not rapidly, in most poor countries. However, it appears that the rate of growth in national income has slowed down in many poor countries in recent years, while the ever-rising pace of population increase insures that income per person is just about static in almost all the poor countries and is even falling in some. The over-all situation can be summed up in a quotation from the United Nations Development Decade Report:

Taken as a group, the rate of progress of the underdeveloped countries measured by income per capita has been painfully slow, more of the order of one per cent per annum than two per cent. Most indications of social progress show similar slow and spotty improvement. Moreover, the progress achieved in underdeveloped countries has often been uneven, limited to certain sectors of the economy or to certain regions or groups of countries. As a result, the disparities in levels of living within underdeveloped countries are often as pronounced as those between developed and developing countries taken as a whole. [11]

---

[10] Cambridge University Press, 1960.

[11] *The Development Decade.* United Nations. Sales No. 62.II.B.2. 1962, pp. 6–7.

Since it is only in recent years that there has been an examination of the effects of technology even in the developed countries, it is not surprising that there has been little attempt to study its effects in the underdeveloped countries. Recently, however, David Morse, Director-General of the International Labour Office, calculated that in the twenty-five-year period 1950–1975 "the number of persons of working age will increase by 800 million" and that "the labour force will be increased by more than 550 million persons—or, in other words, that more than 550 million jobs would be needed." He reckons that the industrialized area, North America, Europe and the Soviet Union, would account, in roughly equal parts, for about 100 million of this increase, while in the underdeveloped areas the increase would be "some 450 million, that for Asia alone being estimated at 580 million . . ." (an increase, he points out, "greater than the total labour force of 340 million in the industrially developed world in 1950"). Seeing the increase in terms of the need for "a lot of new jobs," he presents the dilemma that confronts us in "the fact that the technology, whether in agriculture or in industry, that is most capable of yielding the *greatest increases in production* is least capable of expanding employment." And he sees the world employment problem as a potential source of social and political tension.[12]

Morse suggests that the progress of technology will provide us with the means to solve the productive problem—if we are able to develop new institutions that will make it possible to employ our total technological capacities. Indeed, he goes further and argues that only through the use of the new technologies shall we be able to feed, clothe and provide shelter for the rapidly growing populations of the developing countries. He adds, however, that the use of the new technology may well make it impossible to provide conventional work for the rapidly rising labor force in the poor countries of the world.

---

[12] Speech by David Morse. Sept. 26, 1963.

What policies must we adopt to ensure that we achieve the urgently needed increase in production in the poor countries and to ensure that the lack of job opportunities does not lead to "social and political tension"? I believe that we must recognize now that the rich countries have a responsibility to provide the poor countries with all the resources they can use to help achieve their desired process of development. However, the amount of resources that should be supplied cannot be determined solely on the basis of the maximum feasible rate of economic development that could possibly be achieved but depends, more importantly, on how much economic growth is actually desirable. Our problem today is that we face completely novel social questions to which there are no available answers.

The most crucial questions are these: How are we to provide incomes for everybody if there are not enough jobs to go around? What are people to do with their time when machines can produce more efficiently than men? As we have seen, the present worldwide socioeconomic system is based on the assumption that everybody who wants a job will be able to find one, that the possession of a job will provide everybody with an income adequate to live, that the income will be spent to buy goods and that the demand for goods will provide enough jobs to go around—thus closing the circle.

It has hitherto been believed that the relationships that have existed in the past in the already industrialized countries would prove equally valid in the countries that are only now industrializing. The poor countries have therefore accepted and even welcomed the destruction of their informal "social security" systems which ensured the rather wide distribution of any available production. This process is still continuing, despite the fact that it is now clear that full employment is not a feasible goal in the developing countries and that the method of distributing income at present applied in the industrialized countries cannot be applied to the coun-

168

tries only now industrializing, for it depends completely on the ability to provide a job for everybody who is seeking one.

Different approaches will be required in the developing countries, where extended kinship systems and other informal transfer mechanisms still exist. Each country will have to work out an approach that accords with its own history, economic status and values. In most of the poor countries, however, the most urgent necessity is to prevent the gradual whittling away and even the deliberate destruction of existing informal distributive systems so as to gain time in which new approaches can be developed and accepted.

The development process in the poor countries has so far been conceived as the method by which they could approximate the *present* condition of the rich countries in the shortest possible span of years. Today, we must recognize that this definition is totally inappropriate. Mankind confronts a worldwide challenge, how to live within a technological system and still preserve his humanity. Development can be achieved at an adequate pace only if we use the productive potential provided by technology; but unless man controls the technology we shall find the human being conforming to technological imperatives.

Our problem is not a scarcity of human or material resources; man can be made more intelligent through education, and new material resources can be developed through research. Our problem is a lack of imagination to take the major leaps in understanding and policy that are essential if we are to be able to live in our totally new world. We shall be able to secure development only if we recognize that the technological problems of providing everybody with reasonable standards of living *can* be solved within a generation: and that our problem is therefore to find ways by which to alter our values and institutions to allow us to use this technological potential for the benefit of humanity.

It is not possible to achieve economic growth, let alone social development, without a major change in our approach. We do, however, now possess the means to achieve economic development; our problem is to create the necessary institutions and to ensure their subordination to human and social priorities.

Such a redefinition of the task promises one immediate and substantial benefit. Hitherto, the process of development has been seen as involving transfers in only one direction: from the rich to the poor countries. It has been argued that the poor countries needed to accept not only the technological knowledge but also the social ideals of the West. The poor countries cannot help resenting the inevitable obligation to remain in a dependent role.

The argument of this essay, however, demonstrates that the West has just as much to learn from the poor countries in terms of social values as the poor have to learn from the West in terms of scientific and technological skills. The West needs to discover from the poor countries how it is possible to find satisfaction in life without constant, frenetic activity. It seems more than probable that this cultural lesson, which the West needs to learn in order to live within future conditions, will be less easy to teach than the scientific and technological lessons the poor countries have to learn from the West.

The developing countries have never looked on work as the supreme virtue; this fact has been one of the reasons preventing economic development in the past. Most of those engaged in trying to secure development still believe that they should change the values of the developing countries so that work becomes central. It is hoped that this will make possible a nineteenth-century process of development. We must recognize that this is inappropriate. Instead, we must recognize that many of the present values in the poor countries are highly suitable for a cybernated age. We must preserve them where they are still strong and find ways to introduce them into the countries already rich.

We need a true partnership of all the countries of the world if we are to ensure that we benefit from technology. If we fail to find a viable partnership we must simply await the outcome of rapidly increasing tensions throughout the world. The hopeful and attainable alternative is that a new willingness to work together would make it possible to provide a reasonable standard of living throughout the world by the end of the century.[13]

The Responsibility of the Churches

What is the particular responsibility of the churches in this situation? They have, of course, adjusted themselves to the industrial age and have accepted the evils that were necessary to the operation of the industrial age: exploitation, poverty, materialism, usury. It is only recently that this orientation is being challenged.

The cybernated era is based on the combination of machine power and machine skill, on the combination of automated machinery and the computer. The two major results of this development are already clear. First, it will make it possible to abolish meaningless toil—the machine can toil and free the human being for human tasks. Second, the cybernated age makes it possible to provide enough food, clothing and shelter for every individual wherever he may live.

The barrier to a better society, in which every individual can live with dignity, no longer lies primarily in the economic sphere—we can move, if we so desire, beyond the dismal science. The barrier lies in our unwillingness to reconsider the shibboleths by which we live. The challenge to the churches is clear-cut. The churches can continue to accept the industrial age: acquiescing by default of positive action in the dehumanization of man. Alternatively, the churches can recognize the realities and the challenge of the cybernated era, re-examine their position and struggle to promote the emergence of the new and better socioeconomic order made possible by cybernation.

---

[13] If we are to achieve the needed pace of change there is an urgent need for new institutional structures: I have set out some suggestions in *Technology and Culture,* Vol. III, No. 4. Fall, 1962.

What would this mean? Hitherto, the churches have only inveighed against the evil consequences of the industrial age: they have never been willing to attack its fundamental basis which made these evils inevitable. If the churches are to be effective, they must now attack the values of the industrial age. They might well take as their text a statement of John Maynard Keynes, who was more moralist than economist:

> ... we shall be able to rid ourselves of many of the pseudo moral principles which have hag-ridden us for two hundred years, by which we have exalted some of the most distasteful of human qualities into the position of the highest virtues. ... All kinds of social customs and economic practices affecting the distribution of economic rewards and penalties, which we now maintain at all costs, we shall then be free to discard.

The passage of thirty years has turned Keynes' future possibility into an urgent present necessity. The churches have a major responsibility to bring this necessity to the attention of their members and society in general, and to help to formulate the new policies so urgently required.

8

THE RESPONSIBILITY OF
THE CHRISTIAN IN A
WORLD OF TECHNOLOGY

by HARVEY COX (United States)

IT is doubtful whether technology in its modern form would ever have been possible without the biblical faith. The impact of the biblical faith culminating in the gospel of Jesus Christ constitutes an indispensable precondition without which contemporary scientific technology is unthinkable. Even though the church has very frequently opposed scientific and technological advances—Galileo is the best example—when it does so it is always acting against its own presuppositions and is betraying the very gospel it is called to defend. Technology means "tool," but modern scientific technology is not simply a tool that can be used for good or for evil. It is also a culturally formative power that defines the shape of the world we live in and conditions our way of perceiving that world. It has been contended by some that a technological civilization does not permit the possibility of Christian faith, that it is inherently and essentially anti-Christian. This is not true. The Christian gospel is not the "culture religion" of pretechnological society. Nor is it a particular expression of some general religious spirit that will necessarily vanish when scientific technology has done its work. The Christian gospel, rather, is the Word of God calling men in every age and within any social or cultural ethos to take responsibility for himself and his neighbor in history before the Living God. Far from making Christian faith impossible, in many ways the technologization of our world makes the call of the gospel more unavoidable than ever. It sharpens the issue of obedience or disobedience, maturity or immaturity, response or refusal. It presses the issues of Christian faith more urgently and presents the alternatives more sharply.

We shall begin by showing how the cultural impact of the biblical faith provides a necessary precondition for technology. Three main motifs will be discussed: (1) the "disenchantment" of the natural world, (2) the worth of human work, and (3) the possibility of change.

The Biblical Basis of Modern Technology

1. *The Disenchantment of the World of Nature.* The disenchantment of the world of nature is a cultural prerequisite of technology. No technology can operate where the world is still seen to be holy, where nature is conceived of as the habitat of benign or demonic forces to be wooed or placated. A sharp break between the object of faith and the natural world is a necessary prelude to technological change. The result of the lack of such a break can be seen in some nonwestern countries today, where the mere introduction of modern scientific equipment cannot effect changes so long as forests and streams, fields and rocks are experienced as the locus of deity.

The biblical doctrine of creation de-mythologizes the world of

174

nature. It subjects natural phenomena—sun, moon, stars—to a radical de-divinization. They are no longer to be seen as the objects of religious awe and reverence, but as creations of God placed in the world to serve God's purposes and therefore man's wellbeing. When we compare the Genesis version of creation with the Babylonian myths from which the motifs and figures were borrowed, it becomes even clearer that the Bible makes a distinctive contribution. The world of nature is de-divinized, made available to man for his projects and purposes.

2. *The Worth of Human Work in the Bible.* Aristotle believed that only the slaves should work. He taught that the really mature man, *ho spoudiaos,* should spend his hours in meditation. Work was a lesser activity, directed toward a higher end. Therefore, those who wished to engage in the highest kind of activity should shun work. Aristotle also believed that everything really significant had already appeared and been invented. Man's job involved only the classification and cataloguing of what already was. Invention and the fashioning of the new did not play any role in his world-view.

The Bible, quite to the contrary, viewed man as a being with responsibility for work and achievement in history. No disparaging distinction was possible between the "higher activity" of mental cerebration and the "lower" activity of toil with the hands. Such a distinction could grow only out of a basically dualistic view of man as essentially a spirit more or less imprisoned within a body. But such a dichotomous view is not possible for the Bible. Man was seen as a psychosomatic unity and no disparagement of the body, of work, or of earthly activities was possible.

The biblical view of work is important because it provides one of the key elements in the intellectual structure of modern technology. When science consists of mere speculation and deduction, as it did with most of the Greeks and with the early Renaissance scientists, "modern science" has not yet appeared. Only with the utilization of equipment, with measurement, observation, experiment and laboratory work do modern science and technology appear on the scene. Modern scientific technology is the result of a confluence of unsystematic "tinkering," on the one hand, and untested intellectual hypothesizing, on the other. So long as these two were kept separate by stations in life, by class structure, by separations of "will" and "intellect," no breakthrough to modern technical civilization was possible. But when this basically nonbiblical separation began to be healed toward the end of the Renaissance, when scientists began using equipment and technicians began utilizing scientific theory, the new age had come. An acceptance and respect for human work is an essential element of technology. Without the biblical vision, it might never have been possible.

3. *The Possibility of Changing Things.* Another prerequisite for technological society is that man must believe change is both possible and desirable. He must have some reason for changing things, for initiating projects, for using tools to accomplish some purpose. This desire for change seems natural enough for us, but it would in no way appeal to a man trapped within a fatalistic or cyclic view of history. Only when history is seen as the theater of human response, as the scene of God's call and man's responsibility, does it make sense to try to alter what has been.

A "closed universe" in which everything is already finished, simply waiting to be discovered by man, does not encourage technology. It may encourage speculation or even exploration, but the real animus of the scientific enterprise is an inventive and creative one, that is, to do something new.

In vivid contrast to the deities of the ancient Near East, whose existence was closely associated with the changing of the seasons, the revolution of astral bodies or the annual flooding of the great river, Yahweh disclosed himself in events of social change, principally the Exodus. While the nature gods were thus locked in a circle of cosmic recurrence, Yahweh did things that were utterly new and unprecedented. ("Behold, I am doing a new thing!")

Thus an "open universe" was disclosed, one in which both God and man fashion new things, make innovations, change and alter existing practices.

But toward what end should man do these things? Again the Bible provided an important clue. Man was commissioned by God to name the animals and to tend the garden. Gerhard von Rad reminds us in his famous Genesis commentary that naming was for the Hebrews a kind of command, and that God himself had begun the creation by calling (that is, naming) the light "day" and the darkness "night." Thus, man and God are both involved in the naming and controlling which constitute the creative process. The creation is not finished once and for all, as it is with Aristotle. God does not "rest" until he has created man and enlisted him in the creating process. Thus, for the Bible, creation is "open-ended." It is not finished once and for all, but goes on wherever order is wrestled out of chaos. Man is made responsible for his world.

Naturally we must take the fall of man into consideration. Man is not only God's partner; he is also a rebel and betrayer. But, as Karl Barth has reminded us so clearly in his exegesis of Romans 5, the most basic thing about man is not his sin but his restoration. In Christ man *is* responsible and free; the old Adam has been defeated and displaced. The reality of our existence is our new being as the new Adam, commissioned to care for our brothers, share the world with our fellowman (here especially the woman), tend the garden of the universe and name its phenomena by drawing them into the web of human purpose.

This restoration of man to a position of responsibility for the world, an indispensable prerequisite for technology, is emphasized, as Gogarten has pointed out, in the Galatians figure of sonship replacing tutelage to a schoolmaster. It is again reinforced by the parables of Jesus in which the image of the master who leaves the estate in the care of stewards is constantly repeated. It is made abundantly clear that we are the stewards not only of money, but also of power and responsibility. Thus, the wicked steward who beats and mistreats the servant is judged as harshly as the one who buries his money rather than using it imaginatively.

These then are the basic theological motifs which lie behind and make possible the appearance of technology: man, placed in a natural world that is at his disposal, sensing the value of human work and charged with the responsibility of using the material universe to fashion artifices that will accomplish human purposes. Now let us go on to ask: What are the distorted views of technology that have crept into the theological conversation, some of them under the cloak of religious appeals?

Religious Distortions of Technology

There are many religiously tinged evaluations of technology abroad, most of them false and misleading. We shall touch here only on the three most frequent and most insidious ones: (1) romanticism, (2) utopianism, and (3) conservatism.

1. *Romanticism.* Where men have forgotten, or never adequately known the transcendent God who reveals himself in human events, a pagan reverence for nature may still obtain. It is a residual form of animism or nature worship, structurally comparable in some cases to the Baal worship which the children of Israel met when they arrived in Canaan.

The religious romantic is horrified to see nature used or altered by man. Though he is certainly right in questioning the thoughtless and arbitrary misutilization of nature, the decimation of forests, the pollution of rivers, the destruction of green areas, still he is wrong if he objects in principal to the drawing of nature into the orbit of human responsibility and control. The creation of the world is an expression of God's love for man; so the natural world exists, in a sense, *for* man. But it exists for him not to be bullied and bruised; it exists to be cultivated, enjoyed and shared. There is evidence in the New Testament that the natural world shares in the fall of man and that it too waits for the redemption. This means that nature, as such, is not a source of healing and salvation, but that it shares in both the weal and the woe of man. It means also that its redemption is not prior to man's but takes place only as man is redeemed. The redemption of nature, in short, takes place as nature shares in what God has done for man in Jesus Christ. Nature is redeemed when it becomes an instrument by which man expresses his love for his neighbor. Man loves his neighbor by taking responsibility with him for the shaping and guiding of history.

Biblical faith rejects romanticism as a distortion of the gospel. It therefore rejects any religio-romantic suspicion of technology with its arcadian longing for a more idyllic and elemental life.

2. *Utopianism.* At the opposite extreme is the opinion that through the application of scientific technology all the ills of man can be solved. The machine takes the place of Jesus Christ as the Savior of man. This mistaken notion sometimes takes the form of technocratism, the belief that if technically trained people could be put at the centers of decision making, all political problems would be solved. Such a view is based on a tragically naïve assumption that vastly underestimates the depth and complexity of the political and social issues confronting the modern world. Political decisions have to do with many imponderable factors that are still resistant to the application of the refined measurement demanded by the technological method. Since man is free, human behavior can never be totally predicted. Political leadership is more of an "art" than science, though certain elements of science can help. The political leader must develop the gifts of intuition and even of instinct; he must be able to weigh probabilities and come to a compromise solution in which neither side gets everything it asks for. All this must frequently take place within such a short span of time that the possibility of measuring all factors carefully must often be foregone. The idea of a technocracy is a false and dangerous utopian scheme, and it constitutes a heretical distortion of the Christian hope for the kingdom of God.

But this is not to say that technologists can make no contribution to the political process. They can and do. The valuable suggestions on monitoring and inspecting the testing of nuclear weapons made by American and Soviet scientists without a doubt made a contribution to the achievement of a test-ban treaty. But the point is that after the scientists and technologists had done their work, the political leaders still had to make a decision.

Technologists can both help and mislead political leaders as they forge national policies. One good illustration of both is the use of a "games theory" and computers in policy making. Using the data fed into them by analysts, automatic computers can weigh any number of factors and produce information on the probable result of a particular course of action. The difficulty and danger of this process, however, is the assumption that those who "feed" the machines are always a part of the data fed to them. The selection and weighing of factors finally determines what kinds of answers will be given by the computers. This does not mean that computers should not be used in helping decision makers, whether in agriculture, industry or anywhere else. Computers can be used to explore the *probable* results of the various policies the decision makers are considering. But the computers must not be allowed to *make* the decisions, and the frame of reference within which their thinking and "programing" goes on must always be subject to further criticism and revision. Otherwise the horrible possibility of an atomic disaster touched off by a mistaken bit of programing with an automatic computer moves out of the realm of science fiction and into the realm of possibility.

Technocratism is a kind of gnosticism. It implies that only those with a certain esoteric "know-how" are fit to rule. In democratic societies, however, all the people should share in the decision-making process to the extent that this is possible given the technical problems involved. Technologists have their role to play along with everyone else. They contribute part, indeed an essential part, to the process, but their role should not be determinative.

Technology does not in itself solve any problem. It merely gives to man the means of solving problems he has not been able to solve before; and at the same time it "increases the stakes." It makes it necessary, indeed inescapable, that man accept the maturity and responsibility entailed in tackling these problems. Nuclear energy is merely the most dramatic example of the promise and demand inherent in technology. Now man *can* do constructive and compassionate things for his fellowman that were never possible before; but at the same time man now *must* find ways to settle the differences between different societies without resorting to war since war can no longer result in anything but catastrophic destruction and could not in any sense of the word be "won" by either side.

We can be grateful to technology not only for the tools it has given us to do a better job in caring for the garden of the earth, feeding the hungry, clothing the naked and bringing the entire cosmos into the web of human purpose: we can also thank technology that it has presented us with the challenge to "put away childish things," to leave behind the petty nationalism, jealousy and saber rattling of an earlier period and to accept the fact that the whole world is now one neighborhood. I can now travel from New York to Paris in less time than it took my grandfather to travel from New York to Boston [1]—technology has made us neighbors. The question now is, will we *live* as neighbors?

3. *Conservatism*. Those who wish to see the status quo stay the way it is always oppose technology. They are consistent in doing so. Social change, the setting aside of old ways and the adoption of new ways, often comes on the heels of technological change. The so-called "underdeveloped areas" are the best examples of this fact today. But we all see this in our own countries no matter

---

[1] It is lamentable that despite the astonishing speed and availability of travel, many people cannot utilize them because of restrictions placed on travel by many governments based wholly on political or ideological considerations.

where we come from. When improved travel binds one nation to another, ideas travel along those roads and the social stagnation which comes from ignorance and isolation is challenged. New inventions threaten the power of those whose money and interest is invested in the existing ways of doing things. Thus, those who are dedicated to maintaining things the way they are will frequently find reasons to oppose technological change.

Unfortunately the church has often been on the side of those who were resisting social change rather than on the side of those who were leading it. Since the social basis for this change sometimes rested in new technological, industrial and scientific advances, the church has developed in many instances an antitechnological bias. But the gospel of Jesus Christ is too strong and too incisive to be enveloped forever in spurious religious arguments against science or technology. Galileo, Copernicus and Darwin were attacked by the church or its leaders. But in our time the balance may be righting itself. The call of the gospel is heard and obeyed by people deeply involved in producing social change and in designing the apparatus, equipment and techniques which make previous social arrangements no longer viable. Still a residue of antitechnological conservatism remains.

The chief religious weapon of conservatism is a doctrine of God which draws a straight line from God to the existing political or economic institutions of a society. God becomes the cosmic policeman, sanctifying the existing distribution of power. But the eschatological dimension is lost in this schema; hence, it must be questioned from a theological perspective. Jesus Christ comes as the one who calls us into a new life, into change and movement, into joyous responsibility for the future more than stubborn defense of the past or the present. Likewise the scientific imagination demands flights of fancy and disciplined phantasy. It requires a mentality in which one must envisage something which *is not yet,* something that might be or could be. This the conservative mentality cannot do; hence it is condemned to stagnation.

182

We conserve what is good in the world not by impounding or "pickling" it but by constantly reappropriating it in the light of what today brings and tomorrow promises. The willingness to let go of what "worked" yesterday in order to find something that will work tomorrow is essential in our world today. It is at this point that Christian faith parts company with conservatism and casts its lot with the coming one.

We have rejected romanticism, utopianism and conservatism as valid Christian responses to technology. Now we must ask: What are the real problems and possibilities of a technical civilization and how do we address ourselves to them?

Problems and Possibilities of Technical Civilization

Four specific areas suggest themselves as those in which technology presents modern man with inescapable choices, in which God seems to be saying, "This day, I set before you life or death." The first is modern weaponry; second, food production; third, automation; and fourth, the mass media. We shall touch on each one very briefly, noting the peril and promise it carries with it.

1. *Modern Weaponry.* We have already mentioned nuclear weapons. We are thankful as Christians that a test-ban treaty has been accomplished, but we remain uneasy so long as stockpiles of hydrogen weapons and rocket delivery systems exist. We hope that the test-ban treaty represents only a first step toward the goal of complete disarmament.

But all the attention on nuclear weapons has sometimes distracted our attention from equally perilous developments in weaponry. What about biological and chemical weapons, the possibility of using disease germs, death rays and new types of gases? All these innovations dramatize the fact that effecting a cessation of nuclear weapons testing has in no sense solved the anguishing problem we face. Modern weaponry calls us to a level of maturity heretofore unknown in human history, one in which reason, patience, restraint and compromise must replace bellicosity. The dangers of what military thinkers call "escalation"—beginning with small weapons and moving to larger ones—is possible even in the smallest altercation between global powers. For this reason, provisional solutions to the political tensions and a general improvement in the climate of the international scene are forced on us by modern weaponry.

To choose immaturity and childish brashness in the days of the longbow, the machine gun or the flamethrower was dangerous, but not always self-destructive. Today it can be only catastrophic. This represents a wholly new stage in human history, and it has been brought about largely by technology.

2. *Modern Methods of Food Production.* Our times have witnessed startling discoveries in agronomy and in the scientific management of agriculture and food production. It is possible that the use of atomic radiation on seeds and soil, and the reconstruction of the genetic structure of food animals may produce unprecedented advances in food production in the very near future. Through technology man is about to harvest the teeming food supply of the sea and fashion nutritive substances out of formerly useless material. The construction of synthetic protein, for example, will be accomplished shortly.

But the *availability* of abundance in no way guarantees its distribution. Despite these uncanny technological advances, UNESCO reported last year that the number of starving and undernourished people had increased rather than diminished. The chasm that exists between the rich, highly industrialized nations and the poor, developing nations is widening rather than narrowing. The advances of modern medicine and the consequent decline in infant mortality has accelerated the world's population growth so that many nations, despite a rapid economic growth rate, can barely keep abreast of burgeoning baby statistics.

In short, technology challenges the rich nations to take responsibility, along with the poor nations, to fashion methods of *distri-*

bution that are commensurate with the abundance available. The world has been compared to a cellar in which there are twenty men, and four of them have half the food. This situation is inherently unstable and explosive. It is even more disheartening to see that although some nations must take measures to limit the production of food so that farm prices may be secured, other nations are faced recurrently with famine conditions.

For the first time in human history it is now possible to abolish hunger. Never before was this within the realm of imagination, let alone a possibility. The reason hunger and want have not been abolished is not that the technology is lacking. It is available. The reason is that the economic and political systems of distribution we now have cannot do the job they are supposed to do. Once again, technology calls man to maturity. He could not be blamed for hungry children when the tools for feeding them were not yet invented. But now that these tools have been invented, he is without excuse. It is possible for him to bring clothing, food and housing to "the least of these my brethren," but he has not yet done so.

3. *Automation.* The newest technological breakthrough is the harnessing of electronic computers to automated production equipment, eliminating the need for all but the smallest human role in large segments of the productive process. There are now oil, chemical and even steel plants in which the work force has been reduced to one-tenth or one-twentieth of its previous size by this so-called "cybernation." Automation is the "second industrial revolution," and it comes before we had really adjusted to the first. It brings with it all sorts of new problems and opportunities. Some of them are as follows:

a. "Unskilled work" is disappearing, the kind usually done by uneducated or undereducated persons. Mining, for example, is becoming a technological specialty for university graduates, not a job for untrained workers. The need for a longer period of formal education and for the constant retraining of workers whose skills become obsolescent will become ever more pressing.

b. A shorter work-week, longer vacations and earlier retirement will very soon become the rule. The electrical repair workers of New York City already have a standard work week of thirty hours only. Now what will people do in this increasing leisure time? What will happen to ethics of assiduity and ambition that have become part of a way of life often associated with Christianity?

c. On the positive side, can we so interpret the gospel that it will enable people to live with joy and meaning in a world in which work plays a less and less central role? Aristotle once said that until the harp could play itself societies would always need slaves. His statement was intended as a defense of slavery. However, we now have a society in which the harp *can* play itself, in which a new race of mechanical slaves may take over the toil and drudgery that has often darkened human life. Can we develop a Christian ethic of leisure?

d. We live in a world of nearly instantaneous communication. Through communications satellites it is now possible to watch events happening thousands of miles away. Through television with synchronized translations, Americans will soon be able to sit in on party congresses, and Europeans on congressional committees, all without leaving home. I shall watch the Bolshoi Ballet from my Boston living room. Already we share our films; and it is evident to anyone who has traveled widely in the world that young people of all nations often feel closely drawn together because of a shared familiarity with entertainment, sports and mass media events and personalities. Here again technology has broken down walls between peoples and enabled us to know each other better. What American, for example, who saw "Ballad of a Soldier" or "When the Cranes Are Flying" could avoid having a deeper understanding of the hopes and aspirations of the people of the U. S. S. R.? And millions have seen these films. We should not underestimate the film. It is the first art form produced by the technological era, and

186

it has untold power to mold attitudes and shape opinions. Those who appreciate the film should remember that it is a characteristically modern, technological form of art, that it could not be enjoyed by pretechnological societies.

But how can we be sure that the mass media will be used to strengthen the forces of reason and restraint rather than to stoke the fires of hatred and contempt? How can we know that these new techniques will be used for beauty rather than ugliness, for truth rather than falsehood? Sadly enough, for every true and beautiful film, for every truthful newspaper article, for every balanced and reasonable radio program, we are subjected to many others that are misleading, distorted and propagandistic. Technology provides us with the means by which all men may know and understand each other better. But the same tools can be used to spread falsehood and misinformation.

Again the stakes are now higher. A malevolent newspaper in the nineteenth century could do some damage; today it can do much more damage. The demand for maturity is more pressing. The airways of the world, the ether through which the images of the mass media travel, belong to God. They are made available to us to use responsibly, to tend and care for, not to waste or misuse. Like the stewards of the vineyard in the parable, we should be utilizing these airways in a manner pleasing to the One whose real property they are, to build the basis for world understanding and human community. The TV camera, the communications satellite, the printing press—all these are just as much a part of God's created order as the animals and birds; and it is our task and responsibility to name them, to give them value and significance.

We have now mentioned weaponry, food production, automation and mass media as the areas in which the challenge of the power and peril of technology is most evident, in which the necessity to "put away childish things" is clearest. But all these technical advances tend merely to exacerbate problems we already had. Let us turn now to two main dangers technology brings with it, problems which we did not have, at least in this form, before technology. They are the impersonality of power and the appearance of a utilitarian spirit. These problems might be attributed to what has been called "the technological mentality."

Problems of the Technological Mentality

Technology not only transforms our exterior world. It also greatly modifies the way we think. Man thinks differently in the age of the supersonic plane than he did in the age of the horse and carriage. Technology has influenced our ways of organizing work, of structuring society, of fashioning goals. Two relatively new problems produced by technology are (1) the impersonality of power and (2) the utilitarian spirit.

1. *The Impersonality of Power*. Bureaucracy is the social expression of technology. Bureaucracy organizes people on the basis of rational, logical analysis. It sees them only for what they contribute to the goal for which the bureaucracy functions. Advancement tends to be given to those people who function smoothly within their niche, who enable the program to flow uninterruptedly. Just as the parts of a machine are expected to serve a particular, partial function, so the people in a bureaucracy tend to view their own relationship to the whole in a mechanical, segmented way. The danger of this technological logic is that responsibility tends to be diffused so that no one feels personally responsible for what is happening. There is no one to blame or praise. Everyone has had the unpleasant experience of being confronted with a bureaucracy, personified by a particular bureaucrat, in a situation in which the unique aspects of one's "case" seemed to be overlooked and one was treated as a cipher or a statistic. The problem of how one discovers where decisions are *really* made, where power is *actually* wielded, is a difficult one.

This diffusion of power results in an impersonality of decision

188

which in turn leads to a drift toward inertia-in-motion. A bureaucracy seems to develop a "mind of its own" which drags along those who fill its niches and cancels out human freedom in a very disconcerting way. Acts of destruction on a terrible scale (one thinks of the "final solution" during the Third Reich) become parceled out to thousands of people, each doing one tiny particle of the work, while the responsibility for the whole mechanism is obscured, or lost sight of. Thus Adolf Eichmann could claim that his job was simply "arranging train schedules."

How, in organized, bureaucratic society, does one regain the sense of personal involvement and individual responsibility that is indispensable if the giant structures of modern industrial societies are not to become "principalities and powers" that once again hold man in thrall? Here it is necessary to devise points of conversation and reflection, places and periods in which those involved in bureaucratic organization can become critically aware of the whole complex of which they are a small part, and recognize that what it is doing *is* their responsibility.

2. *The Utilitarian Logic.* The utilitarian logic is another cultural by-product of technology. It teaches people to ask of any person or thing, "What use is it?" Of course there is nothing wrong with subjecting things to this question. To be related to human purpose is, after all, what lends meaning and worth to the phenomena of history. However, the danger of the question of utility is that it is asked from within a narrow frame of reference. It tends to be asked by people who want to know what purpose this thing will serve within *my* purposes and goals.

It is a common failing of technologically trained people that they do not see the "usefulness" of, for example, art and humanistic studies. They tend to believe that any ideas or skills that cannot be applied rather directly to the productive enterprise are not useful and hence are worthless.

This judgment, however, is based on a narrowly provincial view of the meaning of human life. Man is involved in the productive

189

process, but he has often other involvements that transcend this one. Man asks inevitably about the good and the true and the beautiful. He needs poetry and art to be fully human. He has a family and friends and he is part of a cultural heritage that includes music and literature by which his life can be broadened and enriched. It is true that many humanistically oriented people also become stubbornly antitechnological and some even take pride in knowing nothing about modern science. This too is inexcusable; but so too is the antihumanistic bent of some technicians, who reduce the whole world to what fits or does not fit into the immediate technological enterprise. What is needed of course is a reconciliation of what the English writer C. P. Snow once called "the two cultures." The wall between them, like the wall between nations, races, and groups in the modern world, is one of the barriers the gospel of Jesus Christ abolishes. Consequently Christians should constantly be looking for ways to witness to the oneness of the world despite the emergence of two cultures. Just as Jesus Christ breaks down the barrier between Jews and Greeks, today he breaks down the barrier between technicians and humanists, and calls them both to a joyful celebration of what God has done for man and what man can do in response.

The impersonality of power and the utilitarian spirit are two of the distinctive problems of technological civilization. They are problems our grandfathers did not have to face, at least in the way we must face them. But they are not insurmountable problems. They can be solved, and the gospel of Jesus Christ both calls us to find answers to them and provides us with sources of strength and stamina to grapple with them intelligently.

Conclusion

Technology is not just a new tool kit with which to tackle old problems. It has utterly transfigured the world in which we live. It has changed our ways of living, of working, of thinking and imagining. It has placed before us in the most urgent way, problems we might not have had to deal with in the past. Many would prefer to return to the simpler, less formidable difficulties of the pretechnological era. But that is impossible. History is not reversible. It goes forward toward a fulfillment, and within the historical process we can discern, with the eyes of faith, the presence and power of the Living God. He no longer allows us to remain adolescent, tampering and trifling with human life. He now creates for us a civilization in which the only alternatives are maturity or death, responsibility or destruction. Perhaps those who long for the coziness of the nineteenth century or the medieval period are really refusing to grow up, are lingering too long in childhood, are unwilling to shoulder the terrible responsibilities which adulthood always thrusts upon us.

These are serious problems. How can we overcome provincialism in a shrunken world where neighbors whose views are different from ours can no longer be avoided? How do we decide, given the infinite possibilities of technology, what to make and what not to make, what to do first and what to postpone for later? How do we elaborate institutions by which the largest number of people possible can be drawn into the responsibility of making decisions affecting their own destiny? What are the appropriate goals of our shiny technological apparatus? Is it more important to reach the moon than to provide a minimum diet and decent housing for every child in the world?

The once terrifying forces of nature, the thunder clap and the lightning flash, no longer frighten modern man. He has tamed the wild panthers of the natural world and harnessed their energies for his own uses. But now man himself is the cause of terror. His machines and his machine-like organizations can do more damage, or bring more health, than all the thunder and lightning of the aeons put together. But we know that the God and father of Jesus Christ is not just the God of nature. He is also the Lord of history, the supreme sovereign of political and economic life. He is now de-mythologizing the structures of corporate human existence and bringing them under human control, just as he once conquered the natural forces. He continues to dethrone the principalities and powers, making them available to man as his captives, as instrumentalities for the building of human community. The God of Abraham, Isaac and Jacob, is also the Lord of technological man. He holds in his hand a future for this technological man far richer and more brilliant than anything we have yet imagined.

PART III

THE NEEDS
OF THE DEVELOPING COUNTRIES

9

ECONOMIC DEPENDENCE AND INDEPENDENCE — AS SEEN FROM SOUTHEAST ASIA

by A. C. Espiritu (Philippines)

In this second half of the twentieth century man can no longer depend for survival or progress on the traditional structure of nation-states. Not only is the small nation-state politically helpless without the protection of great power; but as an isolated unit it is no longer economically viable and must look to an economic union or regional grouping if it is to develop its economy and make its influence felt in world affairs. And man's needs and desires can no longer be fully satisfied within national boundaries. The fantastic world array of consumer products is fast producing a common mass taste and a universal mass demand. The advances in the technical and scientific fields have further emphasized the interdependence of the modern world.

However, the idea of international union or integrated economy is still far from realization. We still lack the necessary political and social skills. There does not yet exist, in the international context, that sense of solidarity which induces individuals and social groups to accept rules and regulations, some of which are not to their own immediate advantage. Greater internal integration is also needed before any political unit can participate fully in the building of one world.

Economic Dependence: Historical Roots

Because of the wealth of commodities within the region of Southeast Asia trade has always had a large influence in its historical development. Its links with the two big neighbors, India and China, were established over two thousand years ago. Until the end of the first century India traded mostly westward until the pattern shifted and Bengal ships began to make their way through the Malacca Straits to Sumatra and Borneo, and along the Malay Coast across the Siam Gulf to the southern coast of China. Moreover, India's midway position in the Indian Ocean gave her a strategic maritime advantage which was complemented by the spread of the Hindu and Buddhist religions, with their pervasive influence on the culture of the region.

After a slower start, China had developed, by the latter part of the second century, regular trading contacts with the Indianized city-states on the Gulf of Siam, which, before the Christian era, were already its vassals. Commercial exchanges were made at southern Chinese ports of entry, and successive tributary missions completed their leisurely journey to and from various Chinese courts. When the Imperial era was over and the Yang-tze lowlands had been assimilated, China's direct influence extended to the lands bordering the South China Sea; and in the meantime, commercial intercourse increased with all Southeast Asia, with India and Ceylon and with the Near East.

Though the influence of these two giants was to some extent

checked by the arrival of Muslim merchants in the seventh century and by the religious impact of Islam, especially in Sumatra and Java and some parts of the Philippines, many of the greatest achievements in Southeast Asia, whether in the realm of art or of statecraft, were basically of Indian or Chinese inspiration.

The capture of the city of Malacca, at the peak of its commercial prosperity in the early sixteenth century, by a daring band of Portuguese explorers bent on seizing control of the fabulously profitable spice trade to Europe—followed by the Spanish entry into the Philippines and the Dutch control of Java as the hub of a vast trading operation from Persia to Japan—led to the region's subjection to remorseless European rivalry. Trading supremacy fluctuated; and, as that of the Dutch declined, British and French hegemony was established in the Indo-Pacific Peninsula. The continued control of Vietnam, Cambodia and Laos by the French constituted the only serious challenge to the commercial supremacy established by the British at the end of the eighteenth century.

Thus, the countries of Southeast Asia became parts of different imperial groupings under a western dominance, which, though relatively short-lived, brought deep changes to the region, transforming its political and economic life and forging new and powerful ties with the major industrial centers of Europe and the United States.

The achievement of independence after the Second World War has not completely changed the colonial structure of the economies, since, within the former imperial spheres, "special economic ties" have been forged and the lopsided pattern of these countries' foreign trade has been largely maintained. Politically the transformations in international power structures have made of independence little more than a system of alliances and collective defense arrangements; and the sun-and-planet relationship, between the United States and Britain on the one hand and the states of Southeast Asia on the other, has become still further entrenched since China fell to the Communists in 1949.

Political and Economic Instability

The current situation in Southeast Asia is one of political instability and economic stagnation, and the Asian peoples recognize that a long and difficult road lies ahead. During the struggle for independence, the goal was clear-cut and identifiable. Today, the problems are far more complex. Nationalist leaders who were effective as instruments of protest against the colonial regimes have proved less effective as instruments of progressive reform.

In the face of the chronic instability of much of the region, the former imperial powers who now lead the free world feel almost compelled to interfere in the internal affairs of some of these countries. Thus, the desire to keep Vietnam safe from communist invasion, Laos, Cambodia, Burma, Thailand and even the Philippines from the threat of communist infiltration provides the continuing and natural justification for the system of alliances that has grown up in the region. In spite of some grounds for hope, the present pattern of social and political development by no means guarantees the eventual acceptance of democratic institutions. The search for an appropriate political system is a perplexity that, in varying degrees of urgency, confronts each nation. Liberal democracy, as practiced in the West, has not always been acceptable. Though some countries pay lip service to liberal political aspirations, their crucial need is for stability, however this may be achieved politically.

There is little prospect that in their present situations, the countries of Southeast Asia will achieve the modernization of their economies to which they aspire. Their problem is aggravated by the unbalanced structure of their economies, dependent as they are on the western powers for an international market for their exports, which are almost wholly agricultural. Economic aid has only reinforced this dependence.

Foreign Aid and Economic Dependence

It is interesting to note that as a dispenser of foreign aid, the United States has changed the character of its aid from emergency relief to long-term development. Strengthening the economies of the underdeveloped countries has become, with defense build-up, a major purpose of American aid, because of the conviction that economic stability is the best defense against subversion.

But military aid, though it is imperative in emergency situations such as Vietnam, is never really effective in building the foundations of a stable, viable economy. Pouring billions of dollars into the Southeast Asian countries has not liberated them from the age-old problems of poverty and illiteracy. It is, moreover, almost impossible for foreign aid planners to penetrate far enough into a country to make careful and adequate assessments of the social environment and of the apparatus of power. Consequently, much aid has fallen into the wrong hands and has not been widely shared by the masses of people or significantly used.

The magnitude of United States aid to East Asia ($3,500 million in 1964, a substantial portion of which went in military aid to Laos, South Vietnam and South Korea) is indeed impressive. But the tendency to evaluate aid in terms of magnitude, rather than in terms of its positive effects on economic growth, has made the benefits which accrue grossly incommensurate with the amount of funds expended. Foreign aid, whether direct or indirect, has done little to broaden the base of exports in the primary-export economies of Southeast Asia and has, in many instances, perpetuated the old structure of international trade. It has precluded the exporting countries from spreading their imports and exports equally over a large number of countries. Foreign aid is predicated, again, on the lack of external resources, especially capital, technicians and specialists. In fact, in assuming that capital is the missing element, foreign aid programs are doing precisely what colonialism did. Out of his experience as American ambassador to India, Kenneth Galbraith [1] affirms that economic aid cannot be effective unless instituted simultaneously with four other, noneconomic measures: an increase in the literacy rate and the improvement of a higher system of education; the adoption of social justice measures; the creation of an effective system of public administration; and the infusion of a clear and purposeful view of what development involves.

Since it is hardly possible for any country to give aid without increasing its influence over the recipient country, aid programs should be developed on lines that would preclude a further relationship of dependence and influence. There should be increasing provision for fellowships, scholarships and training grants to the nationals of the recipient countries. Some way, moreover, should be found to channel a larger share of foreign aid through the United Nations or its agencies, as has already been done, for example, through the Expanded Program for Technical Assistance (EPTA), the U. N. specialized agencies, the U. N. Special Fund, the World Fund Program and the U. N. Children's Fund (UNICEF). Such agencies as FAO, UNESCO, ILO, WHO, ICAO, ITU, IBRD, IMF, and IFC should all be utilized to minimize interference with national sovereignties.

Increasing Regional Trade

Any increase in the regional trade of Southeast Asia (and of East Asia in general) would lessen dependence on the former colonial rulers. Fortunately, such trade is increasing. As a result of postwar American policy, Japan has re-emerged as a major competitor for the Southeast Asian markets. Its geographical location makes it a natural trading partner for the agricultural countries of the region. The hoped-for expansion of Indian trade with the region has not materialized, but Australia is increasingly active in

[1] "A Positive Approach to Economic Aid," *Foreign Affairs,* April, 1961.

Southeast Asia as a potential market for its manufactured goods. The economy of the Philippines is still closely tied to that of America; but, as these old trading links weaken and the Filipinos begin to solve their own problems, the accidents of history will take second place to the facts of geography. In fact, one might say that the recent attempts at regional economic groupings—the Association of Southeast Asia (ASA), constituted by the Philippines, Malaysia and Thailand, and the Maphilindo (Malaysia, Philippines, Indonesia)—are, in spite of congenital weakness, symbolic of future trends.

Foreign Trade as an Instrument of Power

In the final analysis, the most significant factor in the economic relations of states is to be found in the power structures that are established. As a result of economic inequalities and the differences in stages of development between countries, and also because of the differences in the extent to which they need each other's products, foreign trade becomes an instrument of national power. Take, for instance, relations between the Philippines and the United States. The Philippine Trade Act of 1946, as amended by the Laurel-Langley Agreement, provided for a transition period of twenty-eight years before the final termination of the special trade relations between the two countries, on the assumption that Philippine traditional exports—copra, sugar, abaca, minerals, tobacco— would require such a period to prepare for the eventual loss of a protected position in the American market and at the same time the Philippines could establish a viable, independent economy. But the United States imposed a condition which required the Philippines to confer equal rights on American citizens to exploit the natural resources of the Philippines and to operate public utilities in the country—privileges reserved under the Philippine Constitution to its nationals. In addition, through the Philippine Rehabilitation Act of 1946, the United States Congress made Philippine

201

acceptance of the parity condition for Americans, and the corresponding amendment of the Constitution to that effect, a condition of payment of war damage claims.

The Philippine Trade Act of 1946 did not, however, fulfill the expectations of independent economy, and in fact it made it difficult for the Philippine economy to wean itself from dependence on the American market. There is increasing pressure in the Philippines for parity to be scrapped from the constitutional and treaty commitments of the Philippines, and for the treaty to be allowed to lapse after 1967.

Philippine-American economic relations also illustrate the problems of trade adjustment, when trade relations are not equal. The effect of American economic policy toward the Philippines having been to encourage Philippine overspecialization in a few agricultural exports, among them sugar, the Philippine economy would be seriously dislocated if it suddenly found its sugar exports cut off from the American market. The American economy, on the other hand, could cut off its preferential treatment for Philippine sugar without any disadvantageous effect on itself.

Marshall, the great English economist, was fully aware of this aspect of trade. The rich country, he said, can with little effort supply a poor country with implements for agriculture which she could not make for herself; and the rich country could, without much trouble, produce for herself most of the things that she purchased from the poor nation, or, at all events, could get fairly good substitutes for them. A stoppage of the trade would therefore generally cause much more real loss to the poor than to the rich nation. Moreover, in the classical pattern of colonial relations, "influence" derives from the fact that the trade conducted is critically essential to the underdeveloped country, which therefore grants the former colonial power certain advantages—military, political, economic.

The Struggle for Self-Sustaining Growth

Underdevelopment is the key reality in Southeast Asia. Though, for the moment, in countries like Indonesia and Vietnam basic political issues take precedence, in the long run the vital need is to infuse the economies of the whole region with such a dynamic upward thrust that they will be enabled to take off to self-sustaining economic growth, free from violent swings in foreign exchange and from fluctuations in international markets. Underdeveloped societies have not experienced growth as a built-in, self-sustaining economic process over long periods. Sporadic outbursts of growth and the occasional achievement of great peaks of productivity have been countered by long stationary periods.

Except in Malaysia and to some extent the Philippines, both the momentum of economic growth and the enthusiasm of political leaders for its acceleration have waned. Whereas elsewhere great strides have been made in the 1960's toward doubling national incomes, Southeast Asia shows, by and large, unimpressive rates of economic growth, which have, in any event, been cancelled out by growth in population.

Apart from the need to avoid dependence on former colonial rulers, it is important to achieve economic development on all fronts. Such development demands social, psychological and political changes that are preconditions for the process of economic modernization and also its consequences.

It has been discovered that economic growth is directly related to the existence of an elite entrepreneurial class. The achievement of higher rates of growth seems to depend on the successful activity of some group in society which is prepared to accept innovations. Thus, we are faced with the psychological problem of generating in enough people the motivations, creativity and purposeful sense of innovation required for growth, and at the same time with the economic problems of investing sufficient resources in human capital and of training enough people in public administration and in

203

the managerial and technical skills to operate a modern economy.

It is generally accepted that in most of Southeast Asia, the governments must take the initiative in economic development. But then comes the problem of creating adequate machinery for government-controlled development, since the managerial skills and the sense of efficient and dedicated public service demanded are precisely the qualities that are lacking in public administration in Southeast Asia.

It is fortunate for the underdeveloped countries that they can bypass the trial-and-error period: the clear lessons of waste and error in the economic history of Britain and other countries of western Europe are there for the learning. Moreover, recent experience seems to suggest that modernization is proceeding more by a process of adapting resources, techniques and institutions from the industrialized societies than by innovation. But the overall problem is that of accomplishing in one generation the social, psychological and economic changes that took many decades and even centuries in the western world and of generating, both in the political leadership of Southeast Asia and in the general population, the genuine determination and purpose that are all too often lacking.

The undue concern of Southeast Asia, leaders and people alike, for politics, when the basic issue is beyond all doubt the economic one of liberating people from poverty, is a decisive problem in itself. How are the people to be provided against hunger when they are themselves unwilling to tread with single-minded direction the path to progress? Nor does the problem end there. We can make no progress unless the people learn the most fundamental lesson of all: to sacrifice short-term gains for long-term goals; to create a disciplined society in which everyone, whether in the public service or in private life, is willing to refrain from scrambling for his own advantage, disregarding the welfare of the nation as a whole. The tragedy in the Philippines, which finds a parallel in other countries in the region, especially in Vietnam, is the fragmentation of society into cliques and factions and groups, each seeking to cut the other to pieces and to identify its own narrow motives with the national interest.

Foreign Capital and Economic Independence

W. W. Rostow points out [2] that both Britain and Japan achieved economic maturity without the assistance of foreign capital and that actually, the loanable funds required to finance a country's take-off to self-sustaining growth have generally come from two domestic sources: the shifts in the control of income-flows, including income-distribution; and the ploughing back of profits in rapidly expanding sectors, including that of exports. But foreign loans and investments can help to make good the lack of necessary capital and foreign exchange.[3]

However, attitudes to foreign investment vary as people become aware that their economy is not entirely under the control of nationals. At one extreme, Malaysia is hospitable to foreign capital and has in fact advocated for the countries of Southeast Asia an international charter to regulate the treatment of foreign private investments to be drawn up with the help of the United Nations and in consultation with the U. N.[4] But Malaysia's attitude is explained by the remarkable production and prosperity achieved during the short period of British occupancy of the peninsula. Though the modernization of the economy has been accomplished at the price of British control of a very high proportion of the total tin and rubber production, Malaysia has by far the highest income per capita of any nation in Southeast Asia after Japan.

Though the Philippines, on the other hand, imbibed great po-

---

[2] *Stages of Economic Growth.* Cambridge University Press, 1960.

[3] See, e.g., United Nations, VII, *Economic Bulletin for Asia and the Far East* (No. 1), 1957.

[4] See ECAFE, Annual Report to the Economic Social Council, 1957–58, United Nations Economic Social Council, Official Records: 26th Session, Supplement No. 2.

litical and liberal ideas under the American occupation, it did not get the benefit of an enlightened economic policy. Nor did it achieve the increase in per capita national income achieved by Malaysia, and its foreign trade, communications, banking system, mining industry have all been mainly in the hands of foreigners.

The awakening has, however, come, and Philippine policy on foreign investments now revolves around two mutually antagonistic objectives: a faster rate of economic growth and greater Filipino control of critical areas of the economy. The simultaneous pursuit of both goals often results in tensions that slow down the process of growth. In the Philippines, moreover, there is a tension between the legitimate desire to attract foreign investments and the valid fear that they may dislodge Philippine investments on their own home ground. There is a persistent pressure for industrial development to be promoted only under conditions which give Filipinos the main control and the country the primary benefits of its own economic progress. The policy is therefore to discourage foreign investments in the form of branches of wholly foreign-owned subsidiaries and to expect substantial participation by Philippine nationals, particularly in those ventures concerned with basic industries and the exploitation of natural resources.

The nationalistic impulse involving hostility toward foreign investments has been most clearly manifest in Indonesia and Burma. In Indonesia the Economic Declaration of March 30, 1963, declares that

... the basic strategy of Indonesia cannot be separated from the general strategy of the Indonesian Revolution. According to its basic economic strategy Indonesia, during the first stage, is to build a national and democratic economy, free from the remainders of imperialism and feudalism. The first stage is a preparation which ushers in the second stage, namely, an Indonesian Socialist economy, an economy without the exploitation of man by man.

But the Indonesian economy is only now completing the first stage. "Our duty in the economic field at this first stage," the Dec-

206

laration states, "is to wipe out the remainders of imperialism and feudalism in the economic field; activate all national potentials as an effort to lay the foundation of a national economy and stimulate its growth, which will be free from imperialism and feudalism and which will become the basis for the creation of an Indonesian Socialist community."

In Indonesia, though foreign investment is officially equated with colonialism, many businessmen and professionals are hungering for increased foreign trade, foreign investments and joint ventures; and there is a growing feeling, privately shared even by many government leaders and, ironically enough, encouraged by overly rigid governmental restrictions, that foreign investments are not entirely identical with colonialism and that a planned and well-directed introduction of capital is urgently required. But the trend is toward greater government restriction on foreign investments, and crises over such questions as the government's share in the profits of the three oil subsidiaries, Caltex, Stanvac and Shell, continuously arise. Moreover, Indonesia's withdrawal from the United Nations may even more significantly affect her attitude toward foreign investments.

How much further nationalism and political ends should be pursued at the expense of economic development is the crux of the Indonesia problem. The economy is in a condition of static equilibrium, and it does not look like moving ahead significantly in the foreseeable future. By any standard nothing seems more pressing in the lifetime of this generation than to lay the foundations for initiating a self-sustaining growth. And yet Indonesian leaders are compelled to erase every vestige of western dominance and to create a sense of national purpose.

Nationalism can be turned in different directions. In the main, however, it has taken two definite forms in Southeast Asia: (1) a fierce pride in asserting national sovereignty, accompanied in some instances by an extreme reaction against vestiges of western influence and a loosening of economic ties with the West; and (2) a desire to transfer to indigenous hands the productive assets of the country, which were formerly largely held by aliens, including affluent Chinese and Indian immigrants.

Nationalism and the Idea of Complete Independence

Nationalist feeling is essential both for the development of a sense of national community in young and rising nations and for their drive toward economic maturity. It can be turned outward to remove past injustices suffered under colonialism or to exploit opportunities for national aggrandizement, once the industrializing economy develops sufficient momentum. It is nationalism that provides the social force to unleash individual initiative, creativity and organizational skill for the task of economic, social and political modernization which the old feudal structure had obstructed, in some instances in collusion with the former colonial powers.

In a sense, nationalism is simply a matter of self-assertion and self-affirmation. In this sense it is both natural and necessary. But it is always in danger of distortion and of being made the supreme goal of every activity. The moment nationalism thus becomes an end in itself instead of a means to achieve greater opportunities for development, it leads to destruction.

The dilemma of many Christians in these countries is acute and not easily resolved. Many of them feel that the reawakened national feelings are part of God's plan and that it is only just, in this century of enlightened perspectives, that the people of every nation should shape their own ideals, draw up their own political structures and symbols, manage their own foreign policy and assume primary responsibility for the modernization of their economy. But there is also an obvious need to moderate the more destructive aspects of the change-over, not the least of which is the growth of intolerance, prejudice and hostility.

Nationalism is a reality, and the clamor for a more effective exercise of nationhood has become insistent and compelling. But

208

can there be complete freedom in the context of new developments in power structures and of the reality of Chinese expansionism? Countries that are too small to be militarily self-reliant or economically viable cannot assume that complete freedom comes as a result of liberation from western domination. Indeed, the dominant scene in Southeast Asia is that of countries living under the shadow of China, the colossus of the North, whose influence over the area is now turning full circle and may, in the long run, prove to be more significant and lasting than that of the West.

Structure of World Trade

Southeast Asia's economic dependence has been to some extent perpetuated by the steadily increasing inequalities between developed and underdeveloped countries, a pattern that can be changed only by a structure of trade that reverses the economic trends and insures the poorer countries a share of the world market. They depend almost entirely on a narrow base of primary exports for which the demand is often inelastic and where excessive price fluctuations upset producer expectations. There is also the danger that the decline in commodity prices is becoming a permanent trend. Tied as they are, economically, to their international trade, the underdeveloped countries must boost their trade if they are to achieve higher rates of growth.

One solution might be to fix minimum commodity prices in the world market at approximately the present level, though even this may not be enough. There is much significance in the new concept of aid tied to trade that was propounded by the underdeveloped countries at the U. N. Conference on Trade and Development (UNCTAD) in 1964 (to guarantee the purchasing power of the exports of primary commodities).

It is also encouraging that UNCTAD was able to set up a new organization for the promotion of international trade (The Trade and Development Board, established as an organ of the United

Nations General Assembly)—even if only with the grudging con-
sent of the developed countries and in the face of a lack of genuine concern on the part of the industrial powers, including Japan. Paul Prebisch, secretary-general of UNCTAD, put the case
succinctly:

Many developing countries bear the deep imprint of thousands of years
of civilization. They could do much to ensure that, in our efforts to
control economic forces, we do not subordinate man to the demands
of technology or purely economic process, but enable him to free
himself from economic need, from poverty, and from his inherent ills,
so that he may improve his life and achieve that full existence which,
in the developing countries, has until now been traditionally enjoyed
only by a few.

Conclusion

In spite of the inevitability—and indeed the growing reality
—of interdependence of peoples and nations, our world is still
plagued by the fact of so much plenty in some areas and so much
want in others. The strong and rich nations do not easily compre-
hend their responsibility and they are constantly tempted to use
power without discipline, as we can see in the perpetuation of conditions of dependence in the economic field and of unfair trade
relations. Foreign aid to underdeveloped countries is too often regarded as a painful necessity, given in order to keep these countries out of the communist camp!

Notwithstanding the obvious difficulties involved in reconciling
outside assistance with the understandable pride of newly independent states, it should not be impossible to provide them with a
measure of strength in their struggle for economic progress without
depriving them of the effective exercise of their nationhood. Southeast Asia needs, above all else, a reasonable space of time within
which to work out its own solutions to the vexing problems of
increasing the living standards of its people.

The Southeast Asian peoples are striving to modernize their societies in the full exercise of nationhood, freed as much as possible from the constraints and limitations of dependent relations with the former colonial powers. Western responsibility must see them not as objects of exploitation but as a people for whom the strong bear some burdens not only because every man's suffering is a concern from which there is no escape, but because these people have already suffered for centuries from the injustices of colonial relations.

No task can be more exciting in the interdependent world in which we live than that of closing the gap between rich and poor. But nothing can be more difficult. And yet this is our ultimate responsibility.

10

THE ECONOMIC DEVELOPMENT OF THE MIDDLE EAST IN ITS WORLD CONTEXT

by MUSA NASIR (Jordan)

THIS chapter is concerned with the implications of economic growth in the relations between states, from the point of view of the Middle East. Obviously, these relations depend to a large extent on the internal conditions prevailing within the states involved. It is important, therefore, that the relevant facts pertaining to the Middle Eastern states that may influence these relations, be briefly reviewed as a background for an intelligent understanding of this chapter's theme.

The term Middle East has had different meanings at various times. The widest area which it may cover includes countries in Europe, Asia and Africa. Greece, Turkey, Iran, Afghanistan, Israel, Cyprus, Ethiopia, Somalia, the Arab states of Asia and of Africa, together with the Arab areas which are either not yet independent, or are only semi-independent, may all be covered by the term. This divides the Middle East into two main groups: Arab and non-Arab countries. The Arab countries are again divided into two subgroups: the African and the Asian states. The first includes Egypt, Sudan, Libya, Tunisia, Algeria, Morocco and Mauritania. The latter includes Syria, Lebanon, Iraq, Saudi Arabia, Kuwait and all the nonsovereign Arab countries. In its relations with the other Arab states, Egypt, which is an African state, has one face toward Asia and another toward Africa.

In spite of certain differences and, until recently, in spite of occasional conflicts, the Arab states have many characteristics and aspirations in common, which need not be discussed till later. It would be reasonable, therefore, to think of the Arab states as a group, and to expect each of them to show a genuine desire for cooperation, to a greater or less extent, with the others.

The non-Arab countries of the Middle East, on the other hand, are by no means similar, and have little in common with one another or with the Arab states. It would not be easy, therefore, to think of them as a group, or to expect any of them to show very marked tendencies toward cooperation with the other Middle Eastern states. In the case of Israel, its relations with the Arab states are governed by a precarious truce, which may at any time be suddenly transformed to a shooting war. In view of this, it would be more useful for the present chapter to concern itself only with the Arab Middle East.

Background Information

The facts that we need dwell upon for our present purposes are those relating to the various forces which operate in the Arab Middle East and that influence, or are likely to influence, the attitudes and actions of the people of the area, and of their governments, in matters of economic development and its international implications. These will be briefly reviewed.

213

Religious Forces. With the exception of the small country of Lebanon, the present population of which is approximately half Christian and half Muslim, all the other countries are predominantly Muslim. Religion plays a significant role in the lives of the great majority of Muslims, because Islam is not only a religion, but a way of life. In fact, it started both as a religion and as a political state. For this reason it evokes in its adherents, besides purely religious attitudes, those emotions which tend to insist that any change in the form of government, or in the mode of life, must conform with religious doctrine.

a. *Religious theory.* As a monotheistic religion, Islam has its roots in Judaism and Christianity. Muslims believe that these two religions were originally true and divine, the latter fulfilling the former, but that they have become distorted and have been superseded by Islam, which preserved all that was true in both. This explains the basis for the tolerance so conspicuously displayed by Muslims toward "the people of the Book," as Christians and Jews are termed. Unfortunately, however, this tolerance has not been reciprocated, and Islam has therefore continued to be despised and often abused and attacked by adherents of the other two faiths.

All prophets mentioned in the Bible are recognized as such, and the miraculous birth of Christ is accepted, but his divine nature is denied. It was not he, but someone like him, who was crucified; the concept of redemption and salvation is completely rejected.

b. *Political theory according to religion.* Politically, Islam is neither democratic nor dictatorial. The ruler is given full powers, but he must consult. No special institutions for consultation are prescribed, and present-day parliaments, whatever their form, are variously accepted as sufficiently fulfilling this requirement.

Hereditary rule is frowned upon, and the ruler is supposed to be accepted by elders and responsible citizens. The lack of preciseness in political theory, however, has made it possible for Muslims to acquiesce in various forms of rule, which may represent different grades of compliance wtih religious doctrine or which may some-

214

times appear to contradict the popular understanding of that doctrine. Thus the main criterion for good government has become "unlimited justice," even against one's personal interests. In practice, as long as the actions of any ruler are both just and generally beneficial, his rule remains unchallenged, regardless of the system and method used.

c. *Social theory according to religion.* Socially, Islam has no class or color distinction of any sort. Muslims of every race are brothers, and full intercourse between rich and poor is very common. In theory, Christianity goes to the extreme in emphasizing universal brotherhood. In practice, however, Islam applies the concept to a greater extent. Other points to note in the social structure of Islam are that it demands full legal responsibility for the poor and for orphans and makes obedience to parents and respect for old age common law.

d. *Economic theory according to religion.* Many religious Muslims claim that Islam provides for a special economic system. It is really a capitalistic system, but frowns on the accumulation of too much wealth. It permits private ownership and the exploitation of property, and encourages diligence in economic activity. It also recognizes the need for differences in quality and quantity of work. It provides for tax contribution to the state and requires wealth to be partially used for the benefit of those in need. The general formula for striking a balance between the human urge for worldly riches and the simultaneous desire for a future life in heaven is neatly expressed in the statement: "For the purpose of the future life act as though tomorrow you will die. For the purpose of the present life act as though you never will die." This formula, it is claimed, if applied intelligently, could curb human greed and encourage benevolent action.

e. *Ethical theory.* Islam goes into greater detail than Christianity with regard to ethical behavior, for it lays down specific rules of conduct which are generally noble and compassionate. Theoretically, it does not go so far as Christianity in the matter of

215

forgiveness. A comparison between the corresponding doctrines of Judaism, Christianity and Islam may be of special interest. In Judaism, the law of Moses is "An eye for an eye, and a tooth for a tooth." In Christianity, "If a man strikes you on your right cheek turn to him the left also." In Islam, "If a man trespasses on you, trespass likewise on him, but if you forgive him you are nearer to God." Muslims are equally aware of the extreme loftiness of Christian ethics in this matter, and of the failure of Christians to abide by this ethic, a fact which has made it possible and easy for Muslims to attack Christians bitterly, not necessarily because of Christian lack of forgiveness, but mainly for planned trespass and aggression. A religion, they say, that is unable in practice to narrow the wide gap between its lofty principles and the actions of its followers cannot be of much use to the world.

Geographical Position and Natural Resources. Arabs are now collectively and individually aware of the strategic importance of their geographical position and of the great economic value of the natural wealth of their countries, specially oil. But they realize that the largest benefits from the main source of natural wealth, namely oil, go to foreigners, and that this natural wealth is not equally distributed between the various Arab countries. Furthermore, they realize that although "oil" has made a few people fabulously rich, the ordinary Arab citizen has derived from it relatively very little and has therefore continued at a low standard of living. Small gaps between the rich and the poor which are due to economic diligence are accepted as natural. But wide gaps, because of the grabbing of natural resources or of the abuse of power, are highly resented. The discovery of oil has both widened and changed the color of the gap between the "haves" and the "have nots," as countries and as individuals, and has therefore given rise to deep discontent.

Arab Nationalism. The other forces which influence the area are the attitudes and emotions generated by the contacts with other

216

religions and nations which the Arabs have made throughout their history.

a. *Political attitudes.* For a long period in history most of the Arabs were more or less equal partners in the Ottoman Empire; and although they were never really enthusiastic about that partnership, they were sufficiently contented for a long time because the sovereign was a Muslim, and because Muslim religious law was applied to a considerable extent. After corruption had gradually weakened the empire and it began to decline, some Christian powers seized certain Arab parts of the empire, and Arab Muslims came for the first time under Christian and non-Arab rule. During the First World War, the Asian Arab parts of the Ottoman Empire joined the Christian powers of the West and fought their co-religionists, the Turks, after having been promised support for their desire to create their own national state. When the war ended, the victorious western allies, instead of fulfilling their promises, divided the Arab areas into small states, each under the influence, in one form or another, of one of the victorious Christian powers. One of these states, which eventually became Israel, was presented as a gift to the Zionists. The indignation felt as a result of what the Arabs called "the treachery of the Christian powers" has not yet subsided, and is not likely to do so until the wrongs committed have been put right. It is indeed unfortunate that the effect of the mistakes made after the First World War still persist in the form of major problems in the Arab Middle East. In the process, the reputation of Christianity as such suffered tremendously, and the Arabs learned the hard lesson that they should not rely on foreign friendship and support.

b. *Arab aspirations.* The logical consequences of Arab experience with other nations has been the intensification of the movement for Arab independence, and the addition to it of bitterness which could have been avoided. Most of the Arab countries have now obtained their independence from foreign rule, some after prolonged fighting. The struggle to liberate the remaining areas still goes on, giving unnecessary cause for added bitterness and international misunderstanding.

With independence, however, came the realization that freedom is not a corollary to independence, as had previously been believed. Nor could independence solve all problems. Other forms of struggle have therefore started and are still in progress: one is in search of the best form of government; another is an attempt to secure the maximum individual freedom compatible with the best form of government and with national interests; and a third is to determine the most efficient and just economic system. These are problems common to the whole world, but in the context of the Arab Middle East they acquire special significance. The inherent Arab desire for greater justice in the distribution of income does not stem from the existence of suppressed classes, but rather from the precepts of a religion that regards justice as one of its fundamental cornerstones. Complete equality is not a goal, for variations in abilities and needs are recognized. The elimination of abject poverty, distress and suffering, and the provision of equal opportunities for all are the main objectives. Opinions on how to achieve these ends differ, and the differences may well constitute an important cause of the remaining discord among Arab states.

A basic element in Arab aspirations is Arab unity. Arabs realize that their countries are contiguous, that economically they complement one another and that, unless they unite, they cannot be strong and respected and cannot protect their own rights. How to unite is at present one of the burning questions in the minds of all. The summit conferences have eliminated political differences to a large extent. But economic and administrative differences remain. It is the ardent hope and prayer of every Arab that the Arab League will soon iron out all inter-Arab differences.

A final Arab aspiration is to correct the wrong inflicted on the Arabs of Palestine by the creation of Israel. This aspiration is the strongest single force which is likely to unite all Arabs, and may be sufficiently strong eventually to overcome all forces of internal disruption among them. How to achieve this end peacefully is a major problem confronting, not only the Arabs, but the whole world.

The Broad Issues

The broad issues involved in economic development are not the concern of this chapter. Nevertheless, it would be difficult to discuss the international implications of economic growth without noting these issues, at least to the extent to which they influence action in the Arab Middle East.

One of the main issues may be put as follows: Are human beings in general aware of what they are trying to achieve through economic development, and are they agreed on what they should achieve? Is it maximum individual happiness, or maximum national strength and welfare, or both? Are these two goals necessarily irreconcilable?

In the Arab Middle East, the concept of a world government does not receive much thought or attention. Here, as probably all over the world, ordinary citizens are all trying to advance their own interests, which are usually measured by the amount of income earned from employment or from business.

This much is considered legitimate. Beyond this legitimate activity, however, individual attitudes vary greatly:

a. Some try to achieve their legitimate interests within the framework of national interest as they themselves, or their governments, interpret it.

b. Others are not conscious of national interests and merely follow, willingly, government rules and regulations.

c. A third kind of individual ignores national interests as long as they seem to conflict with his own.

d. A fourth group goes about sincerely, but aggressively, trying to coerce people into making national interest supreme.

219

e. And a final group, by taking shelter behind national interests, tries to obtain power and control.

Unfortunately, the demarcation line between the last two groups is not defined, and we have some sincere and some very selfish people trying to coerce people in some way or other. The confusion is aggravated by serious differences of opinion as to what the national interests are and as to the best means of realizing them. Opinions ranging from extreme right to extreme left, intermingled with Islamic attitudes which would unite state and religion, have their respective supporters, who again may be genuine or who merely use differences of opinion as pretexts for seizing power. This brief analysis should help to explain, to some extent, the multidirection tug-of-war that is going on.

Another main issue is: How much more material development is good for human beings? The general standard of living in the Arab Middle East is so low that the issue is not considered immediately serious, since the Arab Middle East, as a region, has still far to go before it need begin to worry about overdevelopment. Nevertheless, the excessive wealth of some individuals and of some countries is often the subject of comment, and raises various questions as to the final economic goal which should not be passed. Very wealthy people are no happier than those with adequate means and, in view of the generally low standard of living, wealthy persons in the Arab Middle East are beginning to feel a little uncomfortable. They are envied and are usually unpopular and live in a continuous state of apology. They may be respected, not necessarily because of the amount of good that they do, but often because of their power to inflict harm on others. The socialism that is applied in certain Arab Middle East countries is made popular partly by the vengeance that it exhibits toward wealthy individuals.

At this point it may be noted that the Arab Middle East is not even aware of the possibility of economic growth reaching such limits as to create an affluent society with an entirely new set of problems. No thought whatever is therefore given to the implications of such affluence.

Main Problems of the Arab Middle East

In considering the problems of the Arab Middle East, it may be useful to begin by listing as many of them as may seem to concern our present discussion: the low standard of living, the division of the Arab world into separate national states, the economic and political relations with foreign powers and the relations between the Arab states themselves. All these factors present problems which we should examine briefly.

Standard of Living. The standard of living in the Arab world is generally very low, even in countries that have rich sources of natural wealth. These latter countries, with better organization and more efficient administrations, will eventually be able appreciably to raise their standards of living. Many of the remaining countries, like Egypt, are less fortunate, and their prospects for higher standards of living are poor. Because of its size and position, and also because of its political and cultural influences, Egypt's unfavorable economic situation presents a serious problem, not for Egypt alone, but for other Arab and non-Arab states as well. Low standards of living are no longer taken for granted; they cause internal stresses and strains in a country as well as generating pressures which are bound to be felt beyond its borders. Furthermore, the great differences in standards of living that are so obvious, and that can no longer be concealed, bring to the surface the primitive feelings of jealousy that otherwise might remain hidden and that are greatly aggravated by the seeming indifference of the rich toward the poor. With the exception of the dispute between Israel and the Arab world, there is no single cause that can generate a greater number of explosive forces in the Arab Middle East than can this difference between rich and poor individuals and between rich and poor countries.

221

Arab Unity. Since the founding of Islam, about fourteen centuries ago, the Arabs have always felt that they are one nation, with Arabic as their common language and with Islam as the religion of the great majority. The fact that Arab countries are geographically contiguous, that economically they complement one another, and that at one time they formed a major world power which succeeded in effectively spreading its culture and religion over a vast area of the world, intensifies the Arab feeling of "oneness" and gives it a solid foundation. This is a fact that must be reckoned with, regardless of any opinion to the contrary and of any disruptive forces that may appear to exist at any time within the Arab world. It explains the Arab aspirations for unity and their efforts, which may seem at times aggressive, to achieve it.

It also explains any unfriendliness that Arabs may display toward all who had, or still have, anything to do with dividing up the Arab world into separate national states, allowing vested interests to develop within these states as obstacles to the expressed goal of restoring unity.

Arabs, however, do not desire or actively pursue unity as a luxury, or as an end in itself, or as a result of emotions. The political setbacks which the Arabs have suffered during the last few centuries, sometimes with loss of territory, are all attributed to the military and economic weakness that results from lack of unity. Furthermore, it is generally accepted that without economic unity, at least, it will be difficult if not impossible to improve the present economic situation and to raise the standard of living. It is also believed that without political unity, in one form or another, it will not be easy to achieve a satisfactory and adequate degree of economic unity.

Thus, it will be seen that beside the historical, emotional, cultural, linguistic and religious factors that bind Arabs together there are strong basic factors, affecting their very existence and well-being, which give a strong impetus to their aspirations for unity.

Economic Relations—The Oil Resources. The economic rela-

222

tions of the Arab Middle East with other states are based mainly on the following factors:

a. Its vast resources of oil.

b. Its need for grants and/or loans for development.

c. Its need for heavy importation of manufactured consumer and capital goods from industrialized states.

d. Its possession of raw materials, other than oil, which are needed by other states.

e. Its importance, especially the importance of some of its parts, for tourism.

These factors place the Arab Middle East in the category of developing countries, sharing with them all the problems and, perhaps, the blessings of lack of development. The question of oil resources only will be discussed, very briefly, in this chapter.

The oil-producing Arab states have only recently become aware of the high profits of the oil companies and have therefore begun to insist on higher prices for their oil. At the time of writing, negotiations are going on between the governments concerned and the oil companies.

A book recently published in Arabic calls attention to the very low prices that the Arab countries receive for their oil, and yet the oil companies make a minimum profit of 1,380 per cent on their oil dealings. The book, which caused a stir in the Arab world, bases its facts and figures on the statistical reports of the oil companies, and on statements by various western politicians and writers, including Lord Avon. It discusses the immense importance of Arab oil and affirms that in 1961 the Arab states produced one-fifth of the total world production, and that the oil reserves in Arab lands are estimated to be 75 per cent of the total world reserves. Further, the book describes in vivid terms and figures the enormous economic and military benefits derived by the countries of the oil companies from Arab oil, and exposes the meager benefits derived by the Arab states themselves. Finally the book urges

all Arabs to hinge their economic, political and military power on
oil, and suggests that it should be used as a forceful lever to restore
to Arabs their rights in Palestine. In fact, a translation of the
book's title would read: "This is how it (Palestine) was lost, and
this is how it should be regained." [1]

The question of Arab oil is now an extremely sensitive issue,
and it is my sincere opinion that Arab political and economic relations with the West should be reviewed without any further delay
in a spirit of fairness, generosity and understanding.

Political Relations. Arabs divide their international relations
into the following categories:

a. *Relations with Israel.* As we have said, relations with Israel are governed by a truce that may not last long. The Arab
point of view in the dispute is exceedingly simple: The Arabs of
Palestine have been turned out of their country, without any justification whatever; Zionist Jews, imported from Europe and other
parts of the world, have been allowed and helped to take possession of the lands, homes and properties of the original Arab
owners and to establish therein the State of Israel. The Arabs in
general, and the Palestine Arabs in particular, refuse to accept this
situation and are pursuing an active, but so far peaceful policy, to
recover their country and to regain their lost rights. At the same
time, Israel refuses to surrender its gains or any part thereof, and
pursues a similarly active, but sometimes very aggressive policy,
to consolidate her gains and even to expand them, as in the case
of the diversion of the waters of the River Jordan. This is the
essence of the Palestine problem. The refugee question and certain
other economic and political issues, including the Jordan River
problem, are mere offshoots of the basic problem.

The details of why and how all this happened do not concern us here. In fact, the whole problem would have been irrelevant had it not become the cornerstone of most of the political

---

[1] Author, title, publisher obtainable from Musa Nasir.

and economic activity in the Arab Middle East. It has gone far beyond the limits of the Middle East itself and has assumed immense importance, politically and economically for the whole world, involving the United Nations in heavy responsibilities for relief and for keeping peace. No one who has not visited the Arab Middle East can fathom the depth of the emotions that the Palestine problem has piled up in the hearts of all Arabs. It is not merely that they have suffered the material loss of homes and country and the loss of dignity and means of living, but also that they feel themselves punished for the sins of others. Christians persecuted Jews; and Christians atoned for their crimes by allowing and helping the Jews to occupy and take possession of Arab lands. This Christian support of Zionism and of Israel, moreover, may have served other selfish interests of the Christian powers—a fact that increases the gravity of the injustice and makes the reaction even more bitter and more explosive.

b. *Relations with the major states that support Israel.* Arab relations with some of the states that actively support Israel are anomalous. The United States of America, Great Britain and France are considered by the Arabs to be on the side of Israel, since they were responsible for its creation, and are still seriously involved in its maintenance and protection. Nevertheless, many of the Arabs, in view of their great need for assistance, have accepted and are still accepting economic and financial aid from these same countries. This has resulted in very mixed feelings: hatred for the role which these countries played and still play in supporting Israel, and gratitude for the economic and financial aid which they are giving to Arabs. How long these mixed feelings are likely to last will depend entirely on the amount of effective support that continues to be given to Israel. The breaking point may be reached suddenly.

The Arab peoples, as distinct from their governments, are not really happy about the atmosphere that surrounds relations with these western states. Some see the situation as neo-colonialism, which is tactfully trying to absorb the existing deep economic and political discontent. They are suspicious of the outcome, and they express their suspicion and their fears whenever the opportunity occurs.

c. *Relations with the communist states.* Inherently, Arabs are not inclined toward communism. In 1947, when the partition of Palestine was under discussion at the United Nations, Arabs might have received Soviet support against partition if they had sought it. For several years now the communist bloc has been supporting the Arab states at the United Nations in their fight against Israel. They also supported Algeria against France in its war of liberation. Furthermore, the U. S. S. R. offered to assist Egypt in its Aswan Dam project when the U. S. A. withdrew its promise to help. During the Suez crisis, the U. S. S. R. threatened to use force to support Egypt. Very recently Algeria has been promised large-scale financial and economic aid. These and other instances of assistance by the communist states have led the Arabs to change their inherent attitude toward them and to establish with them full diplomatic and economic relations. The last Arab country that decided to enter into diplomatic relations with the U. S. S. R. was Jordan. During the last few years, moreover, the communist states have usually voted with the Arab states at the meetings of various organs of the United Nations.

In the process of their development some of the Arab states —Egypt, Syria and Algeria—have adopted socialism as an economic system, in the belief that it is more efficient for production and in the hope that it will be more effective in the elimination of the huge differences in individual incomes. This socialism brings them nearer in ideology to communism, and is likely to result in the long run in greater understanding between the communist bloc and the Arab states. For those who live in the Arab Middle East, and who can read the writing on the wall, a landslide toward the left seems imminent. The continued support of Israel by the West and the slow rate at which the gap between rich and poor is being reduced will be the two main forces which may bring it about.

d. *Relations with states other than those referred to under a, b, and c above.* Some of these states continuously support the Arabs in their points of view; others support Israel; and a third group may adopt a neutral attitude. For various reasons, the influence of all three categories is relatively small and need not occupy our attention.

Relations Between the Various Arab States. The relations between the various Arab states themselves constitute an important factor in the economic and political life of the Arab Middle East. We have already referred to the universal Arab desire for complete unity, and it would be no exaggeration to say that if a referendum were held, 95 per cent of the people would vote for unity. Why, then, is there no unity at present, at least between those states which are sovereign and which can decide to unite if they really want to do so? The answer is not simple. The form of union, the location of power, the present vested interests in the existing separate states and the extent of power to be given to the states *vis-à-vis* the central authority are matters that must be settled by agreement before union can be achieved. In 1955, Arab alumni from all universities met in conference in Jerusalem to discuss the question. It was agreed unanimously that union should take a federal form, and a committee was appointed to work out details. Soon afterward the Suez Canal crisis flared up, no subsequent conference was held and the committee never reported. Since then, two Arab unions have been created and dissolved, and the Arabs are perhaps a little wiser now as to the necessary prerequisites for unity.

The differences in ideology between the socialist and the capitalist states in the Arab Middle East will probably continue to hinder political union until a generally accepted system is found,

227

or until a formula for uniting irreconcilable economic systems in one political state has been worked out. The discovery of such a formula may need more than one genius. The same would be true, but perhaps to a less extent, of a purely economic union, which is considered the next best thing and an essential first step toward full political union. There is also the difficulty of finding a system that could bring monarchies to unite with republics, without greatly affecting the personal position of the monarchs. But this may be easier to resolve than the difference in economic ideology.

A further factor that retards unity is the gap between the rich and the poor countries. Under existing conditions it is natural that rich countries should not be enthusiastic over a scheme that would make them share their riches with the poorer.

The Search for Solutions

With the exception of the Palestine problem, the problems of the Arab Middle East are by no means unique. They belong to the same categories as those of other regions of the world, though it is doubtful if any other region has them in so many varieties. This makes the search for solutions to the problems both important and interesting, since the results, if successful, could be applied to other areas of the world. The Arab Middle East could reasonably be regarded as a miniature world, presenting samples of almost all the world's existing problems.

Two questions arise at this point:

a. Would non-Christian people accept the principles of Christian ethics for the purposes of solving problems and of regulating international relations, and,

b. Is Christian ethics likely to be sufficiently effective and reliable to solve these problems, if ever it is made to work?

We can answer the first question affirmatively, as far as the people of the Arab Middle East are concerned. They are predominantly Muslims and their real worry is that the Christians of the world seem unwilling in practice to abide by their own ethical principles in their international dealings.

The answer to the second question is not so easy, because there have been no conscious attempts to employ Christian ethics in solving international problems. Lip service is usually offered to the golden rule, but its application to international situations is not consciously given any serious consideration. The fact, however, that Muslims would be willing to apply Christian ethics should suffice to convince Christians that it would be worth while making the attempt. Most of the political and economic problems of the Arab Middle East are so closely linked with foreign Christian powers that a common ethical code for regulating relationships and for restoring mutual confidence needs to be established; and it should not be based on power politics or on merely selfish interest, in whatever form these may be camouflaged.

The first steps would be to determine the real objective of the rule and to give it a practical interpretation over a wide range of political and economic situations. But who should do it? Could any Christian church do it? National churches have often been dominated by the political state, each in its own area. Thus, wars have been blessed, injustices inflicted and human beings exploited with the acquiescence, passive or active, of the organized church.

It would appear therefore that the church as a whole, through its organizations and its institutions, convened in one way or another, should give a clear, practical and unbiased interpretation of the golden rule in the context of modern political, social and economic needs. The doctrines and methods of all economic and political systems which are calculated to produce the greatest good for all human beings should be indicated after thorough study and research by unbiased experts. Only then could the church become the "salt of the earth" and provide the necessary moral leadership which the world so badly needs. Once human beings become fully aware of what is really "good" for them, they will surely move toward that "good" and will eventually reach it. The operation is by no means easy, with vested and selfish interests, at the private and the national level, still to be overcome. This step demands courage and sacrifice, and time will be needed to achieve the final objective. A beginning must, however, be made and as soon as possible.

As regards the most serious problem of all, Palestine, we should attempt to find a solution on the basis of Christian ethics. The problem involves Christian and non-Christian powers, and if the Christian powers refuse to accept this basis for a solution, they are likely to be forever after blamed for the consequences.

Once this problem is solved, the whole political and economic climate of the Arab Middle East will change, and cooperation with the rest of the world in the economic and political spheres will be transformed beyond recognition. Solutions to the remaining problems of the Arab Middle East would automatically follow, and the region would begin to breathe fresh air, free from the poison of hatred and prejudice. The fresh air is bound to blow toward other regions of the world as well.

These are not utopian dreams, for there is no area in the world more favorable to a gigantic experiment in the application of Christian ethics than the Muslim Arab Middle East. It needs Christian leaders with determination and courage. If they are not forthcoming, then Christianity, whether as a religion or as a way of life, is likely to find itself in grave jeopardy. It will have failed to meet the challenges of the modern age.

II

ECONOMIC DEVELOPMENT
AND RACE RELATIONS
IN AFRICA

by SELBY NGCOBO (Rhodesia)

THE problems of the relations between people of different races, colors and culture are found in many parts of the world.[1] But whereas in other parts of the world the tensions arise because of the presence of minority groups, in Africa they concern both the majority group of Africans and the minority group of Asians and Colored persons of mixed racial descent. These people are dominated by a minority white group in several parts of Africa. Race problems are acute in both the United States of America and southern Africa. In the former there are constitutional and legal means of tackling the race problem, but nothing of the kind exists in southern Africa. In this chapter, however, attention will be fo-

[1] See ANDREW W. LIND, ed.: *Race Relations in World Perspective.* Honolulu: University of Hawaii Press, 1955.

cused not on the constitutional and legal aspects of race relations but on the economic aspects.

Wherever races live side by side, there is a complex situation determined by several factors: the exercise of political control by one race over another, interracial economic cooperation or competition, relative living standards and demographic ratios, social interaction between individuals or groups of different races and the interplay of cultures and psychologies.[2] Varying combinations of these factors produce different patterns of race relations. In some, one factor is determinative; in other situations, a different one predominates. Generally speaking, a change in any one tends to influence the others. But in racially structured societies such as obtain in certain parts of southern Africa and central Africa, the extent to which a change can be induced by economic action alone appears to be very limited.

For many generations, the workers and peasants were the underprivileged sections of the homogeneous societies of western Europe of which they were, however, an integral part. But, after a long and difficult struggle, often involving revolts and strikes, they were able to raise their status by the formation of trade unions, consumer cooperatives and agricultural credit banks, and by improving their working skills and agitating for the extension of educational facilities and the political franchise. It has been suggested that underprivileged Africans in white-controlled countries could successfully employ similar economic methods. But in southern Africa the direction of change is determined essentially by the white government and not by anything the Africans can do. This situation is in marked contrast to that of the countries in central and east Africa.

---

[2] *Ibid.,* Introduction.

Patterns of Economic Development in Africa

South Africa, Rhodesia, Zambia and the ex-Belgian Congo all owe their original economic development to the exploitation of minerals. A fairly wide range of manufacturing activity has developed in the former Belgian Congo and in the east African states, but in none of these has industrialization and diversification of the economy been so extensive and intensive as in South Africa.[3] In west and east Africa economic development has come about largely as a result of the production of agricultural crops and some minerals for export purposes. Where peasant agriculture has been the main source of export production, as in Uganda and parts of west Africa, traditional agricultural methods have been modernized to a great extent. In southern and central Africa agricultural exports have come from large-scale farming undertaken by Europeans, with the labor provided by Africans who, however, continue to grow their own food crops by the traditional methods of subsistence farming. In countries where the main impact of the modern economy on the traditional subsistence economy has been in the form of a demand for labor, the effects have been disruptive.[4]

Broadly speaking, two types of economic structure can be distinguished in tropical Africa. In South Africa, Rhodesia, Zambia, and the former Belgian Congo, economic development has involved large-scale foreign settlement, a heavy inflow of foreign capital, and highly developed capitalist techniques of production, resulting in a relatively large flow of workers from the traditional economy into the modern exchange economy. On the other hand, in west and east Africa commercial activities are concerned chiefly with the handling of exports and imports, both of which are essential to the economy. In these countries the level of domestic income, investment and consumption is largely determined by the

---

[3] United Nations, *Economic Survey of Africa Since 1950,* Introduction.
[4] *Ibid.*

demand for their export products in the world market, and government revenue is derived mainly from taxes on incomes from foreign trade transactions. A large proportion of the income from exports tends to be spent on imports because there is little or no local production to satisfy the needs of the recipients. However, some of the income is spent on domestically produced goods and new economic policies aim to increase this domestic economic activity.

The Emergence of Racial Patterns

This pattern of economic development has been accompanied by a racial pattern in the settlement of the country, the occupation and ownership of land, the organization of production and the structure of government and administration. In south, central and east Africa Europeans have been largely responsible for the development of mining, manufacturing and commercial agriculture. Asians have been associated with Europeans in commercial activities. Europeans from the local community or from the metropolitan countries have provided the governors, administrators, judges, magistrates and top civil servants. The Africans, by and large, occupy the manual labor and lower clerical positions in commerce, industry and government.

Except in west and north Africa, the cities and towns are predominantly enclaves of European and Asian settlement. Around these relatively new urban centers African townships have developed, several of which are of considerable size. In most parts of southern, central and east Africa, however, the majority of Africans live in the rural areas. Since the Africans constitute the great majority of the population, they determine the predominant pattern of population distribution. In the colonial era the distinction between the urban area, which was the sector of modern production and money exchange, and the rural area, representing varying

234

stages of the subsistence economy, became of great political, economic and social significance for race relations.

Independence and the Transformation of Racial Patterns

In the countries lying between the Mediterranean and the Zambezi River these patterns of settlement, economic activity and political control have been transformed by the very rapid political changes which have taken place in the postwar era. Beginning with Ghana in 1959, the movement away from colonial dependency toward political sovereignty gathered increasing momentum, so that by the end of 1962 there were thirty-two independent African states, including Liberia and Ethiopia, which were the only two before 1945.

The emergence of African national governments has a threefold significance for race relations. First, African governments have begun to change existing racial patterns and inequalities by using political power to abolish the legal apparatus of racial discrimination in government and administration, employment practices, educational facilities and the distribution of land. Second, since 1950, African governments have devised and adopted new development programs for the acceleration of the economic growth of their countries. These include the establishment of industries, the increase of agricultural and mineral production, especially for export, the modernization of the system of landholding and agricultural production, the provision or increase of power supplies, the extension of road and rail services, and the provision of social services. The implementation of these programs will tend to increase the volume of employment, the level of income, at present admittedly low, and the standard of living of the majority of the people.[5] Gone are the days when policies were designed to maintain a high living standard for only a minority racial group. Third, African gov-

---

[5] See United Nations, *Economic Bulletin for Africa,* Vol. I, No. 1, June, 1961, Ch. B/11.

ernments have substituted new economic and fiscal policies for those which bolstered up racial minority interests. The assumption of new responsibilities for defense, diplomatic representation, the enlargement of legislatures, administration and compensation payments to expatriates consequential upon the policy of Africanization has resulted in increased current expenditure.[6] The demands and expectations of the masses for the tangible benefits of independence and the obligations of leaders to fulfill their election promises have led to the adoption of measures for improvements in the fields of education, health and low-cost housing, and the creation of more remunerative jobs.[7] Although the level of money income and the living conditions of the mass of the people have not yet been appreciably affected, the people and their government have the opportunity and some of the essential means to improve their poor economic circumstances. They are no longer at the mercy of the benevolence of white governments and philanthropic bodies.

The reversal in the economic roles of the different racial groups and the corresponding adjustments in race relations have been painful. In Uganda, African resentment against Asian commercial monopoly has already exploded, and the future is by no means certain. In Kenya, Asians are seriously threatened by measures for the Africanization of the civil service, and there is no reason to believe that the European farmers in the highlands have gladly accepted the land redistribution in favor of the Africans. In Malawi, since independence, European and Asian residents have had to adjust to a new political situation. Even in Zambia there is some uneasiness among expatriates about their immediate future despite the nonracial policy of the government. Recently the government of Tanzania, as part of its new economic policy, has taken over certain Indian-owned business enterprises. According to a

---

[6] *Ibid.*, Vol. I, No. 2, pp. 3–4.
[7] *Ibid.*, pp. 6–7.

three-man Indian Textiles delegation sponsored by the Cotton Textiles Export Promotion Council of India, there was deep-rooted prejudice against Indian suppliers and goods, and throughout East Africa the governments have been very much concerned about the domination of their economic life by immigrants.

The Crux of the Race Problem

South Africa and, to a lesser extent, Rhodesia constitute the crux of the problem of race relations in Africa today. In South Africa the racial patterns established by successive white governments have been powerfully buttressed by a body of discriminatory legislation concerning political rights, landholding, job opportunities and educational facilities. Here it appears that racial patterns will not improve unless the nature or structure of government is changed and made more representative, much of the discriminatory legislation amended or repealed, and artificial hindrances to equal employment and educational opportunities removed. In this context it is well to bear in mind the primacy of securing political rights. It was the desire of African leaders to obtain political power which broke up the Federation of the Rhodesias and Nyasaland in 1962.

In Rhodesia, the approach to race relations has thus far been based on pragmatic considerations rather than on racial dogmas.* This approach has even resulted in a certain liberalization apparent in multiracial hotels, multiracial private schools, and equal facilities for all races in the post offices and on the Rhodesian railways. Parliament itself is multiracial in composition with fifteen nonwhite representatives out of sixty-five members. Unlike that of South Africa, the Rhodesian constitution places no barriers to common citizenship and nationality on grounds of race, color or ethnic affiliation. The declaration of rights applies to all the in-

* This was written before the Unilateral Declaration of Independence in November, 1965.—EDITOR

habitants of Rhodesia. But such are the political realities in Rhodesia today that there is already a white versus black power struggle which has hardened political feelings and race attitudes. The tendency to look for support to the powerful Republic of South Africa may well lead Rhodesia to adopt more or less the Republic's pattern of race legislation and institutions. This remains to be seen. Africans are of course much concerned about existing discrimination. The Land Apportionment Act has operated to the disadvantage of the Africans and has prevented the investment of private capital in the African areas. Loans at low rates of interest are not available to African farmers. Under the act African traders have no real ownership of their trading sites and so are unable to use their lands as security for loans to expand their businesses. In the urban areas, the effect of the Act is to limit African commercial ventures to the African townships. In this manner Africans are deprived of the knowledge, skills and experience which contact with the wider commercial community of the cities and towns would provide.

The Industrial Conciliation Act of 1959 requires a nonracial structure of trade unions, and appears to offer Africans a real opportunity of participating in collective bargaining and so in the improvement of working conditions. But the Africans have responded unfavorably to this act ever since its application in 1960. They find it difficult to think and act nonracially in a situation where there are still considerable differences in status, skills and basic interests between themselves and the white workers; they claim that the provisions relating to office holders and fractional voting virtually protect the whites who form the majority of the skilled workers. They would prefer a horizontal structure of trade unionism, where they could use the weight of numbers in industrial disputes, to the vertical structure provided for in the act. For these reasons several African trade unions have not thus far qualified for registration under the law for purposes of collective bargaining.

238

In the African purchase areas land use is more progressive, and there is a higher level of agricultural production for marketing purposes than in the tribal trust areas. Accordingly, purchase area farmers and their families have higher incomes and a higher standard of living than Africans in the tribal trust areas. The agricultural extension services and the provisions for marketing agricultural produce are available to African rural communities. African traders have emerged in both the rural and urban areas, and some of them have already become businessmen of proved ability and integrity and with a fair amount of capital. Some Africans are successful bus operators and render a useful service by carrying people between the cities or the small towns and the rural areas. Educated young Africans possessing Cambridge School or Senior Certificate or the G.C.E. are able to find white-collar jobs in commerce, finance, banking and industry. Central African Airways, the new Rhodesian Airways, and Rhodesian Railways have begun to take on Africans in certain rather responsible and remunerative positions. The nursing profession offers lucrative employment to European and African girls. A few African graduates have been taken into relatively highly paid employment by the British South Africa Company, Anglo American Corporation and the Rhodesian Selection Trust. The wages of Africans in commercial and industrial employment have risen steadily over the last ten years.[8] All these developments mean that a fair proportion of the African population are able to enjoy the material good things of life.

The Economic Structure of Apartheid

In South Africa since 1948, under an all-embracing political and social theory called apartheid, large-scale social engineering of the different races has been vigorously undertaken.[9] The public life

---

[8] See D. S. PEARSON: "Employment Trends in a Developing Economy: The Case of Southern Rhodesia," in *The East African Economic Review,* Vol. XI, No. 1, June, 1964, p. 18.

[9] See J. E. SPENCE: *Republic Under Pressure: A Study of South African Foreign Policy,* p. 5.

and institutions of the whole country are becoming increasingly organized on the basis of separation according to race and color, and it is a policy to lay down rigid racial patterns. The Africans are being divided into eight ethnic and linguistic groups, and this general pattern will determine their social and political evolution under the paternalistic control of the central government. In contrast to the Europeans who live in a "democratic society" with an economy avowedly based on free enterprise, the Africans are to live in a state-planned economy. The Asian and Colored minority groups are also to have government-provided separate schools, hospitals, housing, beaches and organs of political expression. At the center is the South African government which enforces the maintenance of the separate identities of the various ethnic and racial groups.

In such a situation the possibilities of changing racial patterns by economic or political action, other than in the direction approved by the Republic's white government, are extremely limited. It is the white government that determines where, how and when the African and other nonwhite people may develop. The sequel to the Tomlinson Report on the economic development of the African reserves is one good example of this approach.[10] Since the enactment of the first native urban areas legislation in 1923, it has been government policy to encourage African traders to establish themselves in the African townships, and several have built up fairly considerable businesses there. But now they are required to transfer their operations or create new businesses in the "Bantu Homelands." Thus an element of business uncertainty has been introduced into African commercial enterprises outside the African areas. Within these areas African commercial and industrial development is being encouraged or sponsored by a government-created institution called the Bantu Investment Corporation. Recent legis-

[10] See *South African Government Information Supplementary Fact Paper,* No. 506, Jan., 1957.

240

lation provides that each of the eight Bantu homelands is to have its own Development Corporation. Under South African Common Law, African trade unions are legal and several such unions have been formed. Although these unions encountered many difficulties in securing trustworthy officials, building up or holding their membership, securing funds, and buying, leasing or renting property, they have endeavored to represent the interests of the African workers in a reasonable and responsible manner. But the greatest obstacle to African trade unions has been their failure to secure legal and official recognition for collective bargaining under the Industrial Conciliation Act. The government's attitude has been that such recognition would place a dangerous weapon in the hands of the African people, "a dagger pointed at the heart of the Europeans in South Africa," to use an expression of a Minister of Labor. Under the Native Labor (Settlement of Disputes) Act of 1953, Africans are only allowed to form workers' committees in each establishment, while their disputes with the white employers in commerce and industry are dealt with by the Central Native Labor Board and its Regional Committees.

Many people both inside and outside South Africa are of the opinion that the schemes inspired by the Tomlinson plan for the Bantu reserves, the Bantu Investment Corporation and the Central Native Labor Board could bring about a greater measure of economic uplift for the African population than has hitherto been possible. They point to such things as the rise in African wages and purchasing power. From 1956 to 1963 African purchasing power rose from R200 million to R1,000, which is nearly R3 million per day.[11] Supporters of the South African government also point with pride to the achievements of the Bantu Investment Corporation. Since its creation the Bantu Investment Corporation has granted 422 loans to sixteen manufacturing enterprises, thirty-

---

[11] R1 is equal to $1.40 U. S. A. or 10/-U. K.

eight service industries and 326 commercial concerns all operated by Africans.[12] Certain sections of the African population will of course benefit from the activities of these special agencies. The essential point to bear in mind, however, is that the success of these agencies and their services will further entrench the patterns of race separation or division and the differential status associated with this policy.

It is often asserted that the Africans in South Africa are benefiting greatly from the postwar economic boom in terms of increased employment opportunities, more skilled jobs, increased cash wages and fringe benefits, improvements in standards of diet, clothing and housing, medical facilities and social and civic amenities. Two conclusions are usually drawn from this: First, that Africans in the Republic are economically better off than Africans elsewhere; and, second, that as long as they are given these purely material benefits they will not feel the need to clamor for political or constitutional rights.[13] It is true that the economic expansion which has taken place in South Africa has upgraded many Africans in skills, employment status and pay; and social and economic benefits have mitigated in large measure the hardships caused by the rigid racial patterns.[14] Yet it is precisely the urbanized and educated Africans, presumably those who have benefited most from the economic prosperity, who are in the vanguard of the struggle for economic and political rights. Our Lord's teaching that "man does not live by bread alone" is often disregarded in South Africa.

It would appear that wrong conclusions are being drawn regarding the benefits of the postwar economic boom in South Africa. Though it can be demonstrated statistically that Africans in the Republic do enjoy a higher standard of living than those elsewhere,

---

[12] These figures were quoted by Dr. François J. de Villiers, Chancellor of the University of South Africa, at the Fort Hare University Graduation ceremony held on May 1, 1965.

[13] This is a very popular line of argument in the leading articles of the English press in South Africa and the business interests it represents.

[14] See W. H. HUTT: *The Economics of the Colour Bar*, pp. 81, 82–86.

it should be borne in mind that South Africa is the richest and most industrialized country in Africa, and that in comparison with other sections of the South African population—a more meaningful comparison—the majority of Africans are not very well off. The denial of collective bargaining rights, the industrial color bar, job reservation and the control of the mobility of workers in search of higher pay, limit the extent to which Africans benefit from the expanding economy.[15] Thus, the distribution of wealth and income and the control of economic life and the benefits of economic prosperity are very much to the advantage of the white section of the population.[16]

However, it is not the masses who spearpoint the struggle for political rights. The mass of Africans are acutely aware of the harsh realities and daily pinpricks of apartheid legislation and administration, but they realize the folly of revolutionary action in view of the power of centralized government control and the armed might which the white Republican government could quickly and effectively deploy against them.[17]

The Role and Dilemmas of the Christian Church

In every society where there is private ownership of land and other means of production, inequalities of wealth, income and living standards are bound to occur and to exercise a deleterious influence on the social and political order. This is worse where the line of division between the haves and have-nots, the prosperous and the poor, the owner-employers and the laboring majority is determined by race. In such racially structured societies the division of economic interests and status is reflected within the Christian community. One racial group becomes identified with the de-

---

[15] See W. H. HUTT, *Ibid.*, Chs. 7–11 for a fuller discussion of these aspects and their effects on the economic status and fortunes of the nonwhites.

[16] See article by V. HANCE in the *Rand Daily Mail*, Sept. 4, 1964.

[17] Cf. JULIUS LEWIN: *Politics and Law in South Africa*, London: 1963, Ch. 8.

fense of the political and economic order; the other strives to reform or change it radically. Thus is the body of Christ divided.

Nevertheless, the position of the Christian church with regard to the social and economic order and inequalities or injustices inherent within it is clear. Though the Holy Scriptures and the teachings of the Christian fathers never prescribed any particular social and economic organization as superior to all others, they insisted on the stewardship of the wealthy propertied classes, the obligation to provide for the needs of widows, orphans, and the poor, the duty of the hired man to render faithful service to his master and of the master to give him a just reward. It was such teaching that inspired the Christian Socialists in their attack on the unbridled capitalist system of the nineteenth century and that in our time has led men to work for the elimination of inequities in economic life both nationally and in a world perspective.

The churches in South Africa have, almost from their very beginnings, concerned themselves with policies and legislation affecting the nonwhite races and the social inequalities arising therefrom. One has only to recall here the Christian missionaries' struggle for the legal and political rights of the non-Europeans in the nineteenth century. In the Twentieth Century the Christian churches, though not entirely ignoring matters of general policy and legislation, have tended to concentrate on the amelioration of particular social and economic inequalities.

At a national conference held at Fort Hare in July, 1942,[18] on the general theme of "Christian Reconstruction in South Africa" the bearing of the Christian teaching on the problems of the urban African family, and on the inequalities of wealth and economic opportunity was considered. The trend of the conference was reflected in the findings which clearly indicated the areas of social

---

[18] The Christian Council of South Africa, *Christian Reconstruction in South Africa: A Report of the Fort Hare Conference,* July, 1942, pp. 30–40, 44–51. Lovedale Press, 1942.

and economic life where remedial action was most urgently needed at the time.[19]

In the discussion of race relations in South Africa in recent times, special attention is usually focused on the Dutch Reformed Churches because of their historic role in the rise of the Afrikaans-speaking people and their closeness to the ruling Afrikaaners. These churches generally adopt a cautious and conservative approach on matters of race relations; nevertheless, they have, each in its own way, recognized that race or ethnic separatism within the Christian church is due to historical circumstances, and differences of language and culture.[20] From the various synods and conferences of the Dutch Reformed Churches have come resolutions in favor of mutual respect and cooperation between the races, a search for ways and means by which Christians and church members with a common creed can learn to know each other better, cooperate more effectively and pray together.[21] Though some branches of the Dutch Reformed Church still rigidly uphold separate denominations and separation in worship and sacrament, others have resolved that "on a matter of principle no person will be excluded from corporate worship solely on the grounds of race or colour." [22] The other Protestant churches as well as the Roman Catholic Church have gone much further in recognizing the principle and practice of interracial worship.

Certain ministers and theologians within the Dutch Reformed Church have become more progressive and forthright in their views on matters of race policy. In this connection mention could be made of the names of Rev. Beyers Naudé of the Christian Institute and theologians such as Ben Marais and B. B. Keet. These two theologians have written books questioning and exposing the weak theological and ethical foundations of apartheid and South

---

[19] *Ibid.*, pp. 67–69.
[20] See LESLIE CAWOOD: *The Churches and Race Relations in South Africa.* South African Institute of Race Relations, pp. 24–26.
[21] *Ibid.*, p. 25.
[22] *Ibid.*, pp. 42–44 and 24.

Africa's race policy.[23] A similar standpoint has been adopted by the Anglican and the Roman Catholic bishops.[24] Though men and women of good will may be encouraged by these pronouncements and activities of the churches it is only realistic to note that they have had very little impact, if any, on political trends. This is part of the dilemma of the Christian church and its members.

In Rhodesia, Christian Action, a voluntary association of Christian men and women, has since 1961 been continuously active in making political representations on behalf of the Africans, and also in developing relief services for the families of the political restrictees. The efforts of this body are being complemented by the recently formed Christian Association of Rhodesia. In Zambia and Malawi the Christian churches have been in the vanguard of the movements toward social and political equality between the races.

The church is criticized on two grounds by whites in southern Africa. First, church leaders are frequently admonished to confine themselves to the "spiritual care of their flock and to leave the sphere of politics alone." This popular view seems to be in keeping with the idea that the teachings of Jesus were concerned only with individual confession of sin, repentance and the salvation of souls, and had nothing to say to rulers, the administration of justice, the economic order or the relationship between races and nations. It is not generally realized that most of the ideas underlying contemporary social and economic change spring from Christian concerns for the renewal of society.

The second criticism is that the church is insincere in its protestations against the state's policy of race or color differentiation and discrimination because these same churches have generally adopted such policies and practices in their congregations and schools and also in the stipends of the European and non-European clergy.

---

[23] See B. B. KEET: *Whither South Africa?* Stellenbosch, 1956, Chs. 2–5 and 6. Also, BEN J. MARAIS: *Colour: Unsolved Problems of the West.* Cape Town, 1952, pp. 290–299.

[24] LESLIE CAWOOD: *Op. cit.,* pp. 60–64 and 76–80.

Critics have also pointed out that very often the Christian laity does not support the pronouncements or the actions of its church leaders on matters of race relations. Indeed, many white Christians vote for apartheid policies. Church leaders do not deny these faults or tendencies, but, unlike the state, the churches are trying to move away from practices of race and color discrimination and separatism.

Out of a sense of political frustration and helplessness some Africans are inclined to shrug off the churches as powerless or ineffective in matters of politics; and some churches are accused of being silent or acquiescent in the face of social injustice. Understandable as these attitudes are, they do not fairly represent the feeling toward the churches in southern and central Africa. Africans are greatly appreciative of the Christian concern, the moral support of the churches in matters of politics and legislation and their contribution to the medical, educational and social welfare of the African people.

PART IV

GROWTH IN THE WORLD ECONOMY

12

WORLD ECONOMIC POLICY
AND PLANNING:
AN AMERICAN PERSPECTIVE

by ROY BLOUGH (United States)

World Economic Goals and Planning

BEGINNING with this chapter we focus on relations among nations, and the point of view becomes that of the world as a whole. The central concern continues to be increased economic welfare, achieved through economic development and growth.[1] This concern is justified because for most of the people of the world economic scarcity is a major, and undoubtedly the most keenly felt, factor, limiting richness and fullness of life.

World Economic Goals. Mere economic abundance, however, does not suffice as a goal. In most societies high priority goes also to social justice and personal freedom of choice. With this in mind

---

[1] By economic growth is meant the continuing rise in per capita production; economic development involves also qualitative changes in the kinds or methods of production.

251

the major world economic goals are accepted in this chapter as being the following efforts: (1) rising per capita productivity and production, particularly where these are lowest, thus contributing to (2) greater equality and justice among nations in the distribution of the world's production, while maintaining (3) maximum freedom of economic choice for the individual, both as a consumer and as a producer.

Goals keep getting in each other's way. Because of scarcities of various kinds, the promotion of one goal beyond some point is almost certain to be at the expense of another. Fortunately, the economic goals of higher production, distributional justice and freedom of choice are largely consistent with one another. Yet at times they come into conflict, not only among themselves but with goals that are less exclusively economic in character.

Some people may question whether freedom of economic choice for individuals is an appropriate world goal. But surely our concern is basically for persons, their well-being and their dignity. Freedom of economic choice is an important aspect of human dignity. Since in our time freedom of the individual is ordinarily realized through organization, the relation of the individual to the decisions of the organization, as well as the nature and intensity of the discipline imposed by the organization on the individual, are matters of major concern. In general, the smaller the organization, the greater the role of the individual can be. The preference is clearly for local self-determination wherever possible. Very large organizations may be necessary in order to achieve the maximum alternatives of individual choice.

Economic Planning. The world contains hundreds of millions of economic units, conceptually ranging in size from the individual to worldwide organizations and including families, private groups, business firms, local and provincial governments, national governments and intergovernmental organizations, with the United Nations ideally, though it is not yet in fact, a universal organization. The relationships among economic units include both mutuality and conflict of interest. Mutual benefits are realized from economic cooperation, mainly through increased efficiency of production, either directly in the production process or by means of specialization and exchange, but also often through strengthened bargaining power in dealing with other economic units and groups. The economic conflicts of interest arise mainly over the sharing of the goods and services produced through cooperation, each economic unit striving to secure its maximum share of the total.

Little happens in this direction without planning. Every economic unit plans, with greater or less success, to advance its prosperity and growth. Planning is essentially the systematic exercise of foresight. Planning rests on forecasting. Forecasts are not prophecies; all that can be known must be based on what has already happened. Planning involves two applications of forecasting: the projection into the future of past trends; and the estimation of the probable consequences of measures to influence the future, that is, to modify the realization of those projections. Planning involves the selection of those measures that seem most likely to achieve the maximum degree of progress toward the goals that have been adopted. In a sense planning is but the beginning; only when they are implemented do the plans come to fruition.

Through the mutual benefits of economic cooperation the plans of different economic units are able to support and reinforce one another. Unless the economic units cooperate also in planning, however, many opportunities for mutual benefit may well be overlooked. The conflicts of interests among economic units make it difficult to achieve cooperation in planning. Smooth coordination in planning and production is likely to be realized only when and as some larger unit, within which all the smaller units are comprehended, enters into the planning process.

The philosophical approach to planning may emphasize centralization or pluralism. The emphasis on personal freedom of economic choice indicates a strong distaste for the philosophy of central planning, under which planning starts with the largest and most universal unit and works downward through smaller units only as the complications of implementation require the over-all plan to be decentralized. The strong preference is for pluralistic planning, in which every economic unit, starting with the smallest, is encouraged to plan for itself. Larger and more comprehensive planning units are then required to facilitate cooperation among the smaller units that make them up, to uncover and take advantage of areas of beneficial activity that would not be possible to smaller units and to set rules and provide incentives, so that whatever competition or conflict emerges among the smaller units will be resolved peacefully in support of the total interests of the members of the larger. The process of moving from smaller to larger planning units eventually extends beyond the boundaries of the national state, and at that point comes within the scope of this chapter.

The emphasis on pluralistic planning is not inconsistent with recognition that in many countries, especially the less developed, the national government will have to make the major planning effort. When the planning initiatives of smaller governmental or private economic units are grossly inadequate for the needs, the only way to make progress may be through action at the national level.

Cooperation among countries has great significance for the economic development and growth of them all. Few if any countries do not depend on others for raw materials, foodstuffs or other goods vital to individual and national welfare. Countries differ in their comparative facilities for producing goods and services. Economies of large-scale production in many industries make international specialization and exchange mutually advantageous for all countries.

The less-developed countries,[2] with their narrower industrial

---

[2] It is difficult to find a term to suggest the condition of economic under-development because each new term begins to lose acceptability as soon as it is devised and used. The reference in this chapter to "less-developed

base, are especially dependent on international cooperation. More kinds of goods and services need to be purchased abroad. In particular, capital goods for industrial development must be imported from industrially advanced countries; foreign exchange to pay for them must be earned or otherwise acquired from foreigners.

Planning within the national state can be forcibly coordinated by the government if voluntary cooperation is inadequate. No comparable world government to achieve forcible coordination of the plans of different national states exists; and it is not likely to develop in the foreseeable future. Nationalism would seem to be the strongest emotional force at work in groups of people in the world today; the importance attributed to at least the trappings of national sovereignty has never been so universal and perhaps never so strong.

Nationalism is unlikely to yield just yet to the spirit of world unity without which no world government can emerge, save in the improbable event of one conquering all others. Even a world government would face enormous difficulties in planning and implementing the allocation of resources, industry, markets and, in the last analysis, economic power among the various nations and regions of the world. It would be interesting to speculate on how a world government might overcome these difficulties. The more practicable problem of this chapter, however, is to consider the planning units that are now in existence, their contributions and deficiencies, how they might be improved and what new institutions and arrangements might be added. These new institutions would undoubtedly move in the direction of world government, but with the basic difference that they would have to be established on the cooperation of numerous national states, each maintaining at least a sense of sovereignty, each interested centrally in its own

---

countries" refers only to comparative levels of per capita income and breadth of economic base and has no intended social, cultural or other connotations. A newer term, "developing," has come into use, but regrettably it is for many countries more an expression of hope than of fact.

welfare and none disposed to sacrifice that welfare for the welfare of others.

In working toward world economic goals we encounter both technical and political problems. In the past few decades the techniques of planning for different purposes and at different jurisdictional levels have been greatly improved. They still leave much to be desired, especially for the less-developed countries. It is the view here that the major obstacle to effective planning, particularly at the world level, is political rather than technical. Before the technical planners can be effective the basic goals must be defined and priorities established, which means, among other things, that conflicts of interests must be resolved or subjected to compromise.

Major Agencies of World Economic Planning

Even if a world government existed and were engaged in planning, it would face a great, complex assortment of plans already set in motion. Some of these would be governmental plans at local or national levels or the plans of intergovernmental organizations. There would also be the continuing stream of plans made by private individuals, business enterprises and other nongovernmental organizations. Such planning is going on today, and we shall describe and evaluate below the contributions and possibilities of some of the types.

Private Business. The governmental planning of the mercantilistic era was detailed and rigid. It resulted in repressing rather than promoting economic development and it gave way to a consciously adopted policy of laissez-faire toward individuals and private business, which was, in the broad sense, a form of planning. This policy relied on the "planning of the market" to achieve the objectives both of national and of individual welfare. Business decisions made with a view to private economic gain were relied upon to allocate resources to their optimum uses among industries and geographical regions. Competition was relied upon to

256

stimulate the adoption of improved technology and to distribute the product among the economic cooperators in relation to their contributions to production.

Laissez-faire was found in practice to have many imperfections that led to its partial and in some countries virtually complete abandonment. Two of the imperfections are of particular relevance here. First, it was found that the allocation of resources that brings the greatest private profit does not necessarily achieve the greatest public welfare and indeed may injure it. Second, it was found that the faith in competition was misplaced, because the profit motive frequently resulted not in competition but in its disappearance and replacement by monopolies and cartels.

Private business has made immense contributions to economic growth and development. Its role can scarcely be exaggerated, and it must continue to be relied on as a major instrument of planning. But it failed to bring about a satisfactory development of many less-developed countries. Sometimes this failure was attributable to colonial policies that excluded nationals and corporations of other powers, and encouraged colonies to produce and export primary products and to buy manufactured products from the metropolitan power. But these were hardly the basic causes of slow development. The history of noncolonial less-developed countries and the long delay in industrializing the southern half of the United States strongly suggest that it has been the practice of business firms to expand production at home in order to achieve greater economies of scale, rather than to establish manufacturing industries in less-developed countries in order to take advantage of lower wage rates.

In recent years multinational business corporations have experienced enormous growth; they are in the process of becoming a dominant factor in international business operations. They are viewed by some observers as promising to become valuable institutions for achieving world economic goals because of the worldwide character of their operations. Because their operations in many nations are often integrated into one or a few large units, and because host countries increasingly require them to promote development objectives, the multinational corporations and their managements are tending to shift from a national to an international viewpoint. This tends to reduce their contribution to economic domination by the "home" country. Indeed, some companies can scarcely be identified with any single home country. In many ways this is all to the good; however, the viewpoints of these companies are not those which world economic planning requires. The decisions of private business, whether carried out through multinational corporations or otherwise, generally seek to enlarge private profit. Public policies generally seek to enlarge social product. The goals are different; they may or may not be consistent.

The decisions of multinational business are likely to be in general harmony with the public interest of the countries in which they operate. They cannot safely ignore the opinions and interests of local managers and the local public. More important, when the market system is functioning as it should, the investments that promise the highest rate of profit are generally those which are also the most productive for the economy of the host country. Businessmen will be better judges than governments of the feasibility and profit potentiality of an investment, since governments are likely to be handicapped in their judgments by political pressures and lack of specialized expertise.

It has, nevertheless, repeatedly been found that the decisions of business corporations, however far-flung their operations, are not necessarily fully in harmony with the national interests of the countries in which they are involved. An important reason for this is that in its calculations of costs and returns the business enterprise does not take into account the costs or injuries that may fall on persons or groups outside the company, or the incidental benefits that such persons and groups may receive. The market system can scarcely be expected to allow for this factor. Moreover, there are often, perhaps always, substantial defects in the market situation

258

that distort investment potentialities and profit distribution. Some element of local monopoly is rarely entirely absent. Small countries, and large ones as well, may find themselves increasingly at the mercy of large private business, a situation that they would regard as intolerable despite, and even because of, the international character of the business. They might be expected to react either through repressive national action, taken at the cost of some of the benefits which the businesses could confer upon them, or perhaps, and more probably, by joining in an intergovernmental organization. This would have the function and authority of imposing regulations and providing incentives for multinational corporations, with a view to bringing their actions into harmony with something approaching a world economic interest. Under the watchful eye of such an intergovernmental regulatory agency, the multinational corporation may indeed become a major instrument of world economic planning.

National Economic Planning. In most countries business plans play a major role in determining the allocation of resources and the course of economic development. Business, however, is subject to governmental intervention; and the need for a greater or less degree of such intervention has been indicated. Government may further its objectives for the economy either through requirements and incentives designed to bring business plans into harmony with governmental policy, or by displacing private business enterprise with some form of governmental business.

The diversity of the many national policies adopted toward business may be diagramatically illustrated by arranging them along a line in an orderly fashion, with laissez-faire at one end and the central government planning and operations of communist countries at the other. Numerous intervening points along the line are required to indicate the wide variety of policies actually followed. A few illustrations should suffice. Instead of following a laissez-faire policy the government may adopt tariff and tax policies that will discourage some types of economic activity and encourage others. It may use monetary and fiscal policies to promote economic stability, or go further and use them to encourage economic growth. Quantitative targets for gross national product may be established in the hope that private business will accept them as realistic and put them into effect through investment decisions. To make the implications clearer for specific industries, the targets may be broken down in great detail by economic sectors. A calculation may be made of the extent to which the economy is likely to fail to meet these targets. Governmental action may be taken to provide positive and negative incentives designed to stimulate business to make up the expected investment deficiencies. The government itself may engage in investment in economic infrastructure, or go further and meet deficiencies through the direct establishment of some industries. There are other possibilities, but these will indicate the great variety in forms and degrees of governmental intervention in national economies.

At what point along this range of national policies it is appropriate to say that national planning begins is a matter of opinion. Some might include all policy under planning, all planning under policy. Perhaps the point is reached when the government makes quantitative forecasts and adopts quantitative targets for the performance of various sectors of the national economy, and proposes specific private and governmental action to achieve them.

Policy designed to move the economy in desired directions toward nonquantified goals is an earlier stage and more universal than is planning. Efforts to influence the world economy, as distinct from the national economy, are still almost exclusively at the policy stage and are likely to remain there for a long time. Though some international economic sectors can be subjected to specific quantitative planning long before others, many recalcitrant problems of policy and politics must be solved before it will be feasible to proceed with such planning on any general scale.

Nationalism is a unifying force that enlarges the area of personal loyalty and concern, as well as the size of the market and the

260

potential economic strength of the country. Many of the new nations, notably in Africa, appear to be suffering from an insufficiency of the internal "glue" that holds a people together in national units larger than the family and the tribe. When the national economic units are fragmented into small splinters, per capita production is restricted and economic viability itself may be endangered. In its external aspects nationalism emphasizes separatism from outsiders. Protectionist policies of one small nation against others may be carried to ruinous lengths. Fear of foreign influences may be so strong that useful international cooperation is endangered.

National economic planning should have constructive results with respect both to the internal and the external aspects of nationalism. On the internal or domestic side it should help to create a true national market, with emphasis on high priority investments and improved balance in economic development. On the international side the forecasting involved in planning should result in a clearer understanding of the nation's economic dependence on other countries, thus encouraging international cooperation and a more favorable view toward world planning. But where nations have conflicting interests, national planning may throw the conflicts into even stronger relief.

In developing and pursuing their policies and plans, nations are not willing to allow "natural economic forces," whatever that term may mean, to go unassisted. They use positive measures that other countries may interpret as unfairly or improperly harmful to them. Hardly any significant national policy action has no substantial repercussions on other countries. National governments, however, are prone not only to regard their policies and plans as exclusively their own affairs, but to take an equally self-interested view of anything that other governments do that affects them adversely. The inconsistency of these positions only gradually becomes clear to national governments. Tariff policies have long been recognized as having international significance. Most countries, however, regard immigration policy as strictly their own business, even though a change in that policy may seriously affect the economies of other countries.

A national policy's adverse effect on other countries does not necessarily mean that it should come under international control. An immigration policy that shuts the gates of a country against massive immigration may be justified, despite its adverse effects on other countries, at least as long as the population in those other countries continues to proliferate without so much as a national policy in favor of family planning.

The impact of the policies and plans of other countries on the nation's ability to carry out its own policies and plans has many aspects. A less-developed country, for example, usually depends, in carrying out a national development plan, on the availability in other countries of supplies of materials and capital equipment and on its ability to acquire foreign exchange with which to purchase them. Plans for acquiring the foreign exchange depend, in turn, on foreign markets, foreign investment and foreign aid. The realism of plans for selling in foreign markets depends on production capacity, favorable cost patterns and access to the markets, the last of which at least may be determined by the policies of foreign governments toward international business competition. Plans for foreign investment may depend, in part at least, on the willingness of the government of the capital-supplying country to permit the private capital to be invested. Plans for foreign governmental aid depend on the willingness, as well as the ability, of foreign governments or intergovernmental financial organizations to supply the needed sums.

It may also be noted that the internal effectiveness of monetary and fiscal policies depends partly, sometimes largely, on the monetary and fiscal policies of other countries as they contribute to prosperity, inflation, or depression, with resulting impacts on the balance of payments. Each country both is influenced by and influences other countries. The great good fortune in this respect of being a large country is obvious.

Fortunately, the national policies and plans of different countries do not necessarily conflict, and frequently complement and support one another, especially if, in relation to international trade and investment, they mutually provide needed markets and needed supplies. Inevitably, however, competition comes into the picture. African countries which are newly entering upon or expanding coffee production and Latin American countries at similar stages of cocoa production are increasing world supplies and intensifying competition. The plans of the developing country to establish an import-substitution manufacturng industry may harm that industry in the countries which now supply the goods, just as plans in an industrially advanced country to develop import substitutes for rubber, silk and other materials harm the countries that rely heavily on the production and international sale of those primary products. Again, the balance of payments surplus of one country is the balance of payments deficit of others. National plans to enlarge payments surpluses are almost certain to conflict with similar plans elsewhere.

Powerful countries intent at all costs on promoting their own interests can do great damage to others. The conflict of national policies may cause economic warfare, which may lead to political and armed conflict. National planning obviously is not the answer to the need for world planning. International action is needed to maximize the harmony among national plans, to find areas for greater cooperation and, where conflict of interest is inevitable, to set the kind of rules and incentives that will bring about the greatest possible degree of world welfare.

Bilateral Treaties and Traditional Diplomacy. International arrangements to reduce policy-conflicts among nations are nothing new. In the past, many disagreements have been ironed out by means of traditional diplomacy and bilateral treaties. Because of

263

the benefits to all parties from international economic cooperation, both countries usually prefer compromise to continued hostility. Bilateral treaties of friendship, trade and navigation go far back into history. More recently, many bilateral treaties have been signed with a view to reducing international double taxation and improving fiscal administration. These are only two of many kinds of agreements.

When conflicts concern only two national governments and their enterprises, there is no reason why the problems should not continue to be approached through bilateral diplomacy. It may be that most of the small irritations will continue to be solved in this manner. There are a number of reasons, however, for not relying on it as the major intergovernmental approach to conflicts of interest. What goes on between two national states is often of interest to many others. When a bilateral arrangement affects them adversely, they are likely to become actively involved.

If one of the two countries engaged in bilateral negotiation feels that it is in a weak position in relation to the other, it is likely to seek the help and protection of other countries. Multinational business enterprises may involve so many countries that bilateral diplomacy is unable to encompass the whole range of interests of the enterprise; and when a business enterprise is as wealthy as, or wealthier than, a country with which it is dealing, that country is likely to seek aid at an international level.

Bilateral diplomacy, however, has not in the past solved the major problems of international economic relations. Two world wars in the century, many smaller wars and continued international tensions suggest the need for something more effective. As the world becomes more complex, bilateral diplomacy in world economic planning must be expected to give way to other forms of relationship between governments.

Intergovernmental Cooperative Organizations. Though world government may be only an illusory hope within the foreseeable future, some of its planning possibilities have been realized through

the cooperation of national states in intergovernmental organizations. These organizations are multilateral, and they have become
established institutions, with constitutions, permanent delegations,
regularly scheduled meetings and committees and secretariats for
continuing operation. They thus go far beyond the limits of bilateral diplomatic negotiations.

They function in several ways. First, they provide almost universally for the exchange of information among members—an indispensable necessity if different national plans are to be integrated.
They hold conferences and other meetings and thus provide an
instrument of international communication and help to build international understanding. Group thinking advances the general level
of insight and may result in the negotiation of more adequate
agreements. Policy recommendations are made that, although not
binding, bring to bear the power of international public opinion.

Second, some intergovernmental cooperative organizations engage in mutual aid of various kinds. Technical assistance experts
may be exchanged, and financial resources provided. Projects that
would be impossible or enormously expensive for any one country
to accomplish, such as international weather reporting, may be
readily achieved through international cooperation.

Third, they may deal with international conflicts that reveal
the need for uniform and reciprocal rules of behavior to suppress
arbitrary and discriminatory action. Members are willing to accept
such rules, out of fear of exclusion from the benefits of international cooperation. It is in this rule-making function that cooperative organizations most nearly resemble governments (though
the contracting parties' freedom to withdraw prevents their fulfilling that role). But the greater the number of member countries,
the broader the field of activities covered in the agreement, the
more specific and severe the penalties that members agree to impose on violators and the stronger the organizational machinery
for administering the agreement, the nearer the cooperative ar-

rangement comes to being governmental in character. If, for example, all economic activities that need international arrangements of this character could be comprehended under one grand agreement in the United Nations, so that a member would lose the advantages of international cooperation in all its economic relations if it violated the agreement in any single respect, we should come very close to a world quasi-government that exercised economic sanctions.

Eventually this may be the way in which world government will develop, but national governments are not at present willing to accept it. They may be willing to enlarge the informational collecting and distributing tasks of the United Nations to include national forecasts and national plans, although the author has seen no sign of it, but they have commonly insisted that any international agreement which imposes rules of behavior shall be limited to a rather narrowly prescribed area of activity. This explains the United Nations' multiplicity of specialized agencies, the commodity agreements limited to single commodities and the plethora of other organizations to deal with limited and specific matters.

When acting in their rule-making capacity the international cooperative organizations are developing aspects of international law. The essential nature of international law differs from that of national law in that its creation and enforcement are based on reciprocity rather than on the sanctions of a government. "World peace through world law" at present and for the foreseeable future might well be translated "world peace through international reciprocity."

Traditional international law was developed among the industrially advanced trading countries and reflected reciprocity among them. The less-developed countries had nothing to do with establishing the rules and do not find all of them to their advantage, which at least in part accounts for the breakdown of some areas of international law, for example, that relating to the treatment of foreign investment. The redetermination of areas of reciprocity among developing nations, and between them and the industrially

266

advanced nations, is a prerequisite for world economic policy and planning; let us hope that it can be facilitated by international co-operative organizations.

Before examining the multinational organizations and other arrangements that have emerged in particular fields, we must consider whether regional or worldwide organizations are preferable. There would seem to be no general answer. An intergovernmental organization should be composed of countries that have a common interest in its purposes; there is little to gain and there may be much to lose in extending further the scope of its membership. International arrangements in Europe, for example, are needed to serve some of the purposes automatically achieved in the United States through a national government. It would blur the focus and impair the effectiveness of these European arrangements to add member governments from other regions. The stronger European associations, such as the European Economic Community (EEC), no doubt will in time become regional governments rather than intergovernmental organizations. The Latin American Free Trade Association (LAFTA) has other purposes and other problems; it is not likely to lead in the foreseeable future to a regional government, but it may answer regional planning purposes that would be less well served by a worldwide organization.

Most regional economic organizations, however, deal with problems that have repercussions outside their membership. For this reason, even in the matters dealt with by regional organizations, we need worldwide organizations that can perform the role of coordinating regional policies and plans through the methods of information, mutual aid and rule making. The discussion that follows is limited to selected organizations that have a relatively worldwide membership (although in some of them there is no representation of communist countries).

International Trade. International trade presents several types of problems that call for international cooperative organization. There are those which concern the competition among industrially advanced countries in the marketing of capital goods and consumer goods. Retaliatory increases in tariff rates, the imposition of embargoes and the use of trade discrimination as an economic and political weapon marked the 1930's and the early postwar years. In the light of this experience the General Agreement on Tariffs and Trade (GATT) was negotiated in 1947, in the hope of ending discrimination in trade barriers, preventing unfair competition by governmental subsidization of exports and encouraging the reciprocal reduction of tariffs and other trade barriers. GATT has worked reasonably well for the industrially advanced countries, though it does not deal adequately with certain indirect methods of protection, discrimination and subsidization.

GATT has worked less satisfactorily in the view of the less-developed countries, although its rules have been liberalized to permit them special freedom in protection and trade discrimination. GATT bears no relation to one of the main problems of the less-developed countries, which are also the primary producing countries, namely, the wide fluctuation and inadequate growth of their export earnings on which they must principally rely to finance the foreign exchange requirements of economic development. These countries want from industrial countries more favorable treatment for their trade with respect both to primary products and to the manufactured products that they expect to produce as they industrialize, and more freedom to protect, subsidize and discriminate in their trade. They want an international organization devoted to the promotion of their international trade interests. Demands along these lines were aired extensively in the spring of 1964 at the United Nations Conference on Trade and Development, which made provision for such an organization.

A third problem is presented by international private restrictive business practices, including cartels and other arrangements that interfere with the workings of competition. The United Nations made an extensive study in the early 1950's of such practices, but nothing came of it. The need to improve the quality of competition and to reduce unfair competition and monopolization of trade will undoubtedly increase. At present virtually nothing is being done about it at the international level, except within the EEC; and controversy has arisen over the application of United States laws against restrictive business practices to oversea operations of its own and other companies.

International Private Investment. International private investment, particularly direct business investment, is an important method of promoting industrial development in the less-developed countries. Such developmental requirements as competence in enterprise, marketing, management, worker training and labor relations, as well as the methods and attitudes of industrialization in general, are difficult to secure except along with equity investment. Many nations, however, especially new and weak ones, are sensitive to exposure to undue foreign influence. They often tend to believe that the arrangements which former governments made with foreign businesses are unfair and contrary to the national interest. One reaction has been expropriation and nationalization, limited for the most part to politically sensitive industries, but extending in some countries to foreign investment generally.

A generation or two ago the home government of the expropriated company did not hesitate to use great pressure, including, if necessary, military force, to carry out the rules of international law with regard to expropriation and compensation. Today, the company itself is estopped from taking any action of its own, military action is excluded, the home government of the company frequently is in no position either to prevent expropriation or to assure satisfactory compensation, and no international organization has authority or jurisdiction in the matter. The developing host countries believe that international law, as it applies to expropriation, must be revised to take account of their interests. Thus far, little progress has been made on proposals for revisions of the rules and for new enforcement machinery. The less-developed countries contend also that a code of good behavior should be imposed on large international businesses, and internationally enforced. Any such arrangement will clearly have to be two-sided.

The competition among host countries, and to a smaller extent among the so-called home countries, to promote such investment is another cause of concern. The offering of increasingly favorable tax concessions and other financial inducements may become so important a competitive device as to distort the pattern of investment and to call for international control.

International Payments. In the years between the world wars the world suffered from competitive devaluation of currencies, inadequacy of foreign exchange reserves and other difficulties with the international payments system. At the end of the Second World War the International Monetary Fund (IMF) was established to restrain competitive devaluation and to create a pool of currencies that countries could borrow to tide them over temporary deficits in their balances of payments. The IMF came under heavy criticism for inaction until about the middle of the 1950's. The criticism was perhaps unjust, since the disequilibria in international payments were so great that the resources of the IMF would soon have been exhausted if they had been freely used. United States foreign aid and deficits in the United States balance of payments made available to other countries an expanding volume of dollar deposits, for use as foreign exchange reserves and in carrying on international trade. The European Payments Union (EPU) was an effective means of moving Europe from virtual payments chaos to international convertibility.

After the recovery of Europe and the end of massive disequilibria, the IMF began to fulfill more exactly its intended function. A new problem then arose. The United States in effect had been supplying currency and international reserves to finance trade, growth and development. The accumulated deficit in its balance of payments was a source of concern to the United States and to other governments. What seemed to be needed was a more international method of supplying the volume of internationally acceptable money with which to undergird world economic development and growth. Various measures have been proposed. The problem involves great technical and political difficulties and awaits further consideration and intergovernmental action.

Governmental Aid and Investment. The greater part of governmental aid for the economic development of less-developed countries has come through national "bilateral" program. Numerous intergovernmental organizations have, however, been established to grant such aid, some of them worldwide, others regional in scope. They supply technical assistance, aid for national planning and project development and economic support in the form of grants and loans. The advantages of intergovernmental over national aid are, from a world point of view, substantial. Most countries that receive intergovernmental aid undoubtedly have less fear of actual or apparent dependence on the source from which it comes and appear more willing to carry out needed reforms in fiscal and other matters, when the aid is from that quarter. Such organizations have also the advantage of being able to draw funds from many countries that would not otherwise contribute, and can reduce any imperialistic ideas that donor countries may still harbor.

Governmental foreign aid, whether bilateral or multilateral, falls substantially short of the requirements for accelerated economic development. There seems little need, however, to establish further organizations. If anything, the field suffers from too many, with too few resources being channeled through them.

Other Sectors. The areas of international economic relations discussed in the previous paragraphs are those with which, in the main, intergovernmental organizations are concerned. In addition, there are problems in such fields as labor standards, transport and communications, agriculture and other sectors that have given rise to more or less effective intergovernmental action. At almost every point at which nations come into economic contact a need for some application of intergovernmental cooperative policy and planning arises.

The "American" Perspective

The heading of this chapter promises an "American perspective." To the extent that the author's beliefs and values reflect those which dominate American [4] policy—a matter which it is difficult for him to estimate—the promise has been implicitly fulfilled throughout the preceding analysis, which reflects his personal point of view. The discussion below seeks to indicate more systematically what the author believes to be the major thrusts of American policy on matters that are particularly relevant to world economic policy and planning. It is not his intention either to defend or to condemn them.

There is no such thing as a uniquely American perspective on this or any other subject. What Americans think, feel and do has been, and continues to be, greatly affected by outside influences and in turn affects thought, emotion and action in other countries. Moreover, despite the relatively classless character of American society, the very size and economic diversity of the country give rise to numerous and often contradictory viewpoints and policy positions. The federal government itself, with its relatively independent legislative and executive branches, is not free from major internal differences of opinion and inconsistencies of policy. A statement of American views is inevitably only one person's partial understanding of a reality that, in major respects, is not perhaps entirely what he believes it to be, and in any event is complicated far beyond the possibilities of exposition in this chapter. The reader will have no difficulty in challenging the generalizations given below, as there are always exceptions with which to support any set of opinions.

Outlook on the World. The United States views the world from

---

[4] With apologies to our Latin American friends, the word America is used here to mean the United States, which is unmistakably its meaning throughout most of the world. It is regrettable that no accepted adjective has been developed that refers specifically to the United States.

a position of political and economic leadership which it did not seek. It believes that it has virtually no ambitions for change that would injure other countries or peoples, but its sense of pride makes any loss of economic or political position unpalatable, if not intolerable. Its lack of aggressive ambition has undoubtedly given moral issues and humanitarian motives substantial weight in its policies, but along with this has often gone, some critics believe, a degree of smugness in pressing its views on others.

A central tenet of American policy is peace through strength. The desire for peace and the fear of major war are profound, as is the fear of nuclear contamination of the atmosphere. Any idea that unilateral disarmament or substantial unilateral reduction of military strength, especially of nuclear strength, would lead to anything but quick disaster is universally, with only minuscule exceptions, regarded as an illusion; and persons at home or abroad who subscribed to this illusion would be considered dangerous if there seemed any risk of their becoming sufficiently numerous to weaken resolute national policy in America or among its allies.

In this connection Americans in general view the communist countries as an aggressive enemy who makes it necessary to be ready for defense and resistance at home and abroad, without, it is hoped, armed conflict. The fears of communism, though partly ideological, are for the most part the same fears of aggression abroad and subversion at home that haunt any country. The propaganda of communist countries, with such phrases as "we will bury you" and with its claim that war between communism and capitalism is inevitable and that the United States is run by "capitalistic monopolists" and is colonialist, has been hard to take with complacency. Americans believe, in general, that the promises of a communist country are of little worth, that treaties will be broken whenever it suits the Communists to do so. Undoubtedly a gradual shift of view is taking place, as people begin to recognize that differences have developed between the Soviet Union and communist China and that the Soviet Union has softened its position. But conviction remains strong that the triumph of communism everywhere is its unchanged goal, to be achieved by whatever means seem most promising.

The Americans see themselves as the first anticolonialists and the most sincere exponents of political and social democracy everywhere. They believe that aside from a brief period around the turn of the century, when the "demonstration effect" of European colonial powers resulted in a mild imitation of their behavior, the United States has right from its revolutionary origin to the present day sponsored the cause of the peoples who seek political independence. They are not unconscious—many are keenly conscious —that this has raised two dilemmas which have not been satisfactorily resolved. In the first place, the allies whom America must have if it is to achieve peace through strength have found disengagement from colonialism a difficult task and have often resented American pressures to speed up the process. The second dilemma is that American business interests abroad, in common with those of other countries, require or at least greatly prefer stability of expectations, notably political stability. This preference gives them a stake in the status quo, which is upset by revolutionary change, whether it be to achieve political independence, freedom from foreign economic domination or internal social reform. Moreover, Americans strongly dislike the idea of violence to persons and property. Though the political power of American business is commonly exaggerated in foreign opinion, there can be no doubt that the dilemma for American policy has been a real one.

It has been American policy, over the past two decades, to promote European economic and political unity and strength. The Marshall Plan constituted a major effort toward advancing both strength and unity. The objectives were to restore economic strength to our European friends, to halt the spread of communism, and to end once and for all the internal European crises and conflicts out of which two world wars had developed. A similar policy has been followed, for comparable reasons, toward Japan.

The special interest in Latin America that the United States has also displayed dates back to the early nineteenth century and has expressed itself over the years, among other ways, in political moves to promote and protect the independence of those countries. To some extent a kind of proprietary attitude toward Latin America may have developed on the part of both business and government. The government has seemed to expect political cooperation from Latin America in return for economic assistance, and for fighting Latin American battles for European markets and with competitors on other continents.

American Economic Policies. Despite, however, the special areas of interest, American economic policy generally has been one of nondiscrimination with respect to all countries, save only those in the communist group. This can be seen, for example, with regard to trade policy, which has, since 1934 and especially in the postwar period, promoted the reduction of international trade barriers, the application of most-favored-nation treatment in tariffs and the phasing-out of quotas and other discriminations that have marked colonial and postcolonial trade policies. The United States, however, is generally willing to accept the protection of infant industries and some forms of discrimination on the part of the less-developed countries, although many persons have done so only with reluctance. On the whole, though the policy is changing, the United States has been less than friendly to intergovernmental agreements to stabilize prices and markets for primary products. This attitude is due in part to a general belief in freedom of international markets, but to a large extent also to skepticism regarding the workability of such agreements—a skepticism which rests heavily on experience with agricultural programs at home. The United States is not disposed to accept the theory that there is something exploitative of the less-developed countries in the working of traditional international specialization and exchange.

The United States promoted and has supported GATT, despite congressional reluctance to say so openly, as well as the International Monetary Fund. It has been an active promoter of almost all international organizations designed to introduce an aspect of planning into international economic matters. Many influential Americans are known to be hostile, often emotionally so, to the idea of governmental planning. There is, of course, much planning in the United States, especially by business; and even governmental planning, called by other names, is not uncommon. Opposition to planning has two most likely explanations: the tendency to confuse all planning with central planning as it is carried on in the communist countries, and the general dislike of restrictive governmental action. This dislike has for at least a century been especially strong in the business community, although today many businessmen see much merit in government contracts, subsidies, tax incentives and other promotional devices that do not reduce a private group's opportunities for profitable business. The long "frontier" period undoubtedly exercised a powerful influence on opinion, as did the tradition of local self-government, which stemmed in part from frontier life.

At times the objections to governmental planning have extended even to planning by governments which receive American aid, but here there has been a distinct shift of policy. Under the Alliance for Progress for Latin America, national economic planning, at least for the use of aid, is a virtual requirement for the receipt of substantial aid.

The United States has been in the forefront in promoting the economic development of the less-developed countries, a purpose which has provided a strong motive for giving foreign aid (though in some quarters we must recognize an underlying conception of economic development as the bulwark against communist subversion, guerrilla warfare and violent revolution).

In word, if not in deed, United States policy has emphasized private foreign investment as the preferred method of promoting economic development. In part, this has had a budgetary motivation: tax money would be saved and everyone would benefit. In part,

276

the policy reflected the general distrust of the ability of governments to do anything in the economic field as effectively as private business. Governmental aid was likely, it was believed, to promote government-owned industries, which were certain to be less efficient than private industries—although ideology undoubtedly is responsible for much of this emphasis. United States attitudes may also reflect the fact of its major experience being in Latin America where private entrepreneurship and management capabilities are more in evidence than in many newer economic societies and where examples of government mismanagement of railroads and other industries are not difficult to find.

The United States has helped to form, and contributes substantial financial support to, various international organizations that provide aid in one form or another. Among them are the International Bank for Reconstruction and Development, the International Finance Corporation, the International Development Association, the Interamerican Development Bank, the Central American Development Bank, the United Nations Expanded Program of Technical Assistance and the United Nations Special Fund. But despite this proliferation of organizations, the greater part of American foreign aid, as in large industrial countries generally, has been bilateral in character. The United States is aware of the advantages of multilateral aid, but in proceeding, on the whole, bilaterally, it has been guided in part by the desire to give to specific countries military assistance and related economic support, which no intergovernmental organization would be likely to do. Moreover, the belief prevails, with respect to all forms of aid, that it is easier for the United States than for an intergovernmental organization to formulate its objectives and to distribute aid in such a manner as will best, and most economically, promote them. Though the United States in the 1960's has reluctantly "tied" most of its aid to American exports, because of its balance of payments difficulties, this was not a factor in its choice of bilateral methods, the preference for which goes back long before the tying of aid. There has no doubt been some desire to see the source of the aid recognized and appreciated, though any expectation of gratitude has by now been largely destroyed by experience.

The situation would seem on the whole to add up to a progressive and constructive contribution to world economic policy, including willingness to cooperate extensively. But it gives little encouragement to the belief that Americans are prepared in the foreseeable future to have American economic policy subjected to international planning in any major area. Witness the history of the ill-fated International Trade Organization: the United States negotiators, with those of other countries, worked hard in the late 1940's to bring into being an organization that would provide the instrument to reduce international trade barriers and discrimination in trade. Other countries that were powerfully affected by the domestic policies of such large countries as the United States introduced into the negotiated treaty, the Havana Charter, provisions which suggested the strong possibility of subjecting domestic economic policies to international restriction. The opposition in the United States to such an eventuality was so strong that the Administration abandoned the effort to have the treaty ratified.

Conclusion

We conclude, therefore, that authoritative economic planning by a worldwide body is not feasible for the conceivable future. In the international economy of today the only practicable approach is by pluralistic policy and planning, in which decisions move from small units upward toward the more universal structure. Pluralistic planning is consistent with democratic government and the democratic way of life generally, and can become substantially and increasingly effective.

World economic policy and planning can be improved in several ways:

First, information can be immensely improved in quality and

quantity. Planning, and the forecasting that must precede it, are futile at any jurisdictional level without adequate information. There are many blind spots in our knowledge, some of them because no one able to do so has incurred the trouble and expense to collect, organize and disseminate the available facts, others the result of secrecy. Business planning and investment in America are facilitated by a degree of openness of information about business that does not exist in Europe or elsewhere in the world.

Second, the techniques of planning can be further perfected and much more widely taught.

Third, the goals for a world economy can be clarified and elaborated, and a greater international consensus achieved. This is a major task for the United Nations.

Fourth, through international organization, nations can be increasingly freed from fear of foreign domination. One result should be to soften their nationalism to the point at which they would become increasingly willing to enter into international arrangements that call for orderly procedures and national restraint in those areas of economic relationship which are beset with wasteful international conflict.

A formidable obstacle to economic policy and planning is the challenge of dynamism to the status quo. Economic development inevitably changes the patterns of trade and the location of power, and consequently introduces conflicts. Developing countries must expect to meet resistance to their demands on industrialized countries, especially if they look like reducing the per capita income of the latter. Even when the world's total economic production grows fast enough for all to have a rising level of living, painful adjustments will be necessary in many countries and will be resisted by politically powerful industries.

We have largely bypassed in this chapter the problem of bringing the communist world and the noncommunist world into agreement on the goals and organization of world economic policy and planning. The entry of the communist countries more fully into the world economic system is seriously hampered by differences in methods of economic organization as they affect international trade and investment. The chief obstacles, however, are political. A continuing increase in cooperative action with the communist countries and the development of greater confidence on both sides would represent progress. Confidence, at least on the part of the Americans, is undoubtedly contingent on communist abandonment of the active pursuit of the goal of world revolution.

But in the international field as a whole, the machinery for international cooperation is available and the methods are known. What is needed is to persuade the governments, large and small, that they have more to gain from cooperation than from pressing every competitive advantage they may be able to muster. The strongest countries are in the best position to join in common action, and they should lead the way.

13

A EUROPEAN PERSPECTIVE ON WORLD ECONOMIC PLANNING

by J. TINBERGEN (Netherlands)

DEVELOPMENTS in the technological and political sphere have brought us to a situation that calls urgently for a world economic policy. Technological changes, especially in transportation, have greatly increased contacts between the various parts of the world. Those in armaments have dramatically increased the dangers involved in war. General technological developments, together with other forces, have created an increasing gap in well-being between the rich and the poor countries. Political forces tend to divide the world into blocs: the communist countries, the rich western countries and the developing countries, sometimes called respectively the East, the West and the South.

A world economic policy is needed for two reasons. It is needed for its own sake to counteract the widening gap in well-being between nations and also for the indirect effect it could have in reducing the threat of war by helping to ameliorate political tensions and playing a positive role in the construction of a world order. The desirability of working toward a world economic policy is accentuated by the fact that in this field we know fairly well what can and should be done, in contrast with the politico-military side of world order, where we do not yet know what to do.

In planning a world economic policy we face short-term problems which require intensive effort. But we must not forget the long-term aspects of our task. If we do not think ahead difficulties will take us by surprise. Some of our thinking must be "idealistic" in the sense that even if those who are most involved in the day-to-day problems do not at present recognize all of them, we must try to describe them and search for their solution.

The major aim of a world economic policy must be to reduce the gap in well-being between rich and poor countries. Since it has become abundantly clear that contrary to the thinking of a century ago, there is no automatic mechanism that prevents the gap from growing, it must be the subject of a deliberate policy. The aim can be broken down into several component parts. We need an increase not only in the production of the poor countries, but also in their trade, and more stable prices for their products. We want as many as possible of the unemployed or underemployed all over the world to be absorbed in the productive process, and we hope to reduce income differences within countries.

The idea that something must be done in the field of international cooperation in order to attain these aims is not new. It was expressed at the time of the formulation of the United Nations Charter and even before that, when the International Bank for Reconstruction and Development was established. An impressive volume of work has already been accomplished, but every year we become increasingly aware of its insufficiency and of the inadequacy of its methods. We have to admit that the gap is still widening, that trade impediments of various types persist and that prices of primary goods are out of control.

282

The Need for a Bolder Development Policy

This lack of success has led, in some quarters, to pessimism about the possibilities of realizing our aim. In its extreme form this pessimism finds expression in doubts about whether poor countries can develop at all, in questioning about whether climate or racial differences or the selection exercised by emigration may not prevent tropical countries from ever becoming prosperous. This pessimism is premature. It may be inspired by an unwillingness to help, which is immoral, or by failure to understand the nature of the problem. Increasingly we are discovering that the process of development is much less a matter of course than we Westerners had believed, that we must relinquish some of our deeply rooted ideas, and that it will take much longer than the ten to twenty years which have elapsed since the institutions mentioned began their work. We must recognize the modest extent of the efforts so far made. The financial assistance that the West has given to the developing countries has amounted to less than 1 per cent of its income, and this income is increasing by some 3 per cent annually. Over a ten-year period the West's income has increased by at least 30 per cent, but our help has remained at only 1 per cent. The accumulated income increases over the ten-year period are $3 + 6 + \ldots + 30$, or about 165 per cent, out of which some 10 per cent has been given as help. We could easily increase our financial contribution to 2 per cent per annum without delaying our own progress. Some churches are already urging their governments to increase their aid to 3 per cent of the national income.

The level of the western assistance should be derived from what is needed in order to achieve the aim set out above: to diminish the gap in real per capita income between the prosperous and the poor countries.[1] A stable world society will be possible only if this

---

[1] The precise calculation of what is needed is of a technical character and would lead us too far from our main subject. There is little difference of opinion among economists about the outcome, provided the aim of "closing the gap" is accepted. The main controversies are more sociological or ethical in character, as is indicated above.

gap is reduced. No doubt the first goal must be to lift the level of income of the poor countries to the minimum required for a healthy life; but in the long run this will not be sufficient to produce a satisfactory social structure. It is relative incomes, rather than their absolute level, that are important to human happiness and mutual understanding. People with very different levels of material well-being will not, as a rule, understand each other easily. Moreover, very high incomes, with their corresponding cultural patterns, are of doubtful ethical value. For the time being, however, these considerations must remain purely academic, since for the next ten to twenty years all efforts will have to be concentrated on attaining the minimum needed for a healthy life for all.

We have discovered many difficulties related to the problem of development of which we were unaware ten or twenty years ago; for example, low absorption capacity reflected in the lack of adequate projects to be financed in many developing countries. The solution of such difficulties must be met by further efforts and much imagination, rather than by any tendency to turn back from our development aim as a result of our disappointments. Such a course could lead only to disaster. Because of the present population explosion, if development continues at a modest rate, mass unemployment and severe political upheavals are bound to follow in almost all developing countries. The only way out is to redouble our efforts to design a world development policy that will employ more adequate means than we have so far used. Generally speaking, we must aim at a rate of growth in national production of at least six to seven per cent. The absorption capacity of developing countries can be increased by training planners and administrators.

The main instruments of policy that we must use are investments, education, reduction of trade barriers, market regulations for primary commodities and changes in the social order of the countries concerned. Each of these simple phrases covers a world of varying activities. Thus, investment includes not only the construction of factories or of irrigation dams, but also the supply of food to the workers involved. The supply by the West to the developing countries of so-called surplus goods is an important practical form of investment assistance which should be welcomed for a considerable period of time. However, such investment involves very complicated processes, which require the most efficient possible execution, demanding action by public authorities, private enterprises and individuals at all levels from the local to the international. These activities must be so geared as to avoid possible disequilibrium. For example, if the developing countries are to expand their textile industries, those in developed countries may be threatened with losses and unemployment. Action must be taken to avoid such consequences without giving up the aim of rapid development. How can this be done? This is only one of the many questions for which answers must be found.

There is some divergence of opinion between American and European experts as to the various means to be applied, although this should not be exaggerated. It would perhaps be more correct to say that there are differences between individual experts ranging from the liberals who rely primarily on the operation of spontaneous automatic market forces to those who favor more government intervention. The former view is widespread in the United States, and also in Belgium and Germany; the latter has many supporters in Scandinavia and France.[2]

It is, however, possible to formulate some general principles of a world economic policy all of which have their roots in a desire for efficiency. All available resources should be apportioned and used with this aim in mind. This will imply a division of labor:

---

[2] I believe French politicians have gone in for too much regulation and too many limitations on trade, but the extent of such intervention remains a question for debate.

between countries, between the public and the private sector, between factors of production and between higher and lower levels in the international community.

The division of labor between countries means that each concentrates on the type of activity for which it is best fitted. Countries that have mineral deposits should emphasize their exploitation; those with greater capital resources should engage in capital intensive industries; countries that have scientific manpower should specialize in research and intensive activities; countries with an abundance of labor should emphasize labor-intensive industries, and so on.

The division of labor between the public and the private sector determines the form of the social order. In a liberal order, the private sector is given preference, in the socialist order the public sector. But this ideological controversy seems gradually to be losing its sharp edges: The two systems of the West and the East are converging toward acceptance of a mixed economy with both a public and a private sector. The developing countries have adopted such a mixed system, and are likely to continue to employ it. It may prove most effective to limit the private sector to some types of small or medium-scale enterprise, and to let the public sector engage in activities that, because of external-effect factors, require government initiative or in which private enterprise may not act in the interests of society as a whole. Education, road building, the operation of power plants and a central bank, are examples of the latter.

A correct division of labor between the factors of production means the most efficient apportioning of capital, of many types of labor and of natural resources. The choice within each industry of the "best technology" is a well-known example. Bulldozers may be the best device for moving earth in the United States; wheelbarrows may be better for west Asia, and baskets for east Asia, at least for the time being.

There is also a "best" division of labor between local, provincial, state and federal governments and supranational agencies. The concept of external effects is applicable here also. No authority should formulate economic policy that will influence the well-being of people other than those under its jurisdiction; for the odds are against its exercise of power in the right way since it will not be accountable for all the effects of its policy. For example, the regulation of world markets cannot be left to local or even to national authorities.

The Need for World Economic Planning

Complicated processes, such as those involved in any world economic policy, require prior preparation in order to avoid at least some of the foreseeable inconsistencies that may arise. Planning is just that. Large enterprises have planning departments to ensure that the various stages of production mesh as smoothly as possible. The need for government economic planning has been increasingly recognized since the 1930's. Although the waste of business cycles and overinvestment in railways had been clearly demonstrated in the nineteenth century a strong belief in free market forces persisted in opposition to planning. Only when the great depression demonstrated the absurdity of a completely free society and the terrible waste than can occur under an uncoordinated economic system did it become possible to appraise with some degree of objectivity the relative parts played by free and regulated markets, and by the private and public sector of the economy. In the Soviet Union, the pendulum had swung to the other extreme and led to belief in a society planned in the most minute detail.

The West has now had experience with both a free and a planned economy and has chosen in favor of planning as one of the main instruments of economic policy; and, interestingly enough, the East is discussing the possibility of some relaxation of controls. Even Germany, which, in reaction to national socialism, had paid lip service to complete freedom, returned to some planning during the Marshall Plan period and later, and is now about to introduce it more formally. France, the Netherlands and Norway have had planned economies ever since the Second World War; Sweden and Denmark have followed suit with varying degrees of control. Britain had a period during which planning was decreased, but it has now taken it up again; Italy took some preliminary steps toward planning during the Vanoni Plan and undertook it seriously when the Nenni socialists came into power. Belgium introduced some planning two or three years ago. The gradual elimination of unemployment in western Europe may be seen as the most important single result of planning at the macro level.

What is needed now is the extension of national planning to a world level, with an intermediary level for continents or regions. This process is already underway. Latin America pioneered in national planning, but the uncoordinated beginnings of continental planning were first seen in western Europe. Some planning was necessary for distribution of United States aid under the Marshall Plan. At first this was done almost entirely on the national level, but gradually the Secretariat of the Organization for European Economic Cooperation (OEEC) came to play a more active role, and the 1955–1960 program for a 25 per cent increase in joint production constitutes a good example of international planning activities. The European Coal and Steel Community also engaged in continental planning. Later, the European Economic Community and Euratom expanded these activities into the field of agriculture, power production, and anticyclical policies. These activities are at most "indicative planning," but the experience gained and techniques employed constitute important preparations for the further development of common policies.

Simultaneously the United Nations Secretariat has begun to prepare for world planning. The first goal is to distribute to national and continental planners reliable forecasts and information about other nations and continents as it becomes available. This may later be transformed into a real planning effort, depending a good deal on the degree of responsibility given to the United Nations Economic and Social Council (ECOSOC). A loose form of coordination of government policies in the Annual Meeting of ECOSOC could be a useful beginning and should be based on some forecasts of the development to be expected without such coordination. For the time being the Secretariat is extremely cautious; it mainly discusses the methods of forecasting and planning used by the various national governments in order to learn what is being done in various countries and to discover whether the figures to be combined are actually comparable.

Many governments will, no doubt, oppose the idea of some form of world planning, even without defining precisely what it might involve. There is, to say the least, great caution in both the East and the South. The communist countries reject the idea of giving up even a small portion of their autonomy since, according to their philosophy, they will eventually lead the world, instead of vice versa. Developing countries, especially former colonies, are still overanxious to maintain their independence. The idea that it may be in the interest of all to have some form of economic coordination can only penetrate gradually and will have to be defended with certain qualifications if these groups are not to be alarmed. Similar fears undoubtedly exist in many western countries, although they have manifested greater willingness to surrender small portions of national autonomy. What is needed is some form of cooperation among equals, based on well-defined common interests and mutually acceptable procedures. As an economist, the author is convinced that such a form can be found by discussing common interests in a concrete way and by considering proposals and counterproposals about the procedure to be followed in order to serve these common interests.

World Economic Planning on Behalf of Autonomous Nations

For the time being we have to accept the fact that national governments are autonomous; and that they are free to choose both the aims of their development policies and the means to be used; and we shall have to consider how to avoid some undesirable consequences of these autonomous choices. We shall assume that each government is efficient, in the sense that it chooses a development policy, in the best conceivable way, given its aims and the "available external data." In general, the methods for arriving at such an efficient national policy are known and available through the advice of national and foreign experts.

Each government planning agency has to solve the following problem: Given its aims, it has to make the most accurate possible appraisal of the external data, and, on that basis, decide the extent to which the accepted methods should be applied. The external data are of two types: first, the political means chosen by the other governments and the intensity with which they are applied; and, second, nonpolitical data such as population growth, crop yields, new techniques available and so on.

The controls used by governments may include the regulation of the volume of investment and import duties. Obviously, the economic development of a given country will depend not only on its own volume of investment, its tariffs and its crop yields, but also on the investment levels and tariffs of other governments and on crop yields in the world at large. Therefore, in order to determine its own correct policy—correct in the sense of leading to the aims pursued—the government concerned should also know what other governments are going to do. Their assumptions about the policies of the other governments will be based on past events and on whatever information is available about possible future policy changes. If the assumptions are wrong, the decisions about its own policy will also be wrong and may not fulfill the aims set.

Useful world planning by some international agency on behalf of autonomous nations can take the form of collecting information about the aims and means of individual governments, trying to forecast the consequences for the economic situation in each country, making this information available to all governments and thus inducing them to reconsider their policies. It may also consist of calculating and making available more authoritative estimates of the nonpolitical data—population trends, crop yields and so on. Finally, at this stage, world planning could provide a check on the calculations of national planning agencies. Through these last two activities, it could avoid much of the duplication of work by so many national planning bureaus.

In addition to the collection and distributions of data, world economic planning may also include estimating the effects of the values of the various "means variables" in the economic situation of each country, and more particularly the values of "aim variables." By "means variables" we refer to such phenomena as the investment level or the level of tariffs that constitute the means of development policy; by "aim variables" we mean the phenomena that constitute the aims of policy, such as the national income or the volume of employment. We have restricted ourselves to examples where these phenomena are of a quantitative nature; but they may be of a qualitative nature as well.

The first step would consist in the central agency's sending out to national government agencies, possibly with some regional or continental agencies as intermediaries, questions about their aims and means with answers requested in statistical form where possible. The questions may be accompanied by general information about nonpolitical data, such as population increase, anticipated world crop production, and so on, which may reduce, from the outset, inconsistencies between the aims and means of various national governments that otherwise might operate on differing assumptions.

The second step would be for the governments to submit their answers. Some will not reply, or will not do so on time, and the central agency will have to make its own estimates. Some of the answers will require clarification. The information collected can then be made available to all governments, so that they may revise their first-round planning. The second-round figures may be made available to the central agency, which would then decide whether the changes indicated justify another round.[3]

A more precise approach may be possible at some later stage, such as a division of investments between sectors of the economy. This will pose more difficult questions that will require negotiations between countries. The first-round plans may reveal overinvestment in some sectors, for example, in textiles, and underinvestment in others, such as in electronics. The planning countries will have a common interest in avoiding this disequilibrium.[4]

The Ideal World Economic Policy and Its Planning

From the socioeconomic point of view, complete national autonomy is not necessarily the best political structure to promote the interests of mankind since many autonomous national decisions are wrong from a world viewpoint. We all know the evils such autonomy has caused in the past, quite apart from the evil of war. In the nineteen thirties we saw how the economic policy of one autonomous country damaged the interests of other countries. In analyzing the problem, it is useful to distinguish between those means of socioeconomic policy which have external effects,

---

[3] So far it has been assumed that only a few of the major aims and means are involved and that the policies of the countries concerned are typically "macro-economic," that is, using a few general means of the type given in our examples.

[4] The first-round plans submitted to the OEEC (the Organization for European Economic Cooperation) during the early stages of the European Recovery Program contained inconsistent estimates concerning mutual trade; e.g., France planned larger exports to Germany than Germany planned imports from France. With the disappearance of bilateral payments agreements, these details are no longer a subject of national planning by European countries. The example is less interesting, therefore, than the example about investments in the textile and electronics industries.

and those which do not. The latter—those which do not affect the well-being of other nations—can be handled by national governments without difficulty. Here decentralization is justified. The policies and instruments with external effects should, however, be in the hands of supranational authorities.[5]

This analysis also applies to decisions on production, where a distinction can be made between industries without external effects and those in which a single enterprise has such effects. The former category is typically the kind of industry which Pareto had in mind when he tried to prove that free enterprise will automatically lead to the maximum of well-being. The latter should be carried out by public authorities, either at the local or at higher levels; and planning should be done largely for this type of production.

An Optimum International Order

The analysis above provides us with the concepts necessary to define an optimum international order. National autonomy should be limited to those policies and production sectors without external effects. Decisions on policies and the types of production with external effects should be taken at higher supranational levels. Planning, as the preparation for policy and production, should be organized in a similar way.

The types of economic policy that should be handled at the world and continental level are among the most important. These include the regulation of tariffs and of markets for primary goods. We already have a world organization for trade policy coordination (GATT), and we have created the new U. N. Council on Trade and Development. In Europe we are trying to make trade policies an instrument of the European Economic Community,

---

[5] It may be possible to distinguish more than two levels: those means which can be handled at the local level, others at the provincial (or district) level, still others at the state level, and a number at the continental and world level.

rather than of the single member nations. We also have some commodity agreements (wheat, sugar, coffee, tin). It would, of course, be far better if we had a world political system which could employ stronger forms of coordination.

It has not yet been generally admitted that the instruments of public finance should be handled at supranational levels. It is desirable that more financial power be put in the hands of such supranational institutions as the United Nations and OECD. This does not necessarily imply that all decisions concerning public finance should be handled by some world authority. Inside each country public finance is handled at various levels, the higher levels supplementing and correcting whatever is done in an inadequate way at the lower.

There is a tendency to use the means of public finance at ever higher levels. In many countries local taxes have been reduced, and national taxes increased; local expenditures are increasingly financed out of contributions from the central government made according to carefully formulated and balanced rules. A World Treasury would be a natural development. At first it could finance a limited number of purely international projects such as joint river basin developments or highways, or an international insurance system against declines in export revenues. National contributions could be in proportion to their contribution to the United Nations, or some taxes on international activities, say international transportation, could be levied directly by the United Nations. The immediate importance of a World Treasury would consist in its power to redirect the flow of money to the nations of the world in accordance with the needs of anticyclical policies or of the redistribution of income; and in its capacity to exert pressure on governments to cooperate in other matters of socioeconomic policy. We already have the International Bank for Reconstruction and Development and the International Monetary Fund to handle, at a world level, the transfer of loan capital. But we do not have the more natural institutions for dealing with current expenditures, a more important means of financial policy.

The world institutions here advocated should contribute to the fulfillment of the aims of a world economic policy. Among these aims, the converging growth of incomes and optimum trade under as stable conditions as possible must rank high.

The preparation of joint policies at the national and international levels should be the task of a world planning agency, presumably the United Nations Forecasts and Projections Center, endowed with more means and more power and assisted by the Regional Economic Commissions of the United Nations. In principle, the planning procedure should again be a process of collecting and disseminating information, probably in a few rounds, as described in the previous section. But it should now be begun at the top and with a stronger purpose merely than providing orientation on some nonpolitical data. Here the beginning should be a document—let us call it the "plan outline"—that states clearly some policy aims for the world at large, including those just mentioned, and tentative statistics on such fields as international financial transfers and the numbers of experts to be made available by developed to developing countries. Before being sent to individual governments the plan outline should be discussed, amended and approved by the U. N. Economic and Social Council. This council should also be vested with the power to take decisions committing member governments on some main issues of international economic policy, including income and capital transfers, the approximate size of the inflationary or deflationary gap in public finances, the flow of exports and a number of general trade policy measures.

After approval, the plan outline should be sent to the Regional Commissions of the United Nations for distribution to the governments. These governments, in cooperation with the Regional Commissions, should prepare their own plans and submit them through

295

the Regional Commissions to the Center. Where there are obvious inconsistencies between the general aims and means that have been set and the feasible policies of single countries, governments may propose changes. Moreover, government plans will be much more detailed than the outline, and coordination may be necessary. However, at the outset, weaker forms of coordination may still have to be used, for such questions as investments in particular sectors of the economy. But gradually a procedure should be elaborated. Central decisions can be arrived at concerning investments in those sectors which show external effects. Generally speaking, these will be the international sectors that require heavy investments in capital goods, such as steel, heavy chemicals and international transportation. To these may be added industries such as textiles where there is clearly a danger of overexpansion because of inconsistent national policies.

Activities of this type require a very exact timetable and hence a high degree of discipline of the collaborating agencies. One way to arrive at this discipline may be extensive training and information; another may be to use the center's estimates when figures have not been submitted on time by the governments concerned. It requires little imagination to foresee the numerous conflicts that may ensue, for this will be no easy undertaking.

The Wider Human Impact of Planning

So far we have discussed planning for arriving at a better economic order and policy. This is important enough, yet planning represents something more: It constitutes an instrument of education and reconciliation. It educates people to understand better the conditions under which they live; it helps to reconcile seemingly opposed interests. This more general impact of planning can be intensified by the choice of the right procedures. Above all, it requires that consultation with those whose interests are at stake be part of the planning process.

Experience in both eastern and western Europe with planning provides a number of interesting examples of the educative and reconciliatory role of planning. Since I live in the West, I can speak in only general terms about the impact of planning on human relations in the eastern part of Europe. There it is generally accepted that participation by the employees of an enterprise in the formulation and discussions of its plans represents an important element in the kind of democracy that is typical of these countries and that is less known in the West.

In western Europe, planning plays this role less at the enterprise than at higher levels. Moreover, there are considerable differences in the methods of planning as used in the various western European countries. Some of the closest contacts between planners and private enterprise are to be found in France, where mixed committees regularly discuss the prospects and the aims of development of each sector of the economy. These discussions have not only provided the planners with much information, but have considerably increased the understanding of the use and purposes of planning among employers' and employees' organizations. They have underlined the need to look ahead, to set aims and to coordinate interests. Not so long ago there was little understanding among entrepreneurs that measures had to be taken several years in advance if a supply of skilled or of qualified workers was to be ensured for the future. The planning discussions have made this clear to them.

In the Netherlands, planning has played a lesser role in individual industries, but a correspondingly greater one at the national level. The main lines of socioeconomic policy have been based on analyses and tables prepared by the planning office and discussed in meetings where government officials, trade union and employers' union representatives sit together to advise the government. As a result, many of the difficult problems faced by the country have been much better understood. Reconciliation of conflicting interests has been possible in the majority of cases, including some difficult situations (the inflationary situation in 1951 and 1957 and the deflationary situation in 1953). Understanding of the need to look ahead, to establish aims and coordinate policies has also increased here considerably.

Italy will provide a highly interesting test case. The southern regions of this country have a much lower income level than northern Europe, and its social structure is almost feudal. As a consequence, political controversies are more violent, and distrust more widespread. At various times the country has been on the verge of an irreparable split along class lines. I believe that planning is the way in which greater prosperity and a more equitable income distribution can be achieved in Italy.

Socioeconomic planning can also contribute to a better understanding between East and West; for, like mathematics and physics, the science of economics, and more particularly planning, reduces itself to objective discussion. Such discussion will, of course, run into difficulties over the doctrinaire views that divide East and West. Nevertheless, the solution of this problem may be furthered by (1) common study of economic policy and (2) the objective discussion of the aims and means of the two economic systems, the concrete content of the theory of economic policy.

The Role of Christians

What can Christians do to further the aims and activities outlined above? Should they support these activities?

Christians will find many inspiring tasks in these fields, however technical they may appear at first sight. They can support such activities in a great diversity of ways: as citizens, politicians, civil servants (national and international), teachers and spiritual leaders, industrialists, trade unionists and employers' representatives.

To begin with, Christians may support the immediate aims of a world economic policy: to eliminate suffering in the developing countries and to bring them the minimum of material well-being

298

that is needed for human dignity and happiness. They might also support the ultimate aim of achieving greater equity in the distribution of world prosperity. They should play their part in opposing traditional laissez-faire attitudes if these block the road to a stable world order. There is no relationship whatever between the Christian outlook and the outdated laissez-faire doctrines.

Christians should oppose nationalism and racism, which have contributed so much to human tension and disaster, and stand firm for worldwide cooperation among all peoples and races. More particularly they should oppose narrow materialist attitudes which seek to perpetuate discriminatory practices favoring one nation, to the detriment of the common interests. Above all, they may be the champions of cooperation between West, East and South.

It is desirable that the churches should interpret more precisely the meaning of their universal faith for the economic problems of our world and set before us their understanding of the meaning of human responsibility and solidarity in the face of worldwide economic need and change.

14

AID AND TRADE—
ECONOMIC RELATIONS
BETWEEN DEVELOPED AND
DEVELOPING COUNTRIES

by S. L. PARMAR (India)

INTERNATIONAL economic relations take the form of trade and aid. Exports and imports of goods and services are the main constituents of the former; and grants, loans and technical assistance of the latter. Ideally they should complement each other, and the closer actual trading conditions approximate this ideal, the better the prospects for an expansion of world trade and cooperation, and the emergence of a truly international economy; when they fall far short of it international economic relations are strained and distorted.

When a country's export earnings are less than the import expenditure, it incurs a deficit in its balance of payments or external accounts. If it possesses substantial reserves it can either draw on foreign exchange or gold to cover the deficit, or secure foreign assistance. Under the pressure of efforts for rapid economic growth the foreign trade of developing nations has been characterized by large deficits which necessitate substantial aid. Economic aid to developing nations by the developed nations should be a consequence of trade deficits resulting from efforts at rapid economic growth. Such aid should strengthen their economies and help them to increase their exports, which will enable them to meet their repayment obligations when they fall due. Here, then, is the complementary of trade and aid: Development creates deficits; deficits necessitate aid; aid should stimulate trade.

It is precisely because aid from developed to developing nations has not succeeded in increasing their exports that their economic and even political relationships have become strained. The distinct polarization of views of these two groups at the U. N. Conference on Trade and Development in 1964 brought out the disquieting limitations of existing relationships.

The Urgency of Economic Development

The major preoccupation of countries intent on nation-building is economic development. They are fully aware that political freedom will have meaning for their peoples only if it leads to economic freedom; and that therefore, political power has to serve as an instrument of economic growth.

These nations have a crippling backlog of poverty and economic stagnation. Although they represent two-thirds of the world's population, they produce only 15 per cent of its gross product versus the 85 per cent produced by the developed nations with only one-third of the world's population to support. Such a huge difference in economic performance reduces income. The average per capita income of the developing nations is only one-tenth that of the developed. The range of economic differentials is even wider, with the lowest per capita income, placed at $50, to the highest at

301

$3,000.[1] But economic pressures, political expectations and the logic of technology make rates of growth even more important than growth itself. Time is of the essence.

If a high rate of economic growth is to be maintained, national income must increase faster than population. At the present rate of population growth (2.2 per cent per year) India would have to double its food output by 1980 and quadruple it by the year 2000. Problems relating to employment, capital formation, institutional patterns, welfare needs, and so on, are equally pressing and contribute to the magnitude and urgency of the economic task in the developing nations. Too much has to be done too quickly. If there is to be some improvement in the inordinately low consumption-level in these countries and some capital available for investment, the rate of production increase must be greater than of population increase. India, for example, has set a target of 6 per cent annual increase in national income under the Current Plan. Thus, the large demographic investments necessitated by the population trends in developing nations force them to run in order even to stand still. Real advance calls for a sustained economic gallop.

An awareness of the achievements of other nations, combined with hopes raised during their freedom struggles, has generated a revolution of rising expectations in the developing nations. "If others can do it, so can we" is the prevailing mood. These people do not think of some remote future when their countries will flow with milk and electricity: they expect it in the near future. They are impatient to see their political revolutions take on an economic aspect, and their governments and political systems are under economic duress.

The contact between developed and developing nations does more than make the latter more conscious of their economic disabilities: it promises to bring them the services and benefits of

[1] W. W. ROSTOW: *Economic Development—Some Lessons of a Common Experience.* 1963, p. 5.

modern technology. This possibility merely increases their dissatisfaction with existing conditions. They are determined to achieve economic growth: with the help of developed nations if available; without it if necessary.

Self-Help and Help from Abroad for Economic Development

Because in matters of aid, the initiative rests with the giving nations, stress has been laid on their actions and attitudes. This is not to imply that the receiving nations have no responsibilities: in fact, these are taken for granted. The moment foreign aid becomes a substitute for domestic effort, it undermines development. "Economic growth is primarily a national enterprise. The amount of resources made available from outside can be a critically helpful margin; but it is a margin which will have its effect only to the extent that those receiving aid are effectively committed to the development process as they wish to see it and are effectively mobilising their human and material resources to do the job." [2] Determined self-help and responsible action alone entitle developing nations to assistance.

Often developing nations have been guilty of waste and "capital-consumption" because they were not well prepared to utilize resources secured from outside. They must be willing to accept the obligations imposed on them by international measures for stabilizing or improving the prices of primary commodities. For example, they may have to regulate strictly the production of these commodities, and this is not easy in countries where the economy is insufficiently diversified. They must also adapt technology to their own circumstances. Unquestioning imitation of industrial nations will create more problems than it solves. For example, in economies where labor is abundant, labor-intensive rather than capital-intensive forms of production should be emphasized.

---

[2] ROSTOW: *Ibid.*, p. 9.

Most important of all, the developing nations must work for economic cooperation among themselves and cease futile and wasteful efforts to duplicate each other's economic activities. Though this will certainly not meet their resource requirements, since their economies are not complementary, cooperation will extend trade opportunities, help in coordinating economic policies, especially as regards the production and sale of primary commodities, permit an exchange of experience, develop a sense of solidarity that is a significant noneconomic determinant of development and perhaps improve their bargaining power vis-à-vis the developed nations. One legacy of colonialism is that the developing nations have closer economic links with ex-colonial powers than with each other, and this needs to be corrected.

Regional planning can be more effective than national planning, but it is not easy for new nations that are jealous of their nationhood and sovereignty. Countries with limited resources must achieve an optimal allocation, and this is best ensured by regional economic cooperation and some form of regional allocation of resources. "Regional economic groupings encourage trade, stimulate production, and prevent sterile competition and costly duplication of effort. They make for better utilization of local savings and external capital and the savings they effect in imports is far greater in the early stages than the uncertain profits of difficult exportation to distant markets." [3] The advantages which the establishment of the European Common Market has conferred on European nations is an object lesson for us.

Need for Help from Abroad. Development requires adequate resources in both the quantitative and qualitative sense. Resources can come from two directions. First, internal, in the form of domestic savings; and, second, external, in the form of export earnings (which may be called converted domestic savings, as domestic surpluses are exchanged for surpluses available in foreign markets)

---

[3] Document E/Conf. 46/Sta/8. Speech of the Representative of France at U. N. Trade and Development Conference, 1964, p. 5.

and foreign aid. As mentioned earlier, the need for aid arises when export earnings fall short of import requirements. Such has generally been the case with developing nations over the last decade and a half. For example, the ECAFE region's trade balance which was $ + 427 million in 1938, fell to $ − 396 million in 1948 and $ − 1322 per year for the period 1959–1961.[4]

India's persistent foreign exchange crisis reflects the gravity of the problem. From a deficit of Rupees 3,180 millions for the First Plan, the balance of payments slumped to Rupees—20,590 millions for the Second Plan and is estimated at Rupees—26,000 millions for the Current Plan.[5] Instances could be multiplied by picking out any except the petroleum- or copper-rich countries of Asia, Africa and Latin America. Such huge deficits in the balance of payments have practically denuded the foreign exchange reserves of these nations, and yet foreign exchange alone enables a nation to buy in foreign markets. Even if through extreme austerity more resources are squeezed out of the domestic economy they cannot (unless they result in increased exports) be a substitute for foreign exchange. That is why a higher rate of domestic capital formation, though it is welcome in itself, does not immediately overcome the foreign exchange problem.

Imports in most of the developing nations are high because they have to secure machinery, industrial raw materials and technical know-how from the developed nations. Many of them have cut imports of consumers' goods to the bone in order to divert scarce foreign exchange to the purchase of developmental goods. Their restrictive import policy is forced on them by the exigencies of the balance-of-payments situation rather than by any narrow protectionist instincts. The same cannot be said of the developed nations, which may not have balance-of-payments problems and yet exercise import controls. Simultaneous with import restriction the de-

---

[4] *Economic Survey of Asia and the Far East,* 1962, p. 12, Tables 1, 3.
[5] *Third Five Year Plan: Government of India*—Planning Commission, p. 108.

veloping nations are taking elaborate measures to promote exports.

The continuing strain on their balance of payments prompts developing nations to seek adequate assistance from developed countries. In addition, other forces contribute to their general economic hardships and can be adduced as supplementary arguments for aid.

Strains Resulting from Welfare Programs. Political freedom has been followed by a remarkable extension of welfare programs—health, education, social services, increased opportunities for depressed groups, and so on. From a long-run point of view such "investments in man" strengthen the fiber of the nation; and substantial assistance from developed nations, foreign welfare organizations and international agencies has been available for such programs. But these programs create some short-run problems. Improved health facilities have led to the control or eradication of such diseases as malaria, cholera, and yellow fever. Although the birthrate is unchanged, the infant mortality rate has gone down, life expectancy has increased and the immediate effect has been to increase the rate of population growth. This means a larger share of the social product must be deviated to "demographic investment," which in turn reduces the rate of capital formation.

The only possibility of reducing the population pressure lies in a more rapid decrease in the birthrate than the deathrate. For various reasons, this is not likely to occur in the near future. The forces responsible for reduced deathrate are more effective in the short run than those affecting the birthrate. Consequently, in a discussion of trade and aid relationships, demographic factors must be taken as given data. Welfare activities also tend to slow down public savings because they involve a transfer of income from the richer groups (those with greater ability to save) to the poorer (those with no ability to save). Foreign assistance should be stepped up to meet the dilemma posed by a growth of welfare: improvement in the quality of human capital must be supported by an increase in the quantity of material capital.

Burden of Debt-Repayment. An important aspect of economic development is that there is an appreciable time-lag between investment and the fruits of investment. Insofar as investments call for increased savings they impose a sacrifice of current consumption by the present generation in the interests of a future generation that will enjoy the fruits of the investments. But foreign loans provide a mechanism whereby some of the burden of growth can be transferred to the next generation. Moreover, if today's efforts bear fruit, the level of production will be much greater in the future and the ability to finance debt-repayments will also be greater.

It is clear that foreign aid can play a very positive role in meeting the needs of developing nations. It can ease the balance-of-payment deficits and allow a satisfactory import-surplus to continue; it can ease some of the short-term strains emanating from welfare-oriented activities; it can enable some increase in the level of consumption, which is very necessary for mobilizing public enthusiasm in countries where the vast majority continues to have a submarginal existence; and it can allow a more equitable distribution of the burdens of development between the present and the future. But in matters of giving and receiving, of matching needs and abilities, the initiative rests with those who have resources; and decisions about foreign aid depend upon the developed nations more than upon the developing.

Rationale of Foreign Aid—from the Viewpoint of Developed Nations. What prompts developed nations to extend economic assistance to the developing? Does their rationale provide a stable basis for a relationship of genuine interdependence between rich and poor nations? Or does it suffer from basic limitations that call for radical reformulation?

Three considerations seem to have provided the mainspring for the giving of aid by developed nations. First, large economic differences between the rich and the poor nations are undesirable; the latter should be helped to catch up. Second, only the economic growth of poor nations will provide expanding economic oppor-

307

tunities for the rich; for developed nations are each other's best customers. Third, the continued existence of glaring economic inequalities endangers international stability, since poverty anywhere is a danger to prosperity everywhere. These arguments have some validity but are only half-truths and tend to cloud the real issues.

For example, though we of the developing countries heartily endorse the argument for "catching up," we wonder whether the developed nations are willing and able to carry it to its logical conclusion, and also whether it really has as much bearing on relations between developed and developing nations as is generally assumed.

Developing nations have higher rates of population growth than most of the developed countries. Therefore, even with the same (or even a little higher) rate of growth of national income, their per capita income will increase more slowly than that of the developed; and the economic gap will continue to grow as it has over the last decade.

Three possibilities are open to the developed nations if they are determined to narrow the gulf: they can impose a sufficiently low rate of growth on themselves; they can increase their birthrate so as to counteract their higher growth rate and allow the poorer nations to catch up; and they can fix a ceiling on their growth and transfer all income above that to the needy nations. It would be interesting to speculate on the first two alternatives, but in reality the third is the only live possibility, and even it is very remote.

This line of action would call for a completely new concept of an international economy wherein less developed nations would be treated in the same way that a nation treats its less-developed areas. The rich nations would bear the burdens of development of the poor, just as today in certain western nations the prosperous industrial sectors provide resources for price-support policies and subsidies to the relatively weaker agricultural sectors. International economic policy would take on the appearance of internal fiscal policy with the "haves" being taxed for the benefit of the "have nots." This would mean world economic planning, with all that it implies.

And if a ceiling is to be fixed, at what height? This poses other awkward questions such as these: What is the ultimate objective of economic growth? Where is the pursuit of material progress leading the world? Should human wants be regulated even when resources and techniques are available to satisfy them? Is the present situation, where technology forces its own logic of growth, to be questioned? Personally I should welcome discussion of such issues. We seem to be enslaved in a system where progress, increased consumption and technological advance have become ends in themselves rather than means to human well-being and happiness. Planned obsolescence with its inherent callousness faces planned development with its apparent helplessness, and the idealism or romanticism of the "catching up" argument succumbs to the realities of a hardheaded world.

The central concern of developing nations is to maintain a rate of growth that will lead them from economic stagnation to self-sustained growth. If, in the process, there is a narrowing of the gap between rich and poor nations, that is all to the good and may be taken as a by-product of the developmental effort.

Another consideration is that during the coming period developed nations may grow at a faster rate than the developing and that the gap may widen. While the developing nations are striving to enter the first industrial revolution the developed nations may have a new technological revolution that will multiply their resources rapidly. How are we to insure that no new technological breakthrough is allowed until international economic differences are reduced to the desired level? Technology has its own logic and momentum and, unless its functioning is regulated by some global economic policy, there is no ground to assume that existing differences will not increase.

Philosophy of Growth in Developing Nations

All this, however, should not deter the poorer nations from their efforts to eradicate poverty and misery and to move up from their submarginal economic existence. Whether they reduce the distance between themselves and the developed nations is immaterial so long as they continue to be better off than they were. In effect, each nation competes with itself. Its struggle is against the economic stagnation; its achievement is measured by the speed with which it moves out of it. For this reason, it is very necessary that developing nations have an ambivalent attitude. They need both a philosophy of discontent and a philosophy of content: discontent with economic stagnation and contentment with their relatively less prosperous position vis-à-vis the developed nations. This is not a counsel of passivity and inaction but of realism.

The greater a nation's discontentment with its economic backwardness, the greater will be its efforts to overcome it. No nation can do better than its best. If, having done that, it finds its relative position with regard to others the same as before or perhaps worse, it can only be philosophical and accept the facts of life. Development is central, catching up is incidental. If the two coincide it will be an evidence of international good sense; if they do not, life must go on in its fragmented and inequitable form.

Inasmuch as "catching up" has its origin in some concept of social justice and international egalitarianism, it is a sound objective. But it is important for developing nations to apply it internally before expecting it to operate internationally. Great economic inequality exists within developing nations: their feudal and colonial history has created a small prosperous section while the masses live in deplorable conditions. Efforts at industrialization do not appear to have altered the pattern. Only a few countries have adopted progressive social and economic policies and are reducing economic inequalities; by and large the gap is growing. From the standpoint of both rapid economic development and social justice, it is essential that developing nations follow more egalitarian policies. It is presumptuous for developing nations to press for a reduction of international economic differences if they do not apply the principle of greater equality internally. (Greater egalitarian functioning within a nation strengthens it to propagate similar ideals for international conduct.)

The current obsession of developing nations with "catching up" should not become an escape-channel whereby we blame others for our own failures. This is neither an attempt to whitewash the selfish policies of developed nations nor to justify international inequalities. It is merely a plea for the right perspective.

Whither Material Progress? Acceptance of the "catching up" principle implies approval of the common element in the objectives of the developed nations: increasing consumption. The developed nations are so caught in the coils of progress that they can hardly have any objectivity about it, and it may be for the developing nations to make a virtue of necessity and question the whole modern concept of their material progress. Perhaps only those who have not achieved material progress, and are, therefore, relatively free of its attractions and blandishments can raise the issue. Just as our industrial revolution can benefit from the experience of western nations in order not to repeat their mistakes, should we not, while we can, try to escape the tyranny of technology in its various forms?

All the talk by developed nations about the desirability of narrowing economic gaps, unless it is accompanied by adequate supporting action arouses undisguised skepticism in the developing countries. Some even see in it a reflection of western paternalism—a kind of "white man's burden" in a new garb. (If existing economic differences are paralleled by such wide gulfs between the proclamations and performances of the developed nations, how can one give much credence to the catching-up motivation?) However, the truly humanitarian and fraternal motivations behind certain types of assistance are greatly appreciated by the recipients.

311

Economic Self-Interest of Aid-Giving Nations

Perhaps the strongest economic motivation in developed nations for helping the poorer countries is that in the future they will be good customers. But they are very good customers even now, and would buy much more if they had foreign exchange. So their long-run ability to continue as good customers depends upon their short-run ability to secure foreign exchange. Up to a point, foreign aid is providing this, but if they are to continue as good customers, they must have a continual supply of exchange, which means that they must first repay their loans and thereafter maintain large enough exports to the developed nations. The developed nations must be good buyers, both in the near future when debts are being repaid and in the long run when more purchasing power is being earned.

But today there seems to be a strong unwillingness in the developed nations to increase their purchases from the developing nations. This was the real bone of contention at the U. N. Conference on Trade and Development. The aid-giving nations may subscribe to the idea that development will stimulate trade, but their actions in the crucial determinative period of future trade relations negate the process. If developing nations are expected to be good customers only as buyers and not as sellers, the whole mechanism of international trade breaks down. Today the degree of complementarity between the developed and developing economies is greater than it may be a decade hence, if one can judge from current technological trends, and more sales of traditional products by developing nations should be possible. Also, the size of repayments will grow in the future as interest charges mount and loans mature, whereas today a smaller increase in exports would meet the existing obligations of the debtor nations. Despite these two favorable factors (greater complementarity and desire for smaller export increase) the markets of developed nations are proving increasingly unresponsive. Can this justify optimism about the future?

312

This raises the question whether the assumption that industrial nations are each other's best customers is not an oversimplification. It may be true in a situation where nations have reached a certain plateau of development (for example, that of developed nations today). But what about the interim period when nations on a lower plateau are trying to move up? The exports of a developing Japan were not easily digested by the many available markets of an industrial world. Now when two-thirds of the world is pressing hard toward the same broad goals, and with limited markets to cultivate, can the industrialization-international trade correlation be so easily accepted? After the developing nations have made their economic breakthrough they may become each other's best customers; the existing short-sighted trade policies of developed nations seem to be driving them to this end. If developed nations underwrite large import surpluses in the developing nations now, but are not willing or able to digest their equally large export surpluses later, what kind of trade relations can one visualize for the future? Thus, even this relatively valid motivation for foreign aid goes by the board. This forces us to seek motivations of trade and aid which incorporate the best elements of the standard determinants but with a new dimension which overcomes their negative features, and upon such a new approach to work out tangible forms of economic relationships.

Are Economic Differences Between Nations a Threat to Stability? Too much has been made of the slogan: poverty anywhere is a danger to prosperity everywhere. (This is not to deny the explosive possibilities of economic disorders. But let us be realistic at this point.) Most of the threats to international peace are political rather than economic, and they emanate from the developed nations as a result of the East-West conflict, the nuclear-arms race, balance of power maneuverings, international financial manipulation, resistance to disarmament, military alliances and military aid, vestiges of colonialism or racial strife. (It must be rather convenient for the big powers to blame developing nations for interna-

313

tional instability, when it is themselves who fish in troubled waters and fan dying embers into conflagrations. Assuming that U. S. A. and Russia underwrite world peace today, can minor conflicts grow into international conflicts—other nuclear powers notwithstanding? The threats to international stability are more political than economic: nationalism in the developed world, ideological conflicts at various levels or balance of terror manifestations of large-powers' behavior.) It may be convenient for the big powers to blame the developing nations for international instability, and it is true that their poverty creates some international tension, but they are not the real villains of the piece.

In fact, the shoe is on the other foot. Rather than the economic misfortunes of developing nations being the root cause of conflicts, the political posture of the developed nations accentuates tensions and obstructs the developmental efforts of the former. The competition in evil manifested in the growing defense expenditure of many poor nations grows out of the failure of the big powers to work out some basis for disarmament. The whole economic effort of developing nations would take on a new look if the colossal resources channeled into nuclear armaments were used for peaceful development.

Or witness the inhibiting effects of international finance upon the growth of a sense of real selfhood in a number of developing nations. Without this they cannot embark on nation-building. Consequently, poverty coupled with resentment serves as the raw material for revolutions, which result not so much from economic differences between rich and poor nations as from economic exploitation by international finance. International finance sometimes behaves like a superstate; it makes its own laws; it is not even subject to governments of the nations in which it originates; it makes and unmakes governments in the developing countries. And strangely enough, some developed nations which sometimes question the ethic and motivations of international finance have no scruples in providing it with a protective umbrella when its victims rise up in revolt.

Rightly understood, the idea that the world cannot continue to exist half developed and half underdeveloped, is highly ethical and provides the basis for a one-world approach to economic and political question. But it is not quite valid to claim that the interest by developed nations in the developing flows from such motivations. Ideals do not become realities by constant repetition.

Inadequacy of the "Self-Interest Approach." To conclude this part of the discussion we must bring together the three threads of thought analyzed thus far. First, that economic needs of developing nations make them seek aid and increased opportunities for trade; second, that the initiative for determining economic relationships in this context of need and ability rests mainly with the developed nations; and, third, that the existing basis on which developed nations are structuring their international economic policies requires radical alteration.

So-called "enlightened self-interest" seems to motivate the behavior of nations, and this may be acceptable if it leads to greater cooperation. But there is a snag: if cooperation is a creation of enlightened self-interest, the emphasis is on the latter rather than on the former; it is imperative that the emphasis be shifted from self-interest to cooperation, and this may require the reversal of a number of prevalent political and economic policies. "In the long run, no policy can be sustained by the sole force of cold-blooded self-interest. We do not provide social security to the unemployed simply because it helps to quiet them and makes the possessing classes more secure in their affluence, although social security undoubtedly does contribute to that end. We do it because it is decent and proper, because we feel some sense of responsibility. ... We must recognize that aid is a humane as well as a practical program, that as Woodrow Wilson said of the League of Nations, there is a 'pulse of sympathy in it', and 'a compulsion of conscience throughout it'." [6]

If the best interests of developed nations are served by the rapid economic development of the poor nations, one would expect the former to do three things: to provide an adequate aid to enable a quick economic breakthrough by the developing countries, to provide such assistance on easy conditions and a long-term basis, to accept the logic of developmental aid and to purchase not only more raw materials but also the semiprocessed and manufactured articles that will result from the economic diversification of developing nations. They do none of these, which implies that they are thinking mainly of their short-term interests.

In one sense they give aid in order to provide purchasing power that will ensure adequate markets for their products, and high levels of production and employment in their own economies. No one questions the desirability of full economic activity in developed nations. The crucial question concerns the economic patterns that are followed. If existing patterns of production and sales are continued, how can the borrowing nations hope to diversify their economies and increase their sales? The unwillingness of developed nations to move toward new patterns of specialization and trade blocks the export drive of developing nations. In other words the "self-interest" of aid-giving nations is insular and static and can hardly be termed "enlightened."

If there is to be growth of export earnings commensurate with the growing import needs of the less developed countries, it will have to come in the main from new sources, and in particular from semiprocessed and manufactured products. This means that the less developed countries will have to be persuaded and encouraged to concentrate more of their productive activities on production for export. As a corollary the industrialized countries will have to be prepared to open

---

[6] Senator J. W. FULBRIGHT: *The New York Times,* International Edition, Sat.-Sun., March 27–28, 1965, p. 5.

their markets to this new production from the less-developed countries. The semi-processed and manufactured products from less-developed countries may well cause disturbance to established industries in the industrialized world, calling for structural changes in the economics of the latter countries. Enlightened self-interest would indicate the acceptance of these changes, and economically they would not be disadvantageous since the industrialized countries will no doubt in any case find it more profitable to concentrate increasingly on more sophisticated and complex types of industry. Economic adjustment is, however, never easy, and again an effort of political will is required.[7]

The Importance of the Export Trade for Developing Nations

Strains on the Export Trade. In spite of all these problems, there has been an appreciable increase in the aid given by developed countries and international agencies over the last decade. But, as stated before, if development-induced deficits necessitate aid, such aid should be followed by increased exports from the aid-receiving countries.

"In human terms the objectives of the UN Development Decade are modest indeed. In terms of economic effort they are daunting. They imply, in addition to the maintenance and expansion of financial and technical aid, a major expansion in the export earnings of the developing countries." [8] If conditions for such a basic equilibrium do not exist, the whole trade and aid relationship faces severe strains and will break down unless suitably modified. It is clear that the exports of developing nations are not increasing as they should, and this has created a strain in trade and aid relationships that threatens a breakdown. Developing nations would naturally prefer to earn foreign exchange through trade rather than aid. However, even if conditions were most favorable, it would not

---

[7] "International Trade: The Years of Decision" by E. W. WHITE, Executive Secretary, GATT, GATT Document INT (63), 128.

[8] E. W. WHITE: "Europe and the Trade Negotiations in 1963/64 within the GATT Framework," Article in *EFTA Bulletin*, April, 1963.

317

be possible for them to finance their imports from current export earnings, and hence they must seek more grants and loans. The burden of repayment necessitates increased export earnings, which depend upon the volume of sales and the terms of trade, that is, the price of exports in terms of imports. On both these counts, the developing nations have been facing difficulties.

Primary Commodities. Nearly nine-tenths of the earnings of developing nations comes from the sale of primary commodities, 95 per cent of which go to developed nations. These primary export earnings provide 70 per cent of all foreign exchange including aid and other capital transfers. It has been estimated that in 1970, even under highly favorable conditions, primary export earnings will have to provide 85 per cent of all earnings from exports and 60 per cent of the total foreign exchange.[9]

A number of developing nations depend on one or two commodities for the bulk of their export earnings. This should be corrected by the diversification of industries through the setting up of more import-substitute and export industries to conserve and replenish foreign exchange reserves. However, diversification is possible only through economic development, which in turn depends heavily upon export earnings, that is, on a continuation, for some time, of traditional patterns. Since the prospects for increased trade in primary commodities are not at all encouraging and the possibilities of new export earnings are limited, foreign aid in its present form will prove of limited use. Therefore, it is absolutely essential to evolve new forms of aid and trade.

Primary exports are inhibited by both conditions of supply in the developing nations and of demand in the developed. Over the last decade, trade in primary commodities has been characterized by a fall in its share in world trade, a decline in prices simultaneously with a rise in the prices of industrial goods, an increase

---

[9] "Commodity Export Earnings and Economic Growth" by Gerda Blau, 1964. Paper transmitted by Director FAO to U. N. Conference on Trade and Development.

in the share of industrial countries, and the accumulation of large stocks of important primary commodities.[10]

Three forces have aggravated the supply problem:

1. The lack of alternative lines of production to which resources can be transferred when the world market for primary commodities is not favorable.

2. The long gestation period for tree crops like coffee, tea, cocoa, rubber. Planting is increased when world prices rise, but it takes a few years for the new plantations to yield. By that time prices may have gone down (as happened between 1954 and 1962), and new supplies only cause a glut and aggravate the situation.

3. The introduction of new methods and modern technology in the primary commodity industries in the hope of increasing foreign exchange earnings through increased production. But this has only stepped up the supply and proved self-negating. Other factors such as uncoordinated production and the sales policies of the producers have aggravated the problem: each developing nation has pursued a "go-it-alone" policy to the detriment of all.

There are a number of reasons for the low price-elasticity and income-elasticity in the demand for primary commodities. A decline in prices does not stimulate demand sufficiently to equalize export earnings: more is sold for less. Similarly, a rise in the income of developed nations has not led to a proportionate increase in their demand for primary commodities. A saturation point seems to have been reached. This is due to a combination of factors such as the low rate of population growth, increased use of synthetics, technological changes which result in less raw materials being used for each unit of the finished product, a decline in importance of

---

[10] "Trade as a means of balanced economic development in developing and developed countries." Report by AFRASEC (Afro-Asian Organization for Economic Cooperation), 1964.

industries which are heavily dependent on imported materials and so on.[11]

Paradoxically enough, when prices of primary products increased in the fifties it encouraged developed nations to use new technological methods which try to work with less raw materials. But, when prices declined, the new processes were not checked or reversed because technology generates its own momentum. So the benefits of high prices were temporary and have inflicted long-term injuries to the demand for these products.

According to certain projections for 1970, there will be "a growing excess of world production over world consumption, even on optimistic assumptions concerning the growth of demand in high income countries." [12]

Terms of Trade. The trends in terms of trade present an equally gloomy picture. Since 1954 the primary exporting countries have faced "a slow deterioration in their terms of trade in relation to the prices of manufactures." [13] For example, the coffee-producing countries sold 50 per cent more in 1962 than in 1954, but their exchange earnings were one third smaller.[14] All this made a mockery of increased foreign aid during this period since it has failed to compensate developing countries for the loss in foreign exchange through adverse terms of trade caused by the decline in the price of primary commodities and the rise in that of manufactured articles. It is indeed paradoxical that developed nations are willing to increase aid but refuse to pay better prices for primary exports. This would be a much more strategic method since the developing nations would have the psychological satisfaction of earning their own way and at the same time would escape some of the burden of repayment.

---

[11] "International Commodity Arrangements" by Gerda Blau. Paper transmitted by Director FAO to U. N. Conference on Trade and Development.
[12] *Ibid.*
[13] "Economic Survey of Asia and the Far East," 1962.
[14] "Economic Growth and External Debt—An Analytical Framework." Paper by staff of IBRD, 1964.

Trade Patterns Reflect Selfish Interests of Developed Nations. Such illogical behavior makes the motivations of developed nations suspect. They give aid to serve their own limited, selfish interests. It keeps up the demand for their products and ensures a high level of economic activity in their countries. The donation of agricultural surpluses provides an outlet for embarrassing supplies that, if held, would either depress agricultural prices or force the government to pay larger subsidies to farmers. Though it is true that these surpluses meet needs in some developing countries, through such action the developed nations are helping themselves more than they are others. The crucial test is their attitude to the trade-expanding efforts of developing nations.

The emphasis on diversification is also belied by the fate of industrial exports of the developing nations that face import restrictions in developed markets, despite the fact that their output of such goods is a very small percentage of the total demand of developed nations. "Owing to the developed countries' high levels of income and trade, a small percentage increase of imports from the less developed countries, would, in view of their low levels of income and trade, mean a large proportional increase of their foreign exchange earning." [15]

As a result of such restrictions developing nations have to depend more and more on grants and loans. Grants do not involve repayment, but their share in total aid has been steadily decreasing. For example, the percentage of grants in the total aid received by ECAFE countries decreased from 86 per cent in 1953–1955 to 46 per cent in 1959–1960, whereas that of public loans and private long-term capital investment increased from 7 per cent to 44 per cent over the same period.[16] The trend has been the same in other developing regions.

---

[15] "Commodity Export Earnings and Economic Growth" by Gerda Blau, 1964.
[16] "Economic Survey of Asia and the Far East," 1962.

Pattern of International Loans

Three aspects of international loans are significant: size, maturity and burden of repayment. All three have been unfavorable to the developing nations. A U. N. study estimates that compared to 1959, "the deficit in current account would be quadrupled rising to $20 billion by 1970. Thus, while it had been possible, in 1959, to meet the deficit on current account for the group as a whole by inflows of aid and other net capital transfers of a total of $5 billion, the near-doubling of all such capital inflows to $9 billion in 1970 (a figure based on extrapolating past trends) would not be sufficient to meet more than 40 per cent of the prospective deficit in current account in that year. The remaining 'hypothetical gap' on both current and long-term capital account would amount to no less than $11 billion in 1970, unless new means can be found of reducing it." [17] Of course, if present trends in terms of trade continue, the gap could easily increase by another $4 billion, which was the total amount of debt-service charges in 1959.[18] Even if the 1959 position is taken it is significant that the balance of trade deficit was $1 billion, but the repayment-obligations amounted to $4 billion. This shows the heavy burdens that foreign loans impose.

"In many cases, a dangerously high proportion of export earnings (the prospects for which are themselves clouded) is mortgaged to future debt service. Our own figures show that between 1959 and 1961, a group of 34 countries, accounting for 70% of the population of the under-developed world, more than doubled its total external public debt. Yet over the same period, the export earnings of the same group increased by little more than 15%." [19]

---

[17] "Commodity Export Earnings and Economic Growth" by Gerda Blau, 1964.
[18] *Ibid.*
[19] Statement by the President IBRD, quoted in article by E. W. White

As for the maturities of the loans and the rates of interest charged the position is extremely unsatisfactory for the borrowers. Developmental loans should be long-term loans at low rates of interest. "It is paradoxical that while lending today is overwhelmingly for developmental purposes in which returns flow over a long period, the maturities have contracted." [20] Because countries in a higher stage of development accumulate capital more easily than the less developed nations ". . . lending between advanced and less advanced countries on concessional terms—at low or zero rates of interest and for long terms of repayment—should be considered normal and natural. No one should be excessively impressed by economic aid which is in the form of ten-year loans at 6½%. Few countries in any early stage of development can safely pay the price of purely commercial credits." [21]

Toward a "One-World" Perspective. The main criterion for judging patterns of international trade is whether or not they allow debtor nations gradually to shift from a trade balance of import surpluses to one of adequate export surpluses. If this is to happen developed nations will have to accept import surpluses. But if the U. S. A. and the U. K. have to campaign to increase their exports in the interest of their balance of payments, how can their economies digest import surpluses? Therefore, the only acceptable form of aid and trade relations is one in which the borrowing nations will not be obliged to strive for large export surpluses, and the lending nations to digest large import surpluses. Given a one-world approach to the problem of economic development, such an arrangement is not impossible. It would have two cardinal elements. First, grants would form a steadily rising part of foreign

---

in *EFTA Bulletin,* April, 1963: "Europe and the Trade Negotiations in 1963/64 within the GATT Framework."

[20] "Economic Growth and External Debt—A Statistical Presentation" by staff of IBRD, 1964.

[21] "Economic Development in Perspective" by J. K. Galbraith, 1962, p. 32.

aid, and loans would be reduced. Second, international trade would be regulated in such a way that terms of trade would favor the developing nations.

Grants Rather Than Loans. Grants have an advantage over loans in that they do not require increased exports to permit repayment. The creation of export surpluses is an inordinately difficult task for developing nations with their limited resources and internal scarcities. But far more important is the fact that such surpluses are embarrassing to the developed economies. Therefore, in the general interest of all nations grants are preferable to loans. Such a proposal is likely to be criticized by both sides. Developed nations may feel that they are being asked to give something for nothing; developing nations may feel they are being asked to subsist on charity under a new form of economic servitude. But neither criticism is valid if developing nations are looked upon in the same way as weak sectors of a national economy that are in need of support by more developed areas. The fundamental question is this: Are we prepared to work out in a world perspective relations between nations that are at different levels of economic development?

The sensitivity of developing nations with regard to accepting grants is understandable but not logical. A spirit of nationalism and pride in their sovereign status is characteristic of these nations, and anything which seems even remotely to compromise this sovereignty especially in the economic field is suspect, for the real sting of colonialism was in its economic exploitation. But any form of aid is to some extent evidence of the receivers' less-favored position. If developed nations really believe that development of the poorer nations is essential for international stability, they should encourage it by methods which are least burdensome on the developing nations, and therefore least dangerous to international stability.

Managed International Trade. This suggestion is idealistic and even utopian, and something relatively more workable should be tried. The objective of managed trade would be to increase the export earnings of developing nations sufficiently to enable them to finance their development programs. In effect, the proposed pattern of trade is camouflaged aid. Instead of giving grants that raise psychological and political problems, the developed nations could artificially alter the terms of trade in favor of the developing so that the balance-of-payments gap would be covered. This would mean buying more at higher prices and selling more at lower prices. In the past the industrial nations have not hesitated to dump their manufactured goods in the developing countries, in their own limited interest and to the obvious disadvantage of the economies on the receiving end. Why can they not carry on organized dumping of machines and other goods needed for development in the interest of the developing nations? There would be an element of compensation and even poetic justice in this. And offering higher prices for goods of the developed nations would parallel their internal price-support policies. Contrived equilibrium in the balance of payments of developing nations resulting from such regulated trade would at one stroke eliminate the vexed question of export surpluses and import surpluses.

Choice Between Liberal Politico-Economic Patterns and Rigid Patterns. International economic relations seem to be moving toward a point where either the developed nations will have to agree to underwrite the development efforts of the poor nations or economic relations will break down. Developing nations are determined to grow. If international economic cooperation fails to meet their requirements they will be forced to adopt rigid and authoritarian political and economic patterns to squeeze out the maximum resources from a poor economy. If this happens, it goes against the postwar efforts of building a world community and an international economy. Therefore, it contains the seeds of international instability. Only if adequate economic assistance is forthcoming will developing nations be able to adopt liberal and outward-looking political and economic structures.

325

This is not to imply that existing trade relations cannot or should not be improved. But all such measures require some degree of trade manipulation. If primary exports are to increase, the developed nations will have to avoid deliberately using new techniques that reduce their requirements for imported raw materials. Clearly this means tampering with the processes of technology. Or if international commodity agreements are to ensure favorable prices for primary products, there will have to be deliberate interference with trade-generating forces. Once it is accepted that there is no escaping the need for managed or regulated trade, the proposals for aid in the form of grants rather than loans cease to be as far-fetched as they may at first glance appear.

If it is accepted that positive aid and trade relations require an international approach to economic issues, there is no denying the need to channel aid through international agencies. However, existing politico-economic patterns and trends do not raise much hope that this need will be met in the near future. Often the motivations for bilateral aid are so limited and parochial that instead of strengthening internationalism they undermine it. If aid is used to "sell" particular systems or ideologies or ways of life it serves as an instrument of divisiveness. Here again, the responsibility for devising more positive forms and structures of aid rests mainly on the developed nations.

Internationalization of foreign aid promises a number of advantages:

1. It would eliminate the psychological strains inherent in bilateralism.

"The fundamental difference between bilateralism and multilateralism in foreign aid is psychological. The one carries a connotation of charity, of patron and ward, of arrogance and humiliation; the other has the more dignified connotation of a community organized to meet its common and rightful responsibilities toward its less fortunate members. The one is appropriate to a world of nation states with unlimited sovereignty, the other to a world that is at least groping towards a broader community.[22]

2. It would allow the application of objective economic criteria to projects and programs. Bilateral aid is often determined by non-economic considerations. International agencies can impose the necessary competent technical supervision and obligations on aid-receiving countries without being suspected of political motivation.

3. Internationalized aid would enhance the prospects for regional cooperation. It could stimulate research in forms of technology that are relevant to heavily populated developing economies, and thus provide a starting point for technical cooperation between developing nations.

4. It would create a better climate for the growth of an international economy. Multilateral aid would represent a significant transfer of national economic sovereignty to an international body, and would represent a signal victory for internationalism.

Some developed nations find the system of economic planning adopted by developing nations an obstacle when they come to giving aid. However, most developing nations find that increased state initiative and participation in development is the best way to ensure rapid growth through optimal utilization of all resources, including aid. It is illogical for developed nations to refuse adequate assistance because the structures which promise the best results from the use of such aid do not conform to their ideas. (The logic of development must be allowed to function as the architect of policies in developing nations. If this is granted, it would help to avoid some of the irritants and inconsistencies that have strained relations between some aid-giving nations and planning-oriented developing nations.)

---

[22] Senator J. W. FULBRIGHT: *The New York Times,* International Edition, Sat.-Sun., March 27–28, 1965, p. 5.

Conclusion

It has been argued that relations between developed and developing nations should be built on a global or "one-world" approach. This introduces a moral imperative into economic relations. The task of all men of good will is to help to create a new climate wherein self-interest will give way to sharing and interdependence. Unless this new dimension is introduced, human solidarity will remain a dream. Only if we build a truly international economy shall we be able to echo the optimism of Toynbee: "Our age will be remembered, not for its horrifying crimes or its astonishing inventions but because it is the first age since the dawn of history in which mankind dared to believe it practical to make the benefits of civilization available to the whole human race." Here lies a new frontier for the church.

PART V

CHRISTIAN VALUATION

15

ETHICAL ISSUES IN THE DYNAMICS OF ECONOMIC DEVELOPMENT

by CHARLES ELLIOTT (United Kingdom)

The Economic and Social Factors of Economic Growth

To make a loaf of bread you must take flour, water and yeast and mix them in a specified way. The output of a loaf of bread, then, involves the input of specified materials in specified ratios. In exactly the same way, the output of a whole economy involves the input of certain specified variables. In classical economies, these variables were thought to be land, labor and capital. The economists of the nineteenth century thought that by combining these three factors of production in certain ways you could produce, or you could account for the production of, all the output of an economy.

Within their frames of reference, they were probably right.

331

However, the world has become more complex and the nature of the productive process has become more involved, more technologically advanced and more prolonged. To take account of this change in the nature of production, economists have accordingly redefined the classical factors of production and although they may still use the categories of land, labor and capital, nowadays they are more sophisticated in their account of productive inputs. First, when talking about land, they not only talk about the area of arable land but also, for instance, about the quantities of fertilizer applied to it. In talking about labor they do not take labor as a homogeneous lump but differentiate it according to its skills, its age, its geographical location. When talking about capital, the same process of specification is adopted. Since the war there has been great interest in the analysis of the combination of these inputs to account for outputs or for the rate of growth of outputs. By the means of a technique known as production-function analysis, it is possible to show in what ratio the factors of production have in fact been combined to produce past outputs and also to make recommendations about the future combination to maximize the rate of economic growth.

The outcome of much of this type of analysis has been to show that the classical type of factors of production, even when redefined to take account of the greater technological sophistication of production today, does not fully explain the behavior of the growth of output. Technically, production-function analysis leaves an unexplained "residual" of economic growth that cannot be accounted for by the traditional inputs. By asking what *other* inputs can explain the behavior of output (gross national product), pioneers in this field have started investigating noneconomic changes in a society and their effect on output. For instance, in a study of economic growth in the United States of America, the National Bureau of Economic Research reached the conclusion that the increase of "conventional" inputs went only part of the way toward explaining the rate of growth. Aukrust's study of Norway and

Niitamo's of Finland reach the same conclusion.[1] Economists have therefore begun to explore the nature of the hidden inputs, which, together with the "conventional" inputs, will explain the behavior of these advanced economies. Thus, attention has been focused on what we may call "social inputs."

Put at its most simple the story is this. A well-educated, healthy, happy, politically contented work force is likely to be more productive than an illiterate, undernourished, miserable and politically discontented group of workers. Banal as this may sound, it has important implications. It means that when we are talking about economic growth we must not only talk about aid, or investment, or technology, but also about the quantity, quality and profile of education, about changes in the health provision for the population, changes in nutrition, changes in the infant mortality rate, in the deathrate and in the birthrate. Economists in this field are beginning to recognize the importance of taking into account these social inputs in the analysis of economic growth. So far, however, it has been impossible to define and quantify these inputs with sufficient precision to include them in the conventional mathematical schema used in economic planning.

Having conceded this much, economists well recognize that they will be under pressure from sociologists to concede yet more; for it is not only changes in what we may call the pattern of social development which affect economic growth: it is also in changes in, and the absolute level of, the social structure. Perhaps the best-known example of this is the extended family. To put it in simple terms: if a worker knows that if he works hard, becomes skilled and earns a relatively high wage, his mother and his sister and his cousins and his aunts will demand a share of the higher income, *the incentive* for him to acquire the skill and thereby the

---

[1] ODD AUKRUST: *Investments and Economic Growth.* . . . Copenhagen: 1958.
O. NIITAMO: "The Development of Productivity in Finnish Industry, 1925–1952." *Productivity Measurement Review,* Vol. 15, 1958, pp. 1–12.

wage is reduced. Thus, many commentators on the rate of growth of industrialization in Africa and in India have commented that the extended family system is one of the principal obstacles to improving the quality of the labor force and thereby increasing the national product.[2] This of course is only one example. Others would include the habit which the rural credit survey of India showed so clearly of very great expenditure in certain poor areas on status expenditures. Thus, in India, it is not unusual for a poor cultivator to spend nearly 10 per cent of a year's income on the marriage of a daughter or the funeral of a close relative.[3] With such high status expenditures, productive investment is unlikely to rise.

Another social structural pattern that affects the rate of growth of income per head is the pattern of landholding. It is well-known that in the underdeveloped countries, land is held in many ways, from a peasant owning a number of widely scattered small strips, in aggregate possibly only an acre or two, to the large landowner in Latin America owning huge estates, "haciendas," and farming these extensively and usually inefficiently. In an agricultural community the ownership of land is the very bedrock of the social structure. Yet many agricultural economists consider that the wasteful patterns of land tenure are one of the greatest obstacles to an increase in agricultural productivity—an increase which is a necessary precondition for industrialization.

In some ways similar to the pattern of landholdings is the pattern of income distribution. Economists are divided about the nature of the ideal income distribution. Some point out that the more unequal the distribution the greater the savings, and therefore the greater the potential productive investment and the greater the potential rate of growth of the economy. Others point out that from the fact that there is a rich elite, it does not follow

[2] See, e.g., P. T. ELLSWORTH: "Factors in the Economic Development of Ceylon," *American Economic Review*. Papers and Proceedings. Vol. 43, 1953, pp. 119–121.

[3] Reserve Bank of India. All-India Rural Credit Survey, Vol. I, Pt. 1. Bombay: 1956.

that more is in fact saved—and much less that more is in fact invested. The rich elite may spend vast sums on conspicuous consumption—building palatial homes, owning fleets of expensive cars —and may not encourage the productive capacity of the economy as a whole.

Lastly, it is clear from studies that have been conducted in very many underdeveloped countries that the pattern of religious observance can itself obstruct economic growth. It may be that the poor spend a disproportionate amount of their income in votive offerings or in maintaining some sort of clerical hierarchy. It may be that the religion concerned demands a disproportionate amount of their time. It may be that the religion puts taboos on certain activities—such as fertilizing the soil—which are obviously economically desirable.[4]

The Social Costs of Development

Economists are becoming increasingly aware that these structural obstacles and the social obstacles like lack of education, or high morbidity, or high mortality are as important in the process of economic development as the more conventional economic inputs. From this it follows that economists are coming to see that economic growth involves not only economic or financial cost but also a very considerable social cost. The financial costs of economic development are well-known. First, one must increase the productive capacity of the economy by investment. This involves the postponement of present consumption. The peasant cultivator must eat less today in order that he or his offspring may eat more tomorrow. In the same way, he must forego social benefits that the western

---

[4] G. T. BOUDES: "Point Four and Improved Standards of Living." *Annals of American Academy of Political and Social Science*. Vol. 268, 1950, pp. 140–147. For a different deleterious effect of religion, see MARJORIE TOPLEY: "Capital, Saving and Credit Among Indigenous Rice Farmers and Immigrant Vegetable Farmers in Hong Kong's New Territories," in *Capital, Saving and Credit in Peasant Societies*, R. FIRTH and B. S. VARMEY, eds. London: 1964, pp. 170–172.

countries have come to recognize as indispensable parts of the social order. Because the country must build a dam for a hydro-electric scheme the peasant must forego social security measures such as a national health service or an old age pension. Equally he must forego elaborate education for his children; he must forego an improvement in his housing and environmental sanitation, and also the security that comes with a system of unemployment benefits.

This much is well recognized. But if the peasant cultivator is going to make his contribution to economic growth he must also be prepared to accept the necessary adjustments to the social structure in which he has been brought up. These adjustments may be very far reaching. To take the example of the extended family again, anthropologists have shown that the extended family, so far from being a primitive social organization, is in fact a highly sophisticated, articulated form of social insurance.[5] If a member of the family falls on hard times, he can depend upon one of his relations, and sometimes a quite distant relation, to support him during this time. Within the system there are built checks and balances which guard against, on the one hand, undue wealth—reports from North India show how those who become too wealthy are brought back to the norm by the destruction of their property, not necessarily by jealous neighbors but by their friends and relations [6]— and, on the other, the abuse of the system by the idle and disorderly. Lacking a centralized, actuarially sound system of social security this extended family system vouchsafes to the peasant a degree of security that it would be expensive and administratively complex for the state to provide in a relatively underdeveloped society. Yet it is an obstacle to growth and (economists might suggest) must be superseded.

---

[5] J. L. CONHAIRE, "Economic Change and the Extended Family," *Annals of the American Academy of Political and Social Science.* Vol. 305, 1956, pp. 46–52.

[6] F. G. BAILY: "Capital, Saving and Credit in Highland Orissa, India," FIRTH and VARMEY, eds. *Op. cit.,* pp. 104–132.

The social functions of the marriage feast and death feast are equally intricate. Yet the rural credit survey of India has shown just how much this sort of observance is costing in terms of investment foregone in Indian agriculture. The economist bent on maximizing the rate of growth of income per head—and many regard this as their legitimate function—will therefore give as short shrift to this social institution as he will to the extended family.

He may equally be impatient of the high priority given to independence and leisure by the "peasant" or "primitive." In an agricultural society, the seasons impose a discipline: but, within that discipline, the cultivator can organize his own work so that it fits into the pattern of his whole life in the most congenial way. In a factory or mine, the discipline of the job is more rigorous, more alien and less personal.[7] Politically, too, heteronomy is substituted for autonomy. Instead of the tribal polity, which was often surprisingly democratic and of which each member could readily feel a part, centralized political institutions are established which impose on the country a series of choices. These centralized institutions are absolutely necessary if the rate of economic growth is to be maximized. The conflict is, then, between a form of heteronomy that will, *ceteris paribus,* yield a higher rate of growth, and autonomy, whether economic or political, that can be an obstacle to growth. If autonomy is intrinsically preferable, the choice to maximize the rate of economic development implies the "cost" of heteronomy.

There are other features of society not usually included in accounts of social structure which can also be shown to stand in the way of economic advance. One would be mobility. By mobility we mean not only geographical mobility but also occupational mo-

---

[7] On this theme, see A. O. HIRSCHMAN: *The Strategy of Economic Development.* Yale University Press, 1958, pp. 143–152. For a qualification of autonomy in primitive society, see R. FIRTH: *Primitive Polynesian Economy,* London, 1939. See, too, M. J. HERSKOVITS, "The Problem of Adapting Societies to New Tasks," in *The Progress of Underdeveloped Areas,* B. F. HOSELITZ, ed. Chicago: 1952.

bility. In Africa there have been numerous studies of migration many of which have revealed the strains and disequilibria generated by the recruitment of labor over a vast area for the mines of the Copperbelt and the Rand.[8] Here is an example of the cost of overcoming traditional immobility (in one sense at least) of the native for the ends of economic growth. These costs have been borne by the children and the womenfolk, and to some extent by the migrating laborers themselves, in terms of a disorganization of accepted, familiar patterns.

So far we have been concerned with analyzing and describing some of the costs involved in the process of economic development. These costs, financial and social, must be recognized for what they are. It is an illusion that growth can be had cheaply, or that economic growth and development is a painless and pleasurable experience. From this it follows that if economists, and more particularly Christian economists, put a high priority on economic growth they should be clear that they are advocating the payment of high costs. In another chapter in this volume, the author points out that the rich countries can reduce the costs of development to the developing countries by giving them grants and loans and also by stabilizing and if possible improving the terms of trade of the developing countries. Without the need to dissent at all from this view, it is also true that the proportion of even the economic costs that could be borne by the developing countries in the best of all possible worlds is relatively small; and by the nature of the case the developing countries must bear the social costs themselves.

The Goals of Economic Growth—Secular Redemption

There is here a further point. If costs have to be borne, most people would agree that they should be borne by those best able

[8] For an excellent summary of this subject in Mexico as well as Africa, see W. E. MOORE: *Industrialization and Labor: Social Aspects of Economic Development.* Ithaca: 1951.

to bear them. Until very recently this has not been the typical case. The paradigm example of the costs of development being borne by those least able to bear them was the economic development of Japan after the Meiji restoration. Even today there is no guarantee that the costs of development will be borne by those best able to bear them. Although many of the governments of the developing countries have been swept into power by a popular mandate, these governments often find it extremely difficult to apportion the costs of development on an equitable scale. Thus, it is no surprise to find the income distribution in many underdeveloped countries is very less equal than it is in the U. S. or in the U. K.[9] Perhaps more important both quantitatively and qualitatively than the distribution of income are the social costs of economic development which are usually borne almost exclusively by the lower strata of the society concerned. To return to the example of the extended family, urbanization and industrialization naturally undermine this institution; and the losers thereby are the former peasants (now perhaps unskilled industrial workers) who find themselves cut off from the one source of security that they knew hitherto. To reiterate, economic development involves costs, and there are few reasons for believing that typically they will be borne by those most able to bear them.

This may lead one to question the priority of economic growth. One may ask oneself whether economic growth and economic development is not becoming a new golden calf. The hysterical fascination that the rate of growth of income per head exerts in the U. S., the U. K., West Germany and France is infectious. One detects in successive national plans issued by the planning authorities in the underdeveloped countries an increasing emphasis upon the role of economic growth per se. In other words, there is a danger that economic growth, defined here as the rate of growth of real income per head, is becoming increasingly regarded as the *end* of

9 S. KUZNETS: "Economic Growth and Income Inequality," *American Economic Review*, Vol. 45, 1955.

economic activity. By making the rate of growth of income per head a fetish or a talisman, we are in danger of making it also the ultimate criterion by which everything else is judged. It may be that professional economists are peculiarly guilty of this trait. That is the effect of their discipline, especially perhaps of the more mathematical part of it. To evaluate every part of society by its contribution to increasing the rate of growth of real income per head is to confuse means with ends. The Christian can never agree with a slogan of four per cent per annum *at all costs*.

It is the task of the Christian economist, of the Christian social prophet, to insist that economic growth is a means and not an end. It is a means to what we may call secular redemption: the eradication of the environmental factors that limit and falsify and corrupt the human spirit. Disease, ignorance, superstition, boredom and monotony—these are the cankers of the human spirit which economic and social development should strive to eradicate. Reductions in mortality and morbidity, the availability of higher education (in both technology and the humanities) to all who want it, the satisfaction of a varied, challenging and stimulating job— these are the redemptive ends of economic activity. It is in these directions that the economist and the development planner can go a little toward the re-creation of the fullness of man.

The possibility of imperfect development—that is, a pattern of development in which social development is not commensurate with economic—has already been recognized.[10] The analysis of it, however, is exceedingly complex; for if we are to talk of imperfect development, it is clear that we must have some norm that may be described as perfect development and we must be able to measure the deviation of any one society from the perfect norm. So far this has not been possible. Despite attempts to quantify social variables like education, health and nutrition it has been quite

---

[10] Especially by Prof. JAN DREWNOWSKI of the United Nations Research Institute for Social Development, Geneva. Much of this paper has been illuminated by discussions with him.

impossible to quantify many structural variables that we have already seen are an integral part of the whole process of economic development. So there are here two problems—first, the definition of a norm of development, that is, a definition of a pattern of development in which the growth of social indices is commensurate with economic growth: and, second, the construction of an index of social development.[11]

To these two methodological difficulties is added an analytical one. Work done in connection with the report on the world's social situation of 1961 and the research activity inspired by that report has shown not only that social development is a precondition of economic development—for it is an input as well as an output—but also that the analysis of the relationship between economic growth and social development is complicated, and between leads and lags. There is some evidence, and future research will almost certainly produce more, that in the very early stages of development social inputs, the improvements in education and health, housing and security have no significant effect upon economic development.[12] But there comes a time when the stock of these social indices has built up to such an extent that economic growth becomes possible. Thereafter the rate of economic growth exceeds the rate of growth of the social indices. Ultimately, there comes a time when the social indices, perhaps best viewed now as consumption rather than investment, accelerate and in fact grow faster than real income per head. This is a very schematic and provisional account of the leads and lags in the system. But it does show that given a fairly long view it is extremely difficult to isolate one pattern of imperfect development, for one may wish to condemn as a case of imperfect development an economy in which income per head is rising very fast though the social indices rise only

---

[11] Methodologically, the concept of commensurateness is, of course, far from clear.

[12] See *Report on the World Social Situation*, United Nations. New York: p. 40–62.

slowly. However, it may well be that in this economy it is necessary to hold down the rate of growth of social development at this stage in order that there may be greater wealth in the economy in future as a basis for extending the social development in the ensuing periods.

For these reasons it may be extremely difficult to identify patterns of imperfect development except at the extremes. We have already seen that Japan in the late nineteenth century was almost certainly an example of imperfect development and there are many people who would say that the same was true of Russia in the interwar period. Although figures from China are notoriously unreliable, the evidence we have goes a long way toward suggesting that there too is a clear example of imperfect development, even given the complications of the leads and lags.[13]

This then is one whole series of problems; namely, how to plan development in such a way that it does not put exclusive emphasis on the rate of growth of real income per head but appreciates that the end of economic activity is the liberation of man from the corrupting and distorting effects of poverty in the widest sense. The other big problem that faces economists working in this field today may be dealt with more briefly. Economists have become increasingly aware, as we have already seen, that it is futile to deal with economic parameters in isolation from the social and political structure in which they exist. To give a banal example, it is silly to talk about consumption, investment and wages in the U. S. in exactly the same way as one describes and handles these concepts in the Philippines or in Korea. When the economist takes the wider view outlined above he finds the difficulties compounded, for he is no longer dealing with a manageable quantifiable and analyzable series of parameters that can be fed into a mathematical model which will describe reasonably accurately their operational interdependence: but he is dealing with social and sociological

---

[13] For less extreme variations of social and economic development, see *Report on the World Social Situation, loc. cit.* in preceding footnote.

structural variables that may be quantifiable but that are very much less easy to analyze in terms of interdependence. The experience of educational planning since the war and very recently the experience of health planning have shown to what extent the disaggregation of a society (very useful for analyzing the microproblems in any one discipline) can distort the over-all picture. Take, for example, the eradication of malaria. Most people would say that it is extremely desirable to eradicate malaria from any one region and indeed from the whole world. But a whole series of disequilibria results from the eradication of malaria. Population increases and in an area that is short of land this almost certainly means that income per head falls. *Ceteris paribus,* this results in falling nutrition and therefore increasing morbidity and perhaps increasing mortality. It also results in the impoverishment of a region and therefore in a decrease, perhaps, in the provision of educational facilities and the range of consumer goods available to each family. Or to take another example, this time, from the field of educational planning. Most people, certainly until very recently, regarded the provision of education in underdeveloped countries as a very high priority. As traditionally one of the major providers of education in many underdeveloped regions, the churches responded by increasing the number of primary and secondary schools. In many countries universal primary education became a political rallying cry, with the result that education was provided, but with too little attention paid not only to the needs of the economy but also to the possibilities of suitable employment for the graduates of the educational system. This mass provision of education, though perfectly laudable in one sense, has been catastrophic in another, for the schools have produced literates, and to a lesser extent graduates from higher education, whose value systems have been completely changed by the educational process, and who now despise and reject the life and ambience of their parents. They look for jobs in the cities with a high status value. Not only are these jobs usually of very little economic value: they are also usually in short supply.[14] A very serious problem arises, particularly in Africa and India, of the unemployment of literates and even of university graduates. This sort of imbalance is wasteful of very scarce economic resources. Paradoxically, it is also a direct denial of the brief that the development economist should give himself—namely to increase the level of living of the population or, to put it in more religious terms, to initiate the secular redemption of mankind.

Concerns of the Church in Economic Growth

Now there are many signs that planners and economists, educationalists and public officials are becoming aware of these problems. The worst mistakes in planning of all sorts that have resulted in the sort of disequilibria we have described are unlikely to be made on the same scale. Nonetheless, economists must admit that they have so far failed very largely to forge the analytical tools that enable planners to take account of the fact that a society is a structured organism which demands to be treated as a whole and not as an aggregate of its parts. However, recent advances in the field of econometrics and in the exploration of interdisciplinary studies between sociologists and economists suggest that the sort of analytical framework that is required will be provided in time.

The supreme optimism of the early classical economists about the underdeveloped countries has evaporated in the heat of the economic and political difficulties of these countries since the Second World War. We have come to recognize that economic development implies costs of all sorts for everyone. It is not part of this essay to stress the need for the developed to reduce these costs to a minimum: that is done elsewhere in this volume. We conclude by

---

[14] See B. F. HOSELITZ: "The Recruitment of White Collar Workers in Underdeveloped Countries," *International Social Science Bulletin,* Vol. 6, 1954, pp. 433–442.

pointing out the areas in which the church and Christian laymen should make their influence felt.

First, we suggest that Christian concern should be expressed in an effort to ensure that the costs of economic development are borne (insofar as is consistent with a politically acceptable rate of economic growth) by those who are best able to bear them. This is particularly relevant in Latin America and the Middle East, but it is not irrelevant in Southeast Asia and in Africa—witness the rumpus about the scales of remuneration of the political elite in Nigeria.

A second concern of Christians is the easing of the social pains and stresses involved in the transition from an agrarian, peasant economy to a modern, industrial society. Sufficient has been said of this elsewhere to make further comment superfluous. The position of the Bantu in South African townships and the appalling poverty and squalor encountered by the perceptive observer in nearly every big city in every underdeveloped country has stirred Christian conscience deeply. We must question whether the scale of activity in this field has been even remotely commensurate with the scale of the problem.

Third, reverting to the concept of imperfect development Christians should be concerned to ensure, if necessary by political action, that economic growth—that is, increase in income per head —does not become a fetish but that the increase in the wealth of the community is reflected in increases in the welfare of the community. This is nearly tantamount to saying that Christians should ensure that when an economy begins to develop it is the most needy who are served first from the increasing wealth.

These three issues apply primarily to Christians in underdeveloped countries. Two further points apply to Christians in the developed countries. The first is obvious: it is only repeated here because it is so fundamental. If economic and social development is part of the divine process of secular redemption, then Christians will be anxious to facilitate that development. This means that they will exert every kind of pressure, including concerted political pressure, to ensure that aid from the developed countries to the developing countries is not only improved in terms of quantity but also in terms of quality.[15]

The second suggestion is a little more abstract. Economists and even development economists sometimes find themselves in an ethical vacuum. They realize, sometimes acutely, that they who in many respects are least competent to make value judgments are faced with difficult, normative decisions. It is easy for them to retreat into a world of mathematical formulae in which they can measure the productivity of expenditures in certain fields. To take an example: it may be possible either to improve education or to wipe out malaria. Technically, though perhaps not practically, it would be possible to compute the productivity—that is, the increase in production—brought about by each of these two investments. However, many economists realize the inhumanity and superficiality of this type of approach. What they are often looking for is some kind of ethical criterion by which to judge the possibilities presented to them. Of course, it is not their job in theory to make these decisions; but, because the planning mechanism is becoming at once more complex and less articulated, economists and development planners often find themselves faced with this sort of dilemma. What I am pleading for is a much greater sensitivity on behalf of Christians to the difficulties facing professional economists. This is not, emphatically not, a plea for the "Christianizing" of economics or for bringing God in through the back door of development plans. What is required is a sensitivity to the problems facing people who work in these fields, a readiness to discuss them without laying down dogmatic Christian "answers" and a readiness to accept that the economist, although surrounded by a positive, indicative analytical framework, can yet be, and very often is, an agent of the secular redemption of mankind.

---

[15] For a short but penetrating critique of the quality of aid, see I. M. D. LITTLE: *Aid to Africa*. ODI. London: 1964.

16

THE ROMAN CATHOLIC CHURCH AND ECONOMIC PLANNING—AT THE NATIONAL AND INTERNATIONAL LEVEL

by Abbé François Houtart
and A. Delobelle (Belgium)

*The Question of Economic Planning
in the Roman Catholic Church*

QUESTIONS concerning planning and underdevelopment have only recently been included in the social teaching of the Roman Catholic Church (not at all until the last years of Pius XII, and not substantially until the great encyclicals of John XXIII). Earlier similar concerns were formulated in quite different terms, more closely related to the politico-social structures that existed before 1960.

Within the general setting of the papal doctrine of social justice, we find the first indications of a planned national economic policy in the analyses of the principle of "the fair wage" and of the type of economic order that it requires, in the analyses of an international economic policy, and also in the documents concerning the obligations of the colonizing countries toward the colonized. Admittedly the problems of planning and of mutual aid at the international level still seem to be of secondary importance. But these documents do contain a complete doctrine of economic relationships in national or international life. The problems of the national economy are already examined in the light of technical considerations, whereas the sphere of international economic relations is dealt with only at the level of first principles.

This situation is the sociological outcome of the strong ties that still existed at that time between the Roman Catholic Church and the western world, especially Europe. The economic and social questions dealt with by the Popes were essentially questions which arose out of the industrial societies of the West, with their own particular social pathology and their own characteristics. The economic and social problems in the rest of the world were usually dealt with from the viewpoint of western experience, and the ethical principles applied to them were extensions of the principles applied in the West. Consequently, Roman Catholic social doctrine was primarily derived from the Christian analysis of the position of the wage earners in Europe, and touched only indirectly, when political reports were drawn up by the European colonists, upon what is today called the problem of underdevelopment in other continents. The attention of the Popes seems to have been drawn to this question in the first place in connection with the problem of the indigenous clergy. The question came up again after the Second World War when the former colonial countries in Asia became independent because the ecclesiastical structures had to be separated from the political and economic structures imposed by the colonizing countries.[1]

---

[1] Older papal documents could be quoted, however, concerning the slave trade and the liberation of slaves.

It was on the occasion of the encyclical *Evangelii praecones,* published on June 2, 1950, by Pope Pius XII, that concern for the underdeveloped countries was clearly expressed for the first time. But it was in his encyclical *Fidei donum* of April 21, 1957, that Pius XII definitely and explicitly introduced this question into his teaching. He reverted to it several times in his public addresses.[2] It was Pope John XXIII, however, who brought a new light to bear on the problem in his encyclicals *Mater et Magistra* and *Pacem in Terris,* though the space specifically devoted to underdevelopment is still relatively small and the principles are set forth largely from a western point of view. It is mainly due to the spirit that inspires these two encyclicals that the social doctrine about underdevelopment has been, as it were, renewed and given a fresh start within the Roman Catholic Church. Since then an increasing number of the pastoral letters written by the different conferences of bishops in the underdeveloped countries have taken up the problem and examined it in relation to their various national settings.[3]

Although the theme of underdevelopment has thus been included in the social teaching of the Popes its importance has been greatly strengthened by the changes that are now taking place within the Roman Catholic Church as a general consequence of the spirit of the Second Vatican Council, and especially of the presence at it of many bishops from underdeveloped countries. Consequently the approach of our church to the world can no longer be solely from the West, but will be far more universal in outlook. A social process is going on within the Roman Catholic Church parallel with the process of decolonization in the political world. It ex-

---

[2] See J. Y. CALVEZ and J. PERRIN: *Eglise et société économique. L'enseignement social des Papes de Léon XIII à Pie XII* (1878–1958). Paris: Aubier, 2nd edition revised and corrected, 1961, pp. 139–140.

[3] See Father HOUTART and A. DELOBELLE: "Doctrine sociale de l'Eglise catholique romaine et les problèmes du sous-développement" in *Background Information,* WCC, Geneva, June/July, 1964.

presses at the summit a movement which has been taking place for a long time at the local level, through the creation of indigenous bishops and clergy in the young churches.

On the one hand, therefore, we have a clearly defined doctrine concerning the economic relationships and the social life within the countries based on the pattern of the industrialized countries of the West. On the other hand, we have the first judgments and the expression of certain principles concerning international economic relations and the specific social problems of the underdeveloped countries themselves. In order to be understood, the attitude of the Roman Catholic Church to problems of national or international economic planning must be seen from this sociological, dynamic and historical point of view. This means that, where possible, many problems should be treated by analogy with the situations described in the existing papal documents. But this social doctrine also benefits from the current thinking in the church; many of the documents written by bishops contain preliminary answers, which await the papal sanction. In addition to the teaching of the bishops, the Vatican Council and the Pope, the analytical work undertaken by Roman Catholic experts—clergy or laymen—must be taken into account. Although their conclusions do not enjoy the same authority as pronouncements by the hierarchy, they constitute a basic element of the church's social doctrine, as a part of the dynamic whole in which the authority of the church, the clergy and the laity all have their place.

The Doctrinal Point of View and Planning

In order to simplify the statement of principles, we shall distinguish between the two fields to which they are applied: the national and the international. Although the points of approach remain the same as far as principles are concerned, the ways in which they are discussed and presented are different.

350

A. *The State and National Economic Planning.* National economic planning is joint action, undertaken at different levels and under different names, drawn up by the public authorities and carried out under their supervision, general or direct, with a view to improving the economic and social development of an area or of a whole country. The church has not hitherto directly stated its position with regard to planning and methods of planning; but through the Popes it has stipulated certain conditions and ethical rules that should be observed by the public authorities of all states when carrying out their tasks. These rules, which are inspired by a basic personalism, were laid down in a general way as they applied to states with a liberal or democratic structure, but they also apply to states whose structure is more authoritarian. And whatever the political structure of the country, they remain fundamentally valid for all types of economic planning, from the most rigid systems to the most flexible. The Roman Catholic Church has formulated the rule of subsidiarity (of which we shall speak later) as a fundamental principle which applies to them all.

1. *Conditions for action by the public authorities*

a. *Respect for the common good:* The acts prescribed by the authorities must be

> formally perfect, the content ... must be morally good, or at least capable of being directed towards good. Indeed, since the whole reason for the existence of civil authorities is the realization of the common good, it is clearly necessary that, in pursuing this objective, they should respect its essential elements, and at the same time conform their laws to the needs of a given historical situation.[4]

This general rule also applies both to the public authorities and to all the physical or juridical persons of which society is composed,

---

[4] Encyclical Letter *Pacem in Terris of* POPE JOHN XXIII. Vatican: Polyglot Press, 1963, p. 17.

who are engaged in political, economic or any other form of action. "All individual citizens and intermediate groups are under an obligation to make their specific contributions to the common welfare." [5]

It is also made clear that the common good, which is the common goal of the action of the individual, the social organization and the state, "embraces the sum total of those conditions of social living whereby men are enabled to achieve their own integral perfection more fully and more easily." [6] The social encyclicals of the previous Popes from Leo XII to Pius XII had frequently defined these conditions of social living, and how they should be envisaged from the economic point of view. [7]

b. *Principle of subsidiarity:* In actual fact these general principles draw attention to certain stipulations according to whether one is in a developed or an underdeveloped country. Obviously, in the latter the public authorities have a primary role to play in implanting a modern type of economy, especially in the initial phases. In some of the least favored countries, there is nothing between a few political, social or economic leaders on the one hand and the illiterate masses still living in an independent economy on the other. Between these two levels hardly any social groups exist at all. Owing to this absence of specialized intermediary organizations, and to the rudimentary organization of the leaders and the *elite,* all the problems, whether social or economic, assume a political hue. In most of the underdeveloped countries, therefore, even when the internal structures are more developed, the state exercises an indispensable function in regard to initiative and organization.

None of the papal documents has hitherto dealt directly with the problem, although some of the episcopal letters refer specifically to the necessity for the public authorities to take the initiative in

---

[5] *Ibid.,* p. 17.
[6] Encyclical Letter *Mater et Magistra* of POPE JOHN XXIII, quoted in *Pacem in Terris,* p. 18.
[7] See J. Y. CALVEZ and J. PERRIN: *op. cit.*

certain spheres, especially with regard to agrarian reforms.[8] How ever, in the teaching of the Popes a general rule is found for these matters in which the initiative of the state is dominant; this is the principle of *subsidiarity*. It was affirmed by Pius XI in *Quadra gesimo Anno* (1931) and was stressed again by John XXIII in *Mater et Magistra*.

Although the public authorities have at their disposal methods and instruments that are being increasingly perfected to reduce the economic discrepancies between the different areas of a country, or between different sectors of economic or social life, they are still subject to the rights of the individual.

But the principle must always be reaffirmed that the presence of the State in the economic field, no matter how widespread and penetrating, must not be exercised so as to reduce evermore the sphere of freedom of the personal initiative of individual citizens, but rather so as to guarantee in that sphere the greatest possible scope by the effective protection for each and all, of the essential personal rights; among which is to be numbered the right that individual persons possess of being always primarily responsible for their own upkeep and that of their own family.[9]

In this the Pope fully recognizes the right of the public authorities to take the initiative in the economic field, and to move on to planned development. The important point, in these matters, is not to confuse the end with the means.

c. *The phenomenon of socialization:* The Popes have been dealing with this phenomenon for a long time, but it was John XXIII who drew attention to it by giving it a special name. By "socialization" he means: "A progressive multiplication of relations in society with different forms of life and activity, and juridical institutionalization." [10] This is a specific feature of socioeconomic

---

[8] See, for instance, for Latin America, the documents published by the Bishops in Venezuela, Sept. 16, 1960; in Chile, Sept. 18, 1962; in Paraguay, April 28, 1963, and in Brazil, April 30, 1963.

[9] *Mater et Magistra*, p. 14.

[10] *Ibid.*, p. 14.

development, and the Pope points out that the public authorities side by side with private initiative play an important role in extending it. He recognizes the many social and economic advantages of this assumption by the growing number of organizations in public life. But at the same time the Pope asks that the individual should not be crushed beneath their weight, and that these "intermediary bodies" should enjoy "effective autonomy" in face of the public authorities, so that they can "pursue their own specific interests in loyal collaboration between themselves, subordinate, however, to the demands of the common good." [11]

Such principles are clearly important in evaluating forms of planning in the underdeveloped countries. However, they describe the situation in countries which already enjoy a certain level of development, and in which private initiative is beginning to operate.

2. *Functions of the public authorities*

In his social encyclicals John XXIII also draws attention to the aims of action by the public authorities. The first of these aims corresponds to the primary function of protecting the individual, which is still valid today, but which formerly constituted the essential task of the state. The second aim, the promotion of the person, corresponds to the modern concepts of the state's economic and social role. It is important to affirm this dual function, in order to evaluate the forms of economic planning.

a. *Reconciliation and protection of rights and duties of individuals:*

One of the fundamental duties of civil authorities, therefore, is to coordinate social relations in such fashion that the exercise of one man's rights does not threaten others in the exercise of their own rights nor hinder them in the fulfilment of their duties. Finally, the rights of all should be effectively safeguarded and, if they have been violated, completely restored.[12]

---

[11] *Ibid.*, p. 16.
[12] *Pacem in Terris,* p. 18.

b. *Duty of promoting the rights of individuals:*

It is also demanded by the common good that civil authorities should make earnest efforts to bring about a situation in which individual citizens can easily exercise their rights and fulfil their duties as well. For experience has taught us that, unless these authorities take suitable action with regard to economic, political and cultural matters, inequalities between the citizens tend to become more and more widespread . . . and as a result human rights are rendered totally ineffective, and the fulfilment of duties is compromised.[13]

In this connection the Pope emphasizes that the public authorities have an obligation to concern themselves with the social and economic conditions in their sphere. On this point he mentions the substructure (roads and communications, drinking-water, housing, hospitals, schools, churches, leisure), the insurance systems, all the services which deal with employment (recruitment of workers, fair wages, coresponsibility in enterprises, associations of all kinds connected with work) and cultural services.

3. *Conclusions at the national level*

Although the basic principles for the general evaluation of systems of economic planning can be found in the social teaching of the Popes, we lack certain details required for their application to the developing countries.

We have already shown the extent to which this social doctrine is still largely dominated by the example of the countries in the industrial West. But even so, many of these statements have a certain relevance to the underdeveloped countries, because of their preference for crafts or home industries rather than for gigantic enterprises. However, the papal documents do not always recognize the difference in economic utility between the two, nor the possibility of forming human groupings within such great combines —a development that tends to restore to these latter their human

---

[13] *Ibid.,* p. 19.

dimension. But on this point, if a certain confusion still exists, there are a large number of papal documents which express support for co-management and the transformation of the enterprises and social organizations into associations of responsible collaborators.

There remain, however, certain problems that have been directly tackled by the leaders in the underdeveloped countries, and that have not yet been officially or adequately dealt with by the doctrinal authority of the Roman Catholic Church. Among these are the questions of the concentration of landed property, of the population explosion and of the control of capital and its utilization for the benefit of the country.

B. *The State and International Economic Relations*. The mutual obligation of states to respect one another constitutes an ancient principle in the political doctrine of the Roman Catholic Church, because all men are linked by their common origin, nature and destiny. Moreover, just as a "common good" exists at the national level, so it also exists at the international level. It is a basic principle of social doctrine that the good things of this world are intended for everyone. This approach opens the way to international planning.

One of the consequences of this last principle is precisely that individual economic advantages are subordinated to the common good of the political communities.

These two principles (the community of nations and the fact that the wealth of this world is intended for all men) give rise to two rights: first, the right for people and goods to circulate freely (in the past this has been used to justify certain forms of colonization, on the pretext that political protection and security must be ensured for people and goods); and, second, the duty of the developed countries to aid those which are still underdeveloped. Thus, the universal utilization of wealth which indirectly justified the colonization of certain countries (still incapable of exploiting their own natural wealth) forces the rich countries in a much stricter and more general way to help the poor ones.

356

This doctrine (that the wealth created by God for all men must be equitably available to all, in accordance with the principles of justice and charity), while recognizing that everyone has the right of access to the wealth of the earth, also establishes an equally natural right in international relations—the right to social justice which makes it incumbent upon the more fortunate peoples to help the less fortunate countries. Consequently adequate study of the relations between population-density and means of subsistence must be developed on a world-wide scale, and the problem which it involves can only be solved on the same plane, in the solidarity which operates between all peoples. So that when the artificial barriers which divide them are removed, a more systematic movement of peoples, capital and material wealth may be organized.[14]

Thus, although in the past, when no high international authority existed, the church accepted certain rights of interference by particular states in developing the wealth of underdeveloped countries (without actually going so far as to affirm the right to colonization), its main concern was to formulate the duties of the colonizers toward the colonized countries. These duties included respect for the indigenous culture, since the fact that all men are linked by a common origin, nature and destiny does not mean that anyone has the right to impose cultural uniformity. There is also an obligation to pay fair salaries, by adapting to local conditions the legislation passed in the western countries. Lastly, there is the right of the underdeveloped countries to aspire to independence and the duty of the colonizing states to prepare them for it, in accordance with the general welfare, at the international level.

This social doctrine, inspired by the political supremacy of the West (especially of western Europe) over the rest of the world, remains valid in its basic principles, even after the process of decolonization and the radical transformation of the political scene since the Second World War.

---

[14] MGR MONTINI, at the social week in Palermo. Quoted in G. BLARDONE, P. CATRICE, J. FOLLIET, G. MATAGRIN, R. PADIRAC, R. VOOG: *Initiation aux problèmes d'outre-mer. Colonisation, décolonisation, sous-développement.* Lyons: Editions de la Chronique sociale de France, p. 259.

Something far more important than a change of vocabulary is involved. Behind the basic principles, which remain the same, a vast development is taking place in the social doctrine of the church in relation to the specific problem of underdevelopment. The Vatican Council's schema on the relations between the church and the world have a special section on this question.

Indeed, although the process of political decolonization is almost complete, the economic decolonization of the ex-colonial areas, and especially the radical readjustment of international commerce (in which the influence of western domination is still very strong), are still far from realization. And it is within this context that one can envisage the social thinking of the church taking shape in connection with international economic aid. Just as the church refused to leave the fixing of wages to the free play of supply and demand on the market, so today the church cannot agree to fix the remuneration of the poor peoples in the world simply through the mechanism of an anonymous market. Some of the Popes' previous statements have already been largely on these lines. In *Quadragesimo Anno* Pius XI wrote: "The free play of competition cannot be expected to bring about a well-organized economic régime." [15] Just as the employer has a moral responsibility to fix a fair wage that covers the social needs of the workers, the states that control international commerce have strict moral obligations toward the poorer countries, including the duty to remunerate them adequately so as to ensure their social development.

The doctrinal statements which have already been made by the church, especially by John XXIII, relate essentially to the conditions for, and certain aims of, external aid.

1. *Conditions for external aid*

The encyclicals draw attention to four conditions which should be borne in mind by the more-developed countries, when helping the less-developed:

---

[15] Quoted by J. Y. CALVEZ and J. PERRIN: *op. cit.*, p. 385.

a. *Concern for full development:* Here John XXIII was especially anxious that certain errors committed in the past be avoided, since they had been fraught with serious consequences that influenced the social development of the more developed countries for a very long time. The states must be concerned both about economic and about social development, since the one cannot exist without the other. The process of development must be both harmonious and gradual—a fact that must be borne in mind in the process of development. It will simultaneously affect every sector of economic life: primary, secondary or tertiary. It must produce an equitable distribution of wealth.[16]

b. *Disinterested work:* The bigger temptation with which the economically developed communities have to struggle is that of profiting from their technical and financial cooperation so as to influence the political situation of the less developed countries with a view to bringing about plans of world domination. It is, therefore, indispensable and corresponds to the need of justice that the above mentioned technical and financial aid be given in sincere political disinterestedness.[17]

Otherwise this would be tantamount to neocolonialism and would strike an irreparable blow to the formation of a world community "in which each member, whilst conscious of its own individual right and duties, will work in a relationship of equality towards the attainment of the universal common good." [18] John XXIII attached so much importance to this point of view, and to the need to avoid forms of aid which would be counter to it, that he reverted to it over and over again: "It is vitally important, therefore, that the wealthier States, in providing varied forms of assistance to the poorer, should . . . avoid any intention of political domination." [19] The peoples must be "conscious of their own duties and rights,

---

[16] *Mater et Magistra,* p. 38.
[17] *Ibid.,* p. 39.
[18] *Pacem in Terris,* p. 31.
[19] *Ibid.*

working on a basis of equality for the bringing about of the universal common good." [20] This is a clear reminder, at the international level, of the principle of subsidiarity already stressed at the national level.

c. *Respect for the characteristics of the individual communities:* Respect for others must be observed in international relations, as much as in relations between individuals. That is an old principle which has already been affirmed many times, especially in connection with the relations between colonizers and colonized peoples. The new vocabulary is transposed in view of the new context: "The political communities on the way toward economic development generally present their own unmistakable individuality, due either to their resources and the specific character of their own natural environment, or due to their traditions frequently abounding in human values, or due to the typical quality of their own members." [21] Every people is called upon to make its own special contribution to the world society that is coming to birth. Its own special values must therefore be respected and not destroyed by borrowing from other peoples (whether under compulsion or not).

d. *Respect for the hierarchy of values:* In the process and policies of raising the standard of living by means of economic development or scientific and technical progress, it must be remembered that "scientific and technical progress . . . are not . . . the supreme values . . . but are essentially instrumental in character." [22]

On this point the Pope condemns the neglect, or negation, of spiritual values in the most developed countries, and the way in which these values are sacrificed to scientific, technical and economic factors or to material wealth: "This constitutes an insidious poison, and one of the most dangerous, in the help which the economically developed peoples can give to those on the way to development: people in whom ancient tradition has quite often pre-

[20] *Mater et Magistra,* p. 39.
[21] *Ibid.*
[22] *Ibid.*

served a living and operating consciousness of some of the most important human values." [23] John XXIII has no hesitation in saying, "to undermine this consciousness is essentially immoral." [24]

2. Functions of external aid

On this point the Pope draws a distinction between long-term and short-term objectives and problems.

a. *Short-term aid:* This refers essentially to needs that require urgent assistance, and John XXIII is thinking primarily of the chronic famines in the underdeveloped countries. He contrasts them with the surplus of consumer goods (especially agricultural products) in the more developed countries. However, though fully realizing that a surplus in production (especially in agriculture) may "cause economic harm to a certain portion of the population" in a state, the Pope makes it clear that "this is not a motive for exonerating oneself (in the developed countries) from the obligation of extending emergency aid to the indigent and hungry." [25] The principle that the wealth of the world is intended for all men suffices to explain the moral obligation incumbent upon countries that have a surplus to share it. On the other hand, the principle of subsidiarity could be invoked, to prevent this surplus being distributed in such a way as to destroy the national or local efforts of the poor country to provide for its own needs.

b. *Long-term aid:* This emergency aid is not sufficient "to eliminate, or even to reduce, the causes which . . . bring about a permanent state of want, misery and hunger" [26] in many countries. Other methods must therefore be sought, and the Pope is thinking in the first place of cooperatives.

These cooperatives could give those inhabitants who have the necessary qualifications the technical and scientific advice that they

---

[23] *Ibid.*
[24] *Mater et Magistra*, p. 40.
[25] *Ibid.*, p. 37.
[26] *Ibid.*

need, and the capital required to initiate and to speed up their economic development. But in addition to these forms of basic community development, the Pope also refers to many initiatives (both public and private) begun by the more developed countries for the purpose of helping the less developed. Among these the Pope mentions the granting of study-scholarships to young people from those countries, so that they can come for training to the specialized schools and universities of the more-developed countries. He also mentions the granting of capital by the World Bank, by the wealthy countries or by individuals, and investments effected in the developing countries.

3. *Conclusions concerning international aid*

However, the various forms of external aid (some of which are mentioned in the papal documents) are far from adequate, either in the scope that they have hitherto attained or in their present aims or even in their form. It is not the Pope's task to define what form such aid should take. He can only indicate certain basic moral principles. However, he aptly points out "that the scientific, technical and economic cooperation between the economically developed political communities and those just beginning or on the way to development needs to be increased beyond the present level." [27] And he concludes: "It is our hope that such a development will characterize their dealings during the next decades." [28] This reflection and this conclusion leave the way open for the church's social doctrine to develop significantly in regard to the different problems of underdevelopment and the obligations of the industrialized countries. The insights of Pope John XXIII are like the opening of an entirely new chapter.[29]

---

[27] *Mater et Magistra,* p. 38.
[28] *Ibid.*
[29] On this subject it is remarkable to note that the book of J. Y. CALVEZ and J. PERRIN, mentioned above, still contains, even in the revised edition, only a few paragraphs on economic underdevelopment and the international aid for which it calls.

However, this chapter can take the form only of a dialogue with the actual evolution of international economic relations. And during the next few years these relations are bound to be influenced by the demands of the underdeveloped countries for a fairer system of international trade, in which the industrialized countries will no longer exercise almost supreme authority, and in which the conditions for exchange will not be fixed in such a way as to enrich the developed countries and to drain the poorer countries of their resources.[30]

It is becoming clearer every day that the development of the underdeveloped countries cannot be adequately assured through bilateral financial aid or through international bodies (with or without interest, reimbursable or nonreimbursable). And in addition to financial or technical aid, the mere stabilization of the price of materials is not sufficient, because the resulting returns would themselves be inadequate (in addition to the fact that many of these products can in future be produced synthetically by the industrialized countries themselves). Thus, the policy which must be envisaged is the opening-up of the markets in the industrialized countries to the manufactured products of the developing countries. Having accepted the reform of the political structures, the countries of the West will have to accept the reform of the international economic structures. And this reform certainly cannot take the form of a free market. It will have to introduce some system that will benefit the underdeveloped countries, to the temporary detriment of the more developd, and this will involve planning on an international scale.

The church's social doctrine will have to take all this into account during the coming years, and this will quite normally involve considering the principles and methods to be applied to this

---

[30] See J. Y. CALVEZ: "Justice dans le commerce avec le Tiers-Monde," in *Revue de l'Action Populaire*, Paris, No. 177, April, 1964, pp. 396–408; R. SCHEYVAN: "Pourquoi l'aide aux pays sous-développés est-elle mal partie?" *La Revue Nouvelle*, Tournai, July/Aug., 1964, pp. 3–19.

new joint international economy, i.e. an economy that is planned to an extent, and in ways which are difficult to foresee, but in which the international organizations will play an increasingly important part, in addition to the "zones of preference" that groups of nations may organize among themselves, and the agreements that they arrange separately. The increasing interest shown by the Popes in the great international organizations already points in this direction.

Duties and Rights in Planning

A. *The Acceptance of a Planned Society.* Since the creation (of the world) was not accomplished all at once, but is still being carried out progressively by God in history, man is associated in this process in his own modest way, according to his ability, within his own sphere. And within this historical process there is a kind of principle that is progressively unifying what was dispersed. Whether through competition or through fellowship, on the basis of rights or of duties, men are gradually feeling more and more linked by a common destiny, and are realizing that they are participating in building their own future. Whereas formerly each separate society sought its own destiny, today everything is combining to make them seek together for their common destiny. And whereas in former times the effort to attain a high level of civilization normally took the form of empirical groping (through trial and error), today information has been accumulated so that the way is gradually becoming clearer. God, who gave mankind control over the mineral, vegetable and animal spheres, also gave men the intellectual ability to gain control of their earthly destiny. It is for mankind to overcome the obstacles in their way and to control themselves, in the freedom that God has deliberately granted to them in his love as he patiently waits for them to do so. Thus, mankind responds to God's call both by accumulating information and experience, and by extending its activities, even if original sin does make its efforts ambivalent.

It is within this general perspective that men are called to more extensive planning of societies. Christianity as a whole, and the Roman Catholic Church in particular, cannot withdraw from the struggle. In addition to carrying out its spiritual mission among men, the church has also the indirect mission of helping to bring about the form of secular society best suited to meet the needs of men and to ensure their natural development, as well as their spiritual growth.[31]

B. *The Limits of Planning.* Although men are called to introduce more and more rationality into their societies, certain aspects of their life remain independent of rational calculation (without being irrational). This applies to certain spheres the importance of which is due precisely to the fact that they are worldwide. There is, for example, the function performed by the family in creating balanced personality. Although the family forms an integral part of the worldwide society, through its activities and its dimensions, and must be harmoniously integrated into that society, it is equally true that the family exercises a special function—that of protecting its members and developing them through the wealth of its intimate life. Now socioeconomic planning at this level destroys what is essential for the exercise of these functions, and everything that gives the family universal validity. That is why the principle of subsidiarity (which establishes a kind of ladder of confidence in the social process, and which preserves as its central concern the person, and the elementary forms of social life) must be retained as the guide to economic and social planning.

We must therefore bear in mind the inadequacy of our information, both about the elements themselves that have to be considered and about the criteria for the decisions to be taken. Here again, whatever the value of the previous studies, of the experts called in, or of the executive bodies, the principle of *subsidiarity* retains its full original validity. This is indispensable; for, as the

---

[31] See FR. HOUTART: *Eglise et Monde,* Paris: Editions du Cerf, 1964.

methods and resources available increase, the danger of making mistakes increases also.

C. *The Value of the Person.* The primordial value of man himself in all planning has been sufficiently stressed, and here the church merely emphasizes an essential, absolute principle. But planning is not merely a problem of dominating matter and techniques: Planning also means concerted action to develop the intellectual resources of a society.

Today this is the most serious problem, because of the tremendous technical resources now available for use by the public authorities in planning. Now that they have complete control of all the media of information, both in education and through the mass channels, men are obliged to formulate an ethic of planning much more strictly than in the past. If the principle of subsidiarity (which lays down the principle of autonomy for the intermediary social bodies) cannot, for technical reasons, be respected, the ultimate control of operations and aims must none the less remain in the hands of the individuals who constitute this society and whose welfare is the whole object of planning. It is therefore essential for planning to be controlled on democratic lines, as it becomes increasingly global and important.

There may seem to be a contradiction between the demands of technology and those of democracy, but this is only an alibi. It is the task of political science to find new forms in order to reconcile these claims, which are not really opposed. Many countries must now find new political techniques that will enable them to reconcile the demand for stability and continuity in planning with the need for basic control. On this point too the church will certainly have to draw attention, during the next few years, to certain principles or to formulate new ones.

The future development of the social doctrine of the Roman Catholic Church will therefore take the form of accepting (as a necessary technique) the economic organization of the developed countries, and especially the development of the other countries both at the national and at the international level. Planning, however, is subordinate to certain principles, such as respect for the human person, subsidiarity and democratic control—which implies the rejection of totalitarian planning, and especially of ideological planning.

EPILOGUE

17

ISSUES FOR CHRISTIANS

by PAUL ABRECHT (Geneva)

THE problems of economic justice and order have long preoccupied the ecumenical movement; indeed, they were the main subjects of the first ecumenical conference on social questions in Stockholm in 1925. It is interesting, therefore, to compare the conclusions that emerge from this collection of essays by Christian economists (actually the first volume of its kind in the history of ecumenical social thought) concerning the task of the church in relation to the problems of economic life today with those of earlier ecumenical statements.

This book tends to be dominated by two issues, neither of which has received adequate attention in previous ecumenical studies and conferences on social questions: first, the demands for world economic justice and development created by the needs of the peoples in Africa, Asia and Latin America, and the ethical and social problems of change this produces for them and for the richer nations

371

of the world; and, second, the consequences of the contemporary technological revolution for the organization of economic and social life in our times.

Both issues are world problems, though they clearly pose different challenges and responsibilities to the economically developed and less developed countries. They are interrelated problems. The main hope for world economic progress and prosperity lies in the widespread application of new techniques. Yet, the issues raised by the new technological era go beyond the problem of increasing world economic productivity; they concern the pattern of human living in a world that seems to be increasingly dominated by the spirit of technical change for its own sake and increasingly confused and troubled by the consequences of such change.

It is perhaps worthwhile to try to summarize the points of agreement and disagreement in the interpretation in these essays of the nature of the technological and economic revolutions that confront us and of the Christian response to them.

The Economic Development of the Poorer Nations

The major concern of all contributors to this volume is the depth and extent of the world economic transformation that must occur if the economic and social needs of the developing nations are to be met. All agree that something like a revolution in world economic attitudes must come about if we are to meet the challenge of economic development that is before us today. Though the writers speaking for the West tend to be cautious in their formulation of the issues, they agree that new methods of world economic organization and order are urgently required. Professor Blough, speaking from the perspective of the U.S.A., affirms that the major need today is for effective world economic planning to achieve world economic goals. Though holding that world government may be only an illusory hope, he believes that a useful measure of world planning can be realized through the cooperation of national states in intergovernmental organizations. Professor Tinbergen, speaking as a European expert, believes that cooperation in world economic planning would lead the nations to acknowledge their common interest and to see human needs in a world perspective, thus contributing also to better understanding across ideological and political lines. In his view, Christians must contribute to this evolution by opposing laissez-faire thinking, and all attitudes based on nationalism, racism and other types of economic and political discrimination. The countries of the West must be prepared to make drastic shifts in economic structure that would foster a more efficient world order and the economic interests of all mankind.

The writers from Africa, Asia and Latin America are even more deeply convinced of the necessity for radical and far-reaching changes in the structure of the world economy. Thus, Mr. S. L. Parmar holds that a new concept of international economy is needed, one in which the developing countries would be treated in the same way that a nation treats its own less developed areas. And Mr. Espiritu argues that the old trade structures must be radically altered if the new nations are to advance economically unhampered by the constraints of the richer nations.

Despite the agreement among the contributors about the general principles on which world economic development must proceed, they diverge at three points: in their ideology, in their sense of urgency about the need for changes in world economic structures, and in their feeling of injustice about the present disparities of national wealth and income.

None of the contributors from Africa, Asia and Latin America advocates a particular ideological solution to the problems of economic development in their countries, but all see the problem of initiating it in terms that contrast sharply with the approach to development in the West; and this raises the question whether in

373

fact the presuppositions for encouraging rapid economic development are the same. Professor Sumiya makes this point very clearly.
He emphasizes that the value system of economically developed
societies is foreign to the traditions of developing countries, and
he concludes that often economic development must take place in
conflict with traditional values and without the support of those
particular values that would be conducive to a popular sense of
responsibility for economic growth. Whereas in the early stages
of national independence a common vision supplies the ideological impetus and the cohesion necessary for economic development, as nationalist enthusiasm wanes the sense of unity weak-
ens, and the social conflicts inherent in a situation of fundamental
change become more apparent. This tension, aggravated by the
declining authority of traditional social structures and the poverty
of the mass of the people, constitutes the source of increasing frustration. Professor Sumiya's conclusion highlights one of the important problems of the new nations, and provides what seems to
be a clue to rapid economic development within these nations: "In
the developing countries where the great majority of the people
are poor, one of the most challenging tasks is to organize these
impoverished masses and stimulate them to participate in the building of the new nation-state." This is being done in different ways in
Egypt, Cuba, Brazil, Indonesia, Tanzania, Ghana and elsewhere;
and seldom is the ideological method pursued congenial to the
western countries. The divergence in outlook has been highlighted
by the demands of many businessmen in the West that their governments should follow a policy of development aid that strengthens the institutions of private enterprise.[1]

---

[1] See for example, *Foreign Aid Through Private Initiative*, report of the
Advisory Committee on Private Enterprise in Foreign Aid, Agency for International Development, Washington, D.C., 1965. The theme of this report
is summarized in the statement, p. 8, that in American development policy,
"at every opportunity, we ought to broaden and strengthen the private
sector."

It is evident that the larger western nations do not feel the same sense of urgency about the need for the rapid economic development of the new nations as these countries do themselves. Certainly they are not yet willing to consider the distribution of economic resources according to some supranational principle. The statement of Professor Blough, that the U.S.A. is not "prepared in the foreseeable future to have American economic policy subjected to international planning in any major area," probably applies to most western countries. This attitude is undoubtedly based on some legitimate arguments concerning the risks in handing over responsibilities of economic power to untried international agencies. But this argument only heightens the feeling of the developing nations that their interests will always be secondary in world economic debates. It strengthens their conviction that only through united opposition to the richer nations can they hope to counteract their economic power. This clearly was the strategy followed at the first U. N. World Trade and Development Conference, in 1964, where the 77 poorer nations consistently opposed the 25 richer ones.

The question of world economic justice thus arises in the relations between the rich and the poor countries because there is no structure of world economic order, nor any philosophy of world economic development that takes into consideration the interests of all peoples and countries. The present structures perpetuate the power of the richer ones and their ability to shape world economic development in a manner that suits primarily their own interests, their own philosophy of economic welfare and their conception of world economic progress. In different ways the essays of Mr. Nasir, Mr. Parmar and Mr. Ncgobo point to the sense of injustice which this monopoly of power arouses in the peoples of the poor nations.

The Christian understanding of and concern for justice in the relation of rich and poor countries cannot be activated only by greater contributions in aid and technical assistance. To use an expression of Mr. Elliott, the "secular redemption of mankind" calls for new patterns of world economic relations to ensure that the power of the rich nations does not allow them to determine the pattern of economic development for all.

Unfortunately, the liberal (laissez-faire) view of economic development is not explicitly represented in this book. However, it is still dominant in the thinking of most western countries, especially when they consider their economic relations with the new countries, even though it is rarely explicitly defended. Its advocates hold that the western nations have achieved their economic predominance by virtue of their technological ingenuity and their industriousness. Until the new nations display a similar capacity and concern to make the necessary sacrifices, they cannot expect to share equally in the fruits of world trade and development. Their conclusion is that it is irresponsible to put power in the hands of those who are unprepared for its exercise.

These attitudes suggest a number of difficult but urgent issues for consideration by Christians:

1. Can the convictions of the western nations about the values of private initiative, freedom and personal responsibility in economic life be reconciled with the demand of the developing nations for some type of ideological political control and organization of development? To what extent should the granting of development aid be contingent upon such an agreement? Should the church itself in certain situations try to work out a pattern of economic and social organization in the interests of effective development? In some Latin American countries—for example, Chile and Venezuela—the Roman Catholic Christian democratic parties are experimenting with new forms of political and economic action, and Protestants have been invited to support their programs. There has been great uncertainty in the churches about the right response to this overture. In Africa and Asia the churches often are still struggling with the problem of their involvement in economic de-

velopment, and are only beginning to think about their responsibility for developing new structures.[2]

2. What is the church's conception of world economic justice and welfare, and what are the implications of this for the distribution of economic goods and services? The churches have adopted the pattern of national governments in raising funds for social welfare to meet particular human needs. But is there a form of justice which should replace this essentially paternalistic approach to the developing nations? In the absence of a world government with a concomitant sense of responsibility for world welfare, is there anything the churches can do to produce an "ethical demonstration effect" and to show what a truly international perspective on economic development would mean?

The missing element in the present discussion of economic development in a world perspective is not good will, but a clear statement of the principles that could provide the basis for an alternative to the spirit of altruism in the richer nations.

The Challenge of the
New Scientific and Technological Revolution

Ecumenical study has for too long neglected the social consequences of the contemporary scientific and technological revolution.[3] The chapters by Mr. Theobald, Monsieur Gruson and

---

[2] The Christian Council of Burma in a recent pronouncement on the Christian and the social order in Burma defines the Christian responsibility in these very general terms: "A Christian should be committed to support movements which improve the material conditions of men and women. This he sees as a means to better things, never as an end in itself. If such desire for the raising of man's material living is not there, then man will not attain to spiritual development. A man whose whole concern is whether he is going to find food for his and his family's stomach is not going to have the time or inclination to seek 'spiritual bread' for his soul. The Christian is therefore committed to the building up of a just and equitable social order." *Some Considerations for the Christian Worker in the New Burma.* Pamphlet of the Burma Christian Council, 1965, p. 11.

[3] In the preparations for the first Assembly of the World Council of Churches (1948) Dr. J. H. Oldham made an attempt to introduce a consider-

Professor Cox call attention to some of the potentialities of the technical innovations of our time and the social problems they pose. However, the search for the critical issues has just begun; and much more study of these questions is needed in our churches.

Mr. Theobald in his essay about the character of the new technological era wishes to focus debate on the question: Does mankind realize that it is entering a new scientific and technological era, essentially different in kind from the scientific and industrial era of the past, and one that is bound to require major modifications in socioeconomic systems throughout the world? Without acknowledging the necessity of raising this question we can agree with the fundamental consideration on which he rests his argument, that the new scientific era, through the application of the newest discoveries in electronics to the development of computers, is vastly altering the pattern of work in industrial society, the skills needed in modern industry and the way in which decisions about some of the fundamental problems of welfare and security are made in the modern world. But we need more details, more facts that will indicate the kind of changes to be expected in the coming years and more precise indications of the nature of the society that the new scientific technology is expected to bring about. What exactly is the potentiality of the technological revolution of our times? Will it be realized as rapidly as is often supposed, or delayed because it is not yet either economically practical or politically acceptable? What institutional and social barriers are likely to hinder or at least retard the introduction of new knowledge and new techniques? Until these questions find clearer answers, it is difficult for public opinion and the churches to respond intelligently to the situation.

Such additional facts might help the church to enter more wisely into the debate between those who see primarily the promises of

ation of the issues raised by a technological society. However, the discussion reflected the traditional Christian approach to these questions, and this may explain why it was inadequately followed up.

technological change and those who see only its menacing aspects. The arguments on both sides are compelling. The optimists see the immense possibilities for reshaping society, for developing an economic system that would produce enough goods and services to meet the basic needs of all human beings, or, through the proper use of the new means of mass communication, for encouraging the dramatic speeding up of the educational process and for renewing man and society through the results of the latest discoveries in medicine, biology, and other sciences.

But there are also those who call attention to the dangers: of civilization being carried forward by an irrational dynamic of technological innovation; of techniques accentuating the power of autocratic individuals, groups and parties; of growing human and social confusion and maladjustment because of man's inability to cope with the impact of rapid technical change on work and community. These dangers have been recognized by the pioneers in the study of cybernetics.[4]

Confronted by these contradictory appraisals Christians can do little more than agree with Professor Cox that the scientific and technical innovations of our world should be accepted as a product of the Christian ethos and an expression of the creative power that God has bestowed on man, but recognizing at the same time that like all products of human creativity, they contain possibilities for both good and evil, and are therefore fundamentally ambiguous.

Though modern technical society appears to have its own dynamic, it is a limited or qualified dynamic, because it can be used to serve many different ends, needs and desires as determined by society. A technical elite may emerge as a new leader class in the age of the computer; for, as Norbert Wiener pointed out, although machines are helpless by themselves they "may be used by a hu-

---

[4] NORBERT WIENER: *The Human Use of Human Beings: Cybernetics and Society*. Second Revised Edition. Doubleday, 1954, p. 162. "... the new industrial revolution is a two-edged sword. It may be used for the benefit of humanity.... It may also be used to destroy humanity...."

man being or a block of human beings to increase their control over the rest of the human race. . . . [5]

For the moment, all these concerns and worries tend to remain in the realm of speculation. Even the specialists are not sure where we are going.[6] However, this does not mean that the church can continue to neglect these problems.

---

[5] *Ibid.,* p. 181.
[6] *Ibid.,* p. 162.